TOUGH CHOICES

RISK, SECURITY, AND THE CRIMINALIZATION OF DRUG POLICY

CLARENDON STUDIES IN CRIMINOLOGY

Published under the auspices of the Institute of Criminology, University of Cambridge; the Mannheim Centre, London School of Economics; and the Centre for Criminological Research, University of Oxford.

General Editor: Lucia Zedner
(University of Oxford)

Editors: Manuel Eisner, Alison Liebling, and Per-Olof Wikström
(University of Cambridge)

Robert Reiner, Jill Peay, and Tim Newburn
(London School of Economics)

Ian Loader and Julian Roberts
(University of Oxford)

RECENT TITLES IN THIS SERIES:

Discovery of Hidden Crime: Self-Report Delinquency Surveys in Criminal Policy Context
Kivivuori

Serious Offenders: A Historical Study of Habitual Criminals
Godfrey, Cox, and Farrall

Penal Abolitionism
Ruggiero

Life after Life Imprisonment
Appleton

The Eternal Recurrence of Crime and Control: Essays in Honour of Paul Rock
Downes, Hobbs, and Newburn

Tough Choices

Risk, Security, and the Criminalization of Drug Policy

TOBY SEDDON
LISA WILLIAMS
ROBERT RALPHS

OXFORD
UNIVERSITY PRESS

OXFORD
UNIVERSITY PRESS

Great Clarendon Street, Oxford OX2 6DP,
United Kingdom

Oxford University Press is a department of the University of Oxford.
It furthers the University's objective of excellence in research, scholarship,
and education by publishing worldwide. Oxford is a registered trade mark of
Oxford University Press in the UK and in certain other countries

First Edition published in 2012
Impression: 1

British Library Cataloguing in Publication Data
Data available

Library of Congress Cataloging in Publication Data
Data available

ISBN 978-0-19-969723-6

Printed in Great Britain by
CPI Group (UK) Ltd, Croydon, CR0 4YY

General Editor's Introduction

Clarendon Studies in Criminology aims to provide a forum for outstanding empirical and theoretical work in all aspects of criminology and criminal justice, broadly understood. The Editors welcome submissions from established scholars, as well as excellent PhD work. The CSC Series was inaugurated in 1994, with Roger Hood as the first General Editor, following discussions between Oxford University Press and criminologists at LSE, Cambridge, and Oxford. It is edited under the auspices of the three criminological centres: the Cambridge Institute of Criminology, the Mannheim Centre for Criminology at the London School of Economics, and the Centre for Criminology at the University of Oxford. Each supplies members of the Editorial Board and, in turn, the General Editor of the Series.

In combining extended exploration of contemporary criminological theory with close empirical observation, this book epitomizes the founding aims of the CSC Series. Its specific focus is the 'criminal justice' turn in British drugs policy. This development is characterized by concern about drug abuse as a motor of crime and a determination to deploy the criminal justice system to target and treat drug-abusing offenders with the aim of reducing offending. The 'Tough Choices' of the book's title thus refers to the policy developed under the Drug Interventions Programme to increase reliance upon criminal justice interventions in the treatment of drug users. Perhaps this book's most valuable contribution lies in the analysis of national policy development and the in-depth local studies upon which the core chapters are based. Detailed analysis of policy documents, extensive field observation, and interviews with over 220 individuals (ranging from senior policy makers through service managers and practitioners to drug users themselves) illuminates the issues from the national to local level. In particular, these interviews furnish a wealth of detail about the experiences of drug workers and drug users at three research sites. The result is a textured analysis that provides valuable information and insights drawn from the many different levels at which the research was carried out.

Yet this is no narrowly empirical study. Woven throughout the book is an impressively wide-ranging engagement with important developments in contemporary criminological theory and their implications for understanding recent drug policy. In a conscious bid to apply high theory to substantive developments on the ground, this book provides a valuable exploration of the ways in which broader changes in governance are reflected in drug policy and innovations in practice. The ideas, insights, and conceptual frames of recent criminological theory are put to good use in understanding major changes in drug policy, as well as the challenges faced by those implementing them. These intellectual resources also lay bare the structural, cultural, and political dimensions of policy development, and reveal the complexities involved in the risk management of 'drug-driven crime'. Moving between the macro lens of a 'risk-security nexus' and close observation of the micro-interactions taking place in police stations, courts, and drug treatment services, this study reveals the space between the claims of high theory and the realities of institutional practice. The resulting analysis throws new light on attitudes and responses to a central problem in contemporary criminal justice. *Tough Choices: Risk, Security, and the Criminalization of Drug Policy* is an important and engaging addition to the literature on drug policy and its place within criminal justice practice. The Editors warmly welcome this addition to the Series.

Lucia Zedner
University of Oxford
February 2012

Acknowledgements

The project on which this book is based unfolded over a number of years. The initial idea began to spark in 2005 and a brief encounter between the first author and the late Richard Ericson in the summer of that year in Leeds gave it further impetus. We are very grateful to the ESRC who provided generous funding between 2007 and 2009 (grant reference RES-061-23-0028), which allowed us to carry out the empirical research presented in the book. The bulk of the writing was done in 2011. Inevitably, over this long period, we have accumulated a great number of intellectual and other debts along the way, and we do our best to acknowledge the most important of those here.

First of all, we repeat our thanks to the ESRC for funding. We also thank the School of Law at the University of Manchester for providing us with facilities and support, not least the marvellous John Rylands University Library. The work would not have been possible without the co-operation of the 220 people we formally interviewed, as well as many others in the three local sites who facilitated access to data and people, and we extend a very warm thanks to them all. Our colleague Nishat Hyder provided invaluable research assistance at a couple of key points in the project and Roy Egginton carried out some additional quantitative data analysis on our behalf, which, although it does not directly appear in the book, nevertheless informed some of our thinking. Roy's work was supported by additional funding from the School of Law's Research Support Fund.

Material on which chapter two draws was first presented at a workshop at Keele University in late 2007 and at the Annual International Society for the Study of Drug Policy conference in Lisbon in early 2008, and was later published in the *British Journal of Criminology*. Thanks to Luis Lobo-Guerrero for the invitation to the Keele event and to the editors, referees, and readers of the *BJC* for comments provided. A very early version of parts of chapter five was presented in September 2008 at a 'Regulation and Criminal Justice' seminar in Manchester and at the European Society of Criminology Conference in Edinburgh. We are grateful to participants in those two events for their helpful feedback, especially Barbara Hudson and Clifford Shearing at the Manchester seminar.

Colleagues here in Manchester provided a collegiate and stimulating environment for the work, especially those who have recently come together in the new research centre, ManReg (the Manchester Centre for Regulation, Governance & Security). Our respective families have also provided their usual support and encouragement. Lastly, thanks to Lucy Alexander at OUP for patience and efficiency in helping us to deliver this book.

Toby Seddon
Lisa Williams
Robert Ralphs
Manchester, December 2011

Contents

List of Tables and Figures

Tables

Figures

1

Introduction: Drugs, Crime, and Criminal Justice

We had a healthy drug policy. We don't have one now. Drug policy has now focused down on the link between drugs and crime. If things are done to drug users, it is because of the effect they have on others. We are witnessing the introduction of a punitive and coercive ethos.

[Stimson, 2000: 260]

Introduction

Walk around any police custody suite in England and Wales and something quite remarkable will soon become apparent: the pervasive presence of drug workers. They go in and out of the cells to speak to detainees, they liaise with custody sergeants and detention officers, all the time working from their own permanent office bases in the police station. Visit any magistrates' court building or probation office or prison and you will find drug workers similarly ensconced there.

This would have been unthinkable even 25 years ago, when, for example, drug workers involved in pioneering arrest referral schemes often encountered obstruction and hostility when trying to operate in police custody suites (Dorn et al, 1990). In effect, an entire new infrastructure of drug treatment embedded within criminal justice has been rapidly built up almost from scratch over the last couple of decades.

This growing emphasis on crime and the prioritization of the delivery of drug treatment through criminal justice has led to claims that British drug policy has been 'criminalized' or that there has been a criminal justice turn within policy (see: Stimson, 2000; Hunt and Stevens, 2004; Duke, 2006; Stevens, 2007; Seddon et al, 2008). A central aim of this book is to explore this shift or transformation in policy. Why did it happen? How did it evolve? What exactly does this new drug policy landscape look like? What new ways of dealing with drug-using offenders have been created? With what impact and consequences?

These questions are, of course, of pressing importance and interest to criminologists and policy-makers involved in seeking to study and understand recent drug policy and we hope that the account we present here will have much to interest those readers. But one of the central premises of this book is that this transformation—in shorthand, the 'criminal justice turn'—is of much wider significance, not only for criminology but also for the social sciences more generally. In a nutshell, our thesis is that both the emergence of this new drug policy direction and its implementation in practice can best be understood as part of a broader transformation in governance in which risk-based thinking has become central to the ways in which we seek to address our contemporary insecurities. In this way, we see the book as a contribution to the more general literature on the sociology of punishment and social control in contemporary society, an area of scholarship that has been probably the most vibrant and interesting in criminology in recent decades, encompassing some seminal monographs (eg Cohen, 1985; Downes, 1988; Garland, 1990, 2001; Simon, 2007; Ericson, 2007), as well as some landmark papers (eg Feeley and Simon, 1992, 1994; O'Malley, 1999a; Sparks, 2001; Shearing, 2001; Braithwaite, 2003).

Although we seek to contribute to this literature, we should make clear that we are definitely not attempting to make general claims in this book about the nature of late modernity or neo-liberalism or the risk society (on which, more in a moment). Rather, we are looking at those grand claims from the other end of the telescope. To what extent do the high-level arguments of Garland, Simon, Ericson, and others still hold when we look at a very specific policy area in a specific time and place? It is, in a sense, the shortcomings of those accounts, the tendency to over-generalize, for which, for example, Garland's *Culture of Control* has been criticized (eg Zedner, 2002; Young, 2003a) that we are seeking to correct in our particular case study. We think this focus is appropriate and timely because there have been so many of these 'big picture' accounts that more specific local studies are now needed to point towards ways in which the 'big picture' might begin to be adjusted, revised, and refined. We think, in other words, that at this stage in the development of the field, the advancement of these debates is most likely to come through case studies of the kind we are presenting in this book rather than from yet more sweeping generalized accounts.

This raises a further point about the scope of coverage of our book. This is neither a comparative nor an international study. Our focus, for the reasons above, is on a particular time and place, that is England and Wales from the early 1980s to the present. Nevertheless, it is a significant matter that the criminal justice turn has been an international phenomenon during this period, spanning around the world, from Australia, to Canada, to the Netherlands, including many countries in between. We say a little about this wider international experience later in this chapter when we look at the evidence for the effectiveness of different types of drug interventions in the criminal justice system.

To prepare the ground for the rest of the book, we now turn to three matters that we need to expand on in this introductory chapter. First, we set out our understanding of the broader transformation in governance that has taken place during this period, which we claim provides a vital part of the context for our account. Second, we outline what we mean by the criminal justice turn and review the international research on which it has been based. Third, we describe in brief how this has taken shape in recent decades within English and Welsh drug policy. We conclude the chapter by describing the research methods used in the study on which most of this book is based and outlining the structure of the rest of the book.

Neo-liberal governance

As we have already noted, at the heart of this book is a claim about the significance to this area of drug policy of wider transformations in governance that have taken place over recent decades. We now say a little more here about what we understand these transformations to be. In doing so, we sketch in unseemly brevity what is a vast and complex body of literature that seeks to understand the nature of our contemporary world. Nevertheless, we think it is possible to pinpoint the main contours of these mutations in governance.

Before setting these out, we acknowledge that although most scholars agree that the world has changed dramatically over the last part of the twentieth century, there is major disagreement about terminology. John Braithwaite (2008: 4), for example, one of the surest-footed commentators on these matters on the planet, states baldly that 'those who think we are in an era of neo-liberalism are mistaken'. He prefers the term 'regulatory capitalism', which he borrows from the work of David Levi-Faur and collaborators (Levi-Faur, 2005; Jordana et al, 2011). He argues that this better captures the reality of contemporary governance where the state is very far from being 'hollowed out' and the trend is towards more regulation rather than less (he calls this the 'myth of deregulation').

Within criminology, and influenced by some key sociologists (eg Beck et al, 1994), many have preferred the term 'late modernity', notably David Garland (2001) who suggests that this best serves to indicate 'an historical phase of the modernization process without assuming that we are coming to the end, or even to the high point, of a centuries-old dynamic that shows no signs of letting up' (2001: 77; see also Young, 1999). Yet another variation is the term 'post-modernism' which has resonated particularly within cultural studies and certain areas of social theory (eg Jameson, 1984, 1991) and which conveys, *contra* Garland, the idea that we have indeed left the era of modernity behind and entered into a new phase, albeit one that can still only be defined in relation to its predecessor.

But perhaps the most common label is the one Braithwaite rejects so vigorously, neo-liberalism. Although we are largely persuaded by Braithwaite's demolition of the 'myth of deregulation', nevertheless, neo-liberalism is our preferred term, for several reasons. It helpfully indicates the connection with the tradition of classical liberalism and its valorization of markets. It also encourages us to see the present as the latest mutation within liberal governance, rather than as something entirely new. We recognize, too, that it has become the most widely used term, not only within the academic literature across several disciplines but also in the public sphere. Drawing, then, from what is an eclectic and diverse body of scholarship, we see there being four key, and interrelated, dimensions that define the distinctive characteristics of neo-liberal governance.

(1) The centrality of markets. Neo-liberalism involves a revival of certain elements of nineteenth-century liberal capitalism, in particular the renewed primacy of the idea of the 'free market' as a central mechanism in the effective and efficient operation of a capitalist economy. However, this 'revival' is not simply a 'return to the past', rather, neo-liberalism has a new character (Levi-Faur, 2005: 15), which centres on the way it focuses on competition rather than exchange (Foucault, 2008). *Homo economicus* is now recast as a 'creature whose tendency to compete must be fostered'

(Read, 2009: 28). And with this new focus on competition, the central liberal formula of 'laissez-faire' is transformed. The optimal conditions for competition are not achievable simply by a passive strategy of 'leaving markets alone' and allowing Smith's 'invisible hand' to work its magic. Rather, the conditions of the market need to be nurtured and protected by active intervention. While exchange was something that occurred 'naturally' within markets, competition is an 'artificial relation' that has to be created and then sustained (Read, 2009: 28; Foucault, 2008).

(2) The extension of markets into new realms. The emphasis on competition has spread across diverse fields, including the governmental sphere, and innovations based on market thinking have colonized many new areas—from prisons, to health care, to telecommunications, to transport. As already noted, and contrary to some claims, this has been accompanied by a proliferation of regulatory instruments and technologies, rather than any overall trend towards deregulation (Levi-Faur, 2005; Braithwaite, 2008). This is not as straightforward as just saying that central state oversight and regulation have increased. Regulation now also occurs increasingly beyond the state in private sector and non-governmental agencies, as well as in transnational networks. It is this thickening, extending, and spreading of regulation and governance that is encapsulated in the idea of 'regulatory capitalism' (Levi-Faur, 2005; Braithwaite, 2008).

(3) The consumer society. There has been a shift away from the primacy of production towards a new emphasis on consumption—the rise of the 'consumer society' in shorthand (see: Bauman, 1988; Miller and Rose, 1997; Rose, 1999: 85–9). Choices about consumption have become central to the construction of identities and consumption has become a site for 'symbolic competition' between individuals about lifestyles and identity (Bauman, 1988: 58; Miles, 1998, 2000).

(4) The rise of risk. Recent decades have also seen the emergence of a 'risk society' (Beck, 1992), in the sense that risk has become a central organizing principle for life and hence a 'defining characteristic of the world in which we live' (Garland, 2003: 48). Modes of governance in diverse areas have become more risk-oriented or risk-based (O'Malley, 2004).

For our purposes in this book, a significant matter to draw out here is the way in which neo-liberal subjects are viewed or constituted within these new modes of governance. As Rose (1999: 141) suggests, the concept of choice is central to this, with our entire understanding of human behaviour now reconceptualized as 'calculative actions undertaken through the universal human faculty of choice'. Garland (2001: 190) calls this the shift to an economic style of reasoning. The neo-liberal subject is a choice-maker, a consumer, a 'competing creature', required simultaneously to act *responsibly* by minimizing negative risks (O'Malley, 2004: 71–4) and to be *entrepreneurial* in taking risks in order to innovate (O'Malley, 2004: 57–71, 2011; Osborne and Gaebler, 1992). As we will see in later chapters, this is a critical insight for understanding these new directions in drugs and crime policy.

Drugs and criminal justice: what does the evidence say?

What exactly do we mean by the idea of the criminal justice turn in drug policy? A first and important observation to make is that it is not without historical antecedents. Penal or criminal justice responses to drugs have a long history. In late nineteenth-century Britain, for example, legislation provided powers to the courts for the compulsory detention of criminal inebriates in specialist reformatories (Garland, 1985: 217–18). And, of course, the global drug-control regime that was constructed in the first two decades of the twentieth century has been based since its inception on the use of the criminal law as a tool for regulating the manufacture, distribution, and possession of 'dangerous drugs'. In the United States, for example, the Harrison Narcotics Act of 1914, one of the earliest pieces of national 'prohibition' legislation, provided for fines of up to $2,000 and prison sentences of up to five years for violations of its regulations. The connection then between drugs and criminal justice is not a recent invention. It is embedded in the foundations of drug control. Indeed, we might even go as far as to say that the very concept of 'drugs', in the sense we understand it today, did not exist before the creation of the criminal law regulatory regime (Seddon, 2010a, 2010b).

But the type of fusion of drug treatment and criminal justice that we are interested in here represents a new line of development in this longer story. This integration of the two systems is built around a single central purpose: to do something about the problem of drug-driven crime. It is based on three linked assumptions:

(1) *Drugs cause crime.* Drug-driven property crime—'addicts stealing to fund their habit'—is a major driver of local area crime rates, especially in deprived neighbourhoods.

(2) *Identification and targeting.* The criminal justice system can be used to target these drug-motivated offenders and channel them into treatment.
(3) *'Treatment works'.* Treatment can lead to significant reductions in their offending.

As we will see in chapter three, the development of the criminal justice turn has been closely linked with the development of a research evidence base. Here, we summarize and review some of the key elements of this research foundation. We begin by looking at the evidential foundation for these three assumptions.

Assumption 1: Drugs cause crime. The behavioural model underpinning this first assumption is straightforward: users of addictive drugs like heroin and crack cocaine, who tend to have limited sources of legal income, are driven to commit income-generating property crime in order to fund their drug purchases. Its empirical basis is the well-established finding that there is a strong correlation or association between heroin/crack use and involvement in property crime (eg Gandossy et al, 1980; Nurco et al, 1985; Johnson et al, 1985; Parker and Newcombe, 1987; Holloway and Bennett, 2004; Bennett et al, 2008). If we take samples of offenders, we find very elevated levels of heroin and crack use. For example, research on arrestees in England and Wales has found rates of recent heroin use that are around 10 times higher than in the general adult population (Holloway et al, 2004; Boreham et al, 2006). Similarly, if we look at samples of heroin and crack users in treatment, levels of involvement in property crime are also high (Harocopos et al, 2003; Jones et al, 2007). Further, there is evidence that heavier and more frequent use of heroin or crack is associated with higher rates of property or acquisitive offending (Hammersley et al, 1989; Best et al, 2001). A recent paper by Trevor Bennett and colleagues provides perhaps the definitive account of this evidence by presenting a meta-analysis of data from 30 published studies from around the world, concluding that there is a 'significant positive association between drug use and crime' (Bennett et al, 2008: 112). This was concentrated most strongly among crack and heroin users, and the association was strongest for a particular set of offence types (shoplifting, theft, robbery, burglary, and prostitution) (2008: 114–15).

What is far less clear is the extent to which drug-related crime really does drive neighbourhood crime problems. In other words, how big a problem is drug-related crime in the context of the crime problem in general? In recent years, British drug policy-makers have consistently claimed that up to a half of all property crime is drug-driven (Home Office, 2008: 8). Yet there are good reasons to suggest that this may be a considerable exaggeration (see Stevens, 2008). A study by Dorn et al (1994), for example, based on data from the early 1990s, estimated that rather than 50 per cent, the proportion actually lay between 1 and 21 per cent. The answer to the question also depends on how we define 'property crime'. Increasingly, the 'crime of choice' for heroin and crack users in Britain is shoplifting, rather than burglary or robbery (eg Jones et al, 2007) and it is a moot point whether public and political anxieties about drug-driven crime extend to concern for the profits of high street retail stores.

While the drug–crime association is well established, the nature of that link is highly contested. We have referred so far to 'drug-related' and 'drug-driven' crime, other terms include 'drug-motivated' crime, but there is considerable uncertainty and disagreement about what is meant by 'related', 'driven', or 'motivated'. There is a voluminous literature on this and we direct readers to some of the better and more interesting contributions (eg Auld et al, 1986; Parker and Newcombe, 1987; Simpson, 2003; Seddon, 2000, 2006). The criminal justice turn is based on what has been described as the 'economic necessity' or 'drugs cause crime' model: property crime provides a means of financing expensive drug habits for people with limited legitimate income (eg Parker and Newcombe, 1987). However, this has been much criticized as an over-simplification of what is in fact a more complex causal picture (see Seddon, 2000, 2006). An alternative account is the 'informal economy' or 'crime causes drugs' model: people experiencing socio-economic disadvantage encounter drugs as commodities within the semi-criminal informal economies they operate in (eg Auld et al, 1986; Seddon, 2008a). In other words, it is the need for marginalized groups to engage in economic activity that brings drugs and crime together. Others have suggested that drugs and crime are highly correlated because they are both causally connected to a third common factor (eg poverty) or else form part of a complex causal web (Seddon, 2006). Bennett and Holloway (2007) argue that there is no single drugs–crime link but rather a series of specific drug–crime connections.

Overall, then, the evidence suggests that this first assumption is built on some shaky foundations. Perhaps the only point on which most would agree is that there is a strong association between (consumption of certain types of) drugs and (particular types of) crime. Beyond that, the picture is less clear and there are good reasons to doubt the accepted policy view of 'drug-related crime'.

Assumption 2: Identification and targeting. At the heart of the second assumption is the idea that the criminal justice system is a good place to find these drug-using offenders. The premise here is that a sufficiently high proportion of this group are apprehended at some stage and brought into the system. Given the uncertainties described above in measuring the extent of drug-related crime, this assumption is very difficult to assess. We know that the best estimates of the number of heroin and crack users in England put the figure at around 330,000 (Hay et al, 2008). It is uncertain, however, what proportion of that group are involved in property crime. A recent large-scale English study found that only 43 per cent of treatment entrants had committed an acquisitive offence in the previous four weeks (Jones et al, 2007) but extrapolating from that sample may be misleading as we know that at least one-third of the heroin/crack-using population are not in treatment at any given time (NTA, 2010). In the absence of better data, we could perhaps estimate very crudely, and no doubt imprecisely, that there may be around 165,000 heroin/crack users who are currently engaged in property crime. So how many of that group does testing at the police station manage to identify? Again, this is not straightforward to estimate. There are approximately 240,000 tests conducted annually, around one-third of which give positive results. However, some of these 80,000 positive tests will involve repeat tests of individuals who have multiple visits to the police station during the year, so the annual figure of people identified will be somewhat less than that. This suggests, then, that a rough estimate would be that perhaps between one-third and one-half of the drug-using offender population is picked up by drug testing in the police station.

There are two broad reasons why so many of this target population may slip through the net. An unknown proportion may simply not be arrested and taken to a police station in a given year. In other words, they may successfully evade capture for sustained periods of time. A second reason is that, even for those people who are captured and end up in police stations, testing itself may be an imprecise identification tool. The evidence for its efficacy is certainly mixed. In the piloting of drug testing in England and Wales, there was continual concern expressed both by testers and arrestees about its accuracy (Matrix & Nacro, 2004: 12–13; Seddon, 2005). We examine this issue further in chapter four. An earlier and much-cited review of (largely US) research on drug testing by Wish and Gropper (1990) was a little more positive than this, although they noted that the most serious shortcoming of testing is that it offers only a binary result (positive or negative) and gives no indication either of the severity of drug problems or of drug-related behaviours.

We might conclude then that using the criminal justice system as a site for finding this group is a strategy likely to be only partially successful. Certainly, many drug-using offenders will be found there but a substantial proportion will not. We explore this further in subsequent chapters, chapter four in particular, when we look at the question of attrition through the criminal justice process.

Assumption 3: 'Treatment works'. The third assumption is that individuals who enter and then stay in treatment will reduce their level of offending. The supporting evidence for this assumption comes from a series of longitudinal studies of treatment outcomes that have been undertaken in several different countries around the world (eg Gossop et al, 2001; Hubbard et al, 2003; Jones et al, 2009). The evidence here is quite compelling at one level. For example, the Drug Treatment Outcomes Research Study (DTORS) conducted in England found that the percentage reporting involvement in acquisitive offending nearly halved after three to five months in treatment (Jones et al, 2009), replicating the findings from the earlier National Treatment Outcome Research Study (NTORS) (Gossop, 2005). A large-scale study of the impact of the prescribing of opiate substitutes found similar reductions in crime (Millar et al, 2008). Other international studies paint a similar picture in terms of the crime-reduction benefits of treatment.

One caveat we should highlight here is the problem of drop-out. Clearly we can only talk of treatment 'working' for those people that treatment services manage to keep in touch with. Retention rates vary quite considerably between treatment types or modalities as well as between different services. Recent data for England, provided by the National Treatment Agency, suggest that just under 80 per cent of new treatment entrants are successfully retained for three months (NTA, 2010).

A further question posed by delivering treatment through criminal justice concerns whether treatment can be effective for

individuals who are pushed into it through the leverage of the criminal justice system. Drug users 'coerced' into treatment, so the argument goes, cannot be compelled to change if they lack the motivation. Somewhat counter-intuitively, the research evidence from the United Kingdom (McSweeney et al, 2007), Europe (Schaub et al, 2010), and the United States (Farabee et al, 1998) points to the opposite conclusion: treatment is no less effective for 'coerced' clients than it is for those who enter voluntarily (see also Stevens et al, 2005a). As we will see, this is an absolutely critical finding for the criminal justice turn (for a discussion of some of the explanations for the finding, see Seddon, 2007a). The *ethics* of coerced treatment is a different question that we do not consider here but interested readers are referred to the discussions in Seddon (2007a), Stevens et al (2005b), Caplan (2006), and Urbanoski (2010).

Drug interventions in criminal justice

So there are clearly some weaknesses in the evidence base for these three assumptions. Nevertheless, a series of drug interventions within the criminal justice system have been tried out in countries around the world over the last 30 or more years. Perhaps the first significant step along this road was Robert DuPont's ill-starred 'Operation Tripwire' proposal in 1977 in the United States (see DuPont and Wish, 1992). DuPont was the first Director of the National Institute on Drug Abuse (NIDA) between 1973 and 1978 and the second White House 'drug czar' between 1973 and 1975. Despite DuPont's powerful and influential position, Tripwire was never implemented. Nevertheless, its key components—the use of drug testing as a screening tool and for the monitoring of compliance, coupled with the systematic integration of treatment and criminal justice—set the template for much of what has followed over the last 30 years.

Early pioneering projects in the United States, on which DuPont drew in formulating his ideas, included the civil commitment programmes in California (see McGlothlin et al, 1977; Anglin, 1988) and New York in the 1960s and the TASC initiative (Treatment Accountability for Safer Communities—previously Treatment Alternatives to Street Crime) first established in 1972. An interesting review by Webster (1986) describes now largely forgotten programmes from the 1970s as far afield as Singapore, Hong Kong, and Sweden. But it was in the 1980s and 1990s that these developments really gathered pace and began to extend in a significant way beyond the United States. By the first decade of the twenty-first century, we can certainly say that the fusion of drug treatment and criminal justice had become a genuinely worldwide phenomenon (see Stevens et al, 2005a). But what do we know about the effectiveness of this fusion? Here, we begin by summarizing the research on the two principal community-based models for dealing with drug-using offenders: drug courts and treatment sentences.

Drug courts

Perhaps the single most well-known and widely adopted model for responding to drug-using offenders is that of drug courts (see: Belenko, 2001; Fischer, 2003; Wilson et al, 2006). The first drug court was established in Miami, Florida, in 1989. In the following years, others were set up across the United States and then around the world, including in Australia, Canada, England, and Scotland. There is no single drug court model but there are some common features:

(1) *Specialism.* Drug courts are specialist courts that are designed to deal exclusively with drug-using offenders. The aim here is to ensure that those involved in the court process—such as judges, lawyers, and clerks—develop high levels of expertise. In some versions, speeding up case processing is central to the operation of the courts.

(2) *Integrated treatment.* Drug courts offer access to a range of treatment and related support services. Treatment and criminal case processing are integrated. This requires a significant degree of co-ordination and partnership working between judges, court clerks, lawyers, probation officers, treatment workers, and others.

(3) *Drug testing.* Frequent testing is used to monitor participants' compliance. Rigorous testing procedures (eg direct observation of the collection of samples) ensure that the results can be used within the legal process.

(4) *Judicial monitoring.* The judge takes a central role in reviewing progress and draws on information provided by others, notably the treatment agency that reports on attendance and drug-test results. The judge is also central in rewarding positive progress (eg by praise or suspending imprisonment) and punishing

non-compliance (eg by warnings or increasing testing frequency). Some models also emphasize the importance of judicial continuity, that is that the same judge maintains contact with an individual participant.

The evidence on the impact and effectiveness of drug courts is mixed. Some studies, and indeed some reviews of research, have found that drug courts reduce reoffending (Wilson et al, 2006; Shaffer, 2006; Rossman et al, 2011), while others have suggested their impact on reoffending is marginal or unproven (Granfield et al, 1998; McIvor, 2009). In Sherman's language they can probably be best described as 'promising' (Sherman et al, 1997). Nevertheless, drug courts are the most widespread model for court-ordered treatment across the world.

Treatment sentences

The second main model of interventions is community sentences that include a drug-treatment component. These can operate within the framework of drug courts or simply as standalone sentences. Again, there are many varieties here but there are some common features:

(1) *Attendance requirements*. At the heart of treatment sentences is a requirement by the court for the offender to attend appointments at a treatment agency.

(2) *Supervision*. Offenders on these sentences are usually under the close supervision of probation or parole officers who manage and co-ordinate their case.

(3) *Drug testing*. Testing is often used for the purpose of monitoring progress and compliance with treatment.

(4) *Alternative to imprisonment*. Treatment sentences are typically intended to be community-based alternatives to imprisonment, although breaches for non-compliance often lead to incarceration.

Examples of this type of court-ordered treatment sentence are many and varied. In the United States, TASC, which we have already mentioned, is one of the oldest, dating back to the early 1970s. Other US examples include DTAP (Drug Treatment Alternatives to Prison), established in New York in 1990, which involves referral to residential treatment in lieu of a prison sentence, and California's

Proposition 36, initiated in 2001, which allows first- and second-time non-violent drug-possession offenders the opportunity to receive drug treatment instead of incarceration. Evaluations of TASC (Anglin et al, 1999) and DTAP (Belenko et al, 2004) show some evidence of positive impact on reoffending, although findings for TASC are a little more equivocal, reflecting the wide variations in local arrangements for case management and monitoring. The evaluation of Proposition 36 has found quite mixed outcomes for reoffending (Urada et al, 2008).

A British example of a treatment sentence is the Drug Treatment and Testing Order (DTTO), now restyled as the Drug Rehabilitation Requirement (DRR). DTTOs were found to have very poor completion rates and little or no impact on reoffending, apart from the small proportion (30 per cent) who finished their orders successfully (Hough et al, 2003). More recent innovations have seen new court interventions introduced that mirror treatment sentences but that apply at the pre-sentence stage, typically making treatment attendance a condition of bail. This has been introduced, for example, in Australia with the CREDIT (Court Referral and Evaluation for Drug Intervention and Treatment) programme (Heale and Lang, 2001) and in England with the Restriction on Bail (RoB) provision (Hucklesby et al, 2007).

Again, as with drug courts, the evidence base here is a mixed bag. Some interventions show promise, others do not. In an insightful review, Mike Hough (2002) highlights one of the reasons for this patchy performance, namely the sheer difficulty of implementing drug-treatment interventions in the criminal justice context. Getting health services and criminal justice agencies to work together effectively requires levels of partnership working that are not easy to achieve in practice, given the different philosophies, goals, and values of the two sectors. In Hough's view, while the underlying approach behind channelling drug users into treatment as they pass through the criminal justice system is sound, implementation remains problematic.

More recently, a new model for drug-crime interventions has started to emerge in the United States, which may indicate a new direction in this area. Project HOPE in Hawaii, piloted initially in 2004, is based on the idea that not all drug-using offenders require treatment to desist from offending and drug use and that the prevailing model of assessment followed by mandated treatment is therefore highly inefficient. HOPE provides a model for managing drug-involved offenders on probation in which the emphasis is on the application of swift and certain sanctions for *all* violations or breaches (that is all missed appointments or positive drug tests or other relevant 'misbehaviour'). It is claimed that for most offenders, this regime is enough to secure compliance. Only the small number who continue to 'fail' are deemed to require treatment. Hawken (2010) terms this a 'behavioural triage' model, in the sense that it is an offender's observed behaviour (eg continually providing positive tests) that signals their need for treatment or other services. Initial results from the evaluation of HOPE have certainly been impressive (Hawken and Kleiman, 2009). In a nice echo of the first steps along this path, Robert DuPont, the architect of the Operation Tripwire proposal in the late 1970s, has become a prominent cheerleader for the Project HOPE model as the best bet for the next phase of drugs-crime interventions.

The criminal justice turn in British drug policy

Here, we describe what the criminal justice turn has involved in the British context, beginning with a potted history (to which we will return in more detail in chapter three). The story begins in the mid-1980s, when a series of experimental arrest referral schemes were developed, initially involving the handing out of information about drugs and drug services to detainees in police stations (Dorn et al, 1990; Dorn, 1994; Turnbull et al, 1995; Edmunds et al, 1997, 1998). Over time, these schemes moved away from the early 'information-giving' model to involve drug workers screening and assessing detainees *in situ* in custody suites and attempting, where appropriate, to refer them on to community drug services (see Sondhi et al, 2002; Oerton et al, 2003). A key problem with these schemes was attrition: a very small proportion of those contacted in police stations ended up going through the doors of a drugs service in the community.

In the early 1990s, attention began to focus on the court stage. There were some short-lived experiments to replicate the arrest referral model in magistrates' courts, although these appeared to have only a limited appeal and impact (Dorn and Seddon, 1996; Webster, 1996). But the most significant developments concerned attempts to bring drugs work into the mainstream for probation officers (ACMD, 1991; Lee, 1993, 1994; Nee and Sibbitt, 1993; Hart and Webster, 1994; Rumgay, 1994; Dorn and Lee, 1995; Lee and Mainwaring, 1995; Sibbitt, 1996; Hearnden et al, 2000). One focus for this was the introduction under the Criminal Justice Act 1991 of a power for the courts to attach a requirement to undergo drug or alcohol treatment to a probation order. Although these orders, known as 1A(6) orders, turned out to be little used in practice (Lee, 1993, 1994; Lee and Mainwaring, 1995; HMIP, 1997), they paved the way for what was to become a flagship element within the new criminal justice approach, the Drug Treatment and Testing Order (DTTO), which we have already briefly mentioned above. The DTTO was a standalone community sentence introduced under sections 61–64 of the Crime and Disorder Act 1998, which required offenders to attend treatment, to submit to regular urine tests, and to undergo periodic court reviews of progress. It was piloted in 1998 (see Turnbull et al, 2000) and subsequently rolled out nationally.

The prison end of the system also saw developments in the 1990s. A programme of mandatory urine testing was piloted in 1995 under section 151 of the Criminal Justice and Public Order Act 1994 and then extended nationally the following year (Edgar and O'Donnell, 1998; Singleton et al, 2005). In 1999, the CARAT (Counselling, Assessment, Referral, Advice, Throughcare) service was introduced across the entire prison estate, with the aim of ensuring a more consistent response to drug-using prisoners (May, 2005).

Following the piloting of drug testing in police custody suites and within certain parts of probation work from 2001 to 2003 (Mallender et al, 2002; Matrix and Nacro, 2004), a pivotal moment was the introduction in 2003 of what was known initially as the Criminal Justice Interventions Programme (CJIP) and subsequently re-named as the Drug Interventions Programme (DIP). The aims of CJIP/DIP were to bring together the range of drug interventions that had been accumulating up to that point in a relatively piecemeal fashion and to provide more co-ordinated and joined-up provision to drug users going through the criminal justice system. A key mechanism here was the introduction of local Criminal Justice Integrated Teams (CJITs), which were tasked with delivering this co-ordinated case management for drug users going through the system.

In 2006, an extension of the more coercive elements within DIP was launched under the title 'Tough Choices'. This consisted of a set of measures contained in the Drugs Act 2005: the introduction of Testing on Arrest (which had previously been after charge only), the introduction of the Required Assessment (in effect, a type of coerced arrest referral), and the national roll-out of the Restriction on Bail. The 'Tough Choices' measures aimed to curb further the levels of attrition and drop-out between individuals being identified and actually arriving in treatment. A study by the Home Office tentatively indicated it had some impact on this (Skodbo et al, 2007).

The hyperactivity of national policy-makers tailed off at this point and the key elements of DIP have become relatively stable. We summarize its main components below, in order to provide a guide for understanding later chapters where we describe the operation of DIP and related criminal justice interventions.

At the police station

Drug testing

The process begins after an individual has been arrested and brought to the police station for detention in the custody suite. Under section 7 of the Drugs Act 2005 (amending the Police and Criminal Evidence Act 1984), detainees aged 18 or over who have been arrested in relation to a set of offences known as 'trigger offences' are required to undergo a drug test to detect whether they have opiates and/or cocaine in their body. Refusing to be tested without good cause is a criminal offence carrying a maximum penalty of three months' imprisonment and/or a fine of £2,500. The list of 'trigger offences' was initially set out in the Criminal Justice and Court Services Act 2000 but has since been amended and added to by subsequent legislative orders. Broadly, they include the types of acquisitive crimes believed to be connected to the use of heroin and/or crack. The list in operation throughout most of our fieldwork period is set out in Table 1.1 below (see also appendix one).

In addition, where an individual has been arrested for a non-trigger offence and brought to the police station, they may be required to be tested if an officer of at least the rank of inspector believes that their use of Class A drugs may have caused or contributed to their alleged offence. This is known as testing under 'inspectors' discretion' or 'inspectors' authority'. As we will see, in practice, this discretionary power has been little used.

Table 1.1 'Trigger offences'

Act	Offence
Theft Act 1968	Theft (section 1) [plus attempts] Robbery (section 8) [plus attempts] Burglary (section 9) [plus attempts] Aggravated burglary (section 10) Taking motor vehicle (section 12) Aggravated vehicle-taking (section 12A) Handling stolen goods (section 22) [plus attempts] Going equipped for stealing (section 25)
Misuse of Drugs Act 1971	In respect of Class A drugs only: Production and supply (section 4) Possession (section 5(2)) Possession with intent to supply (section 5(3))
Fraud Act 2006	Fraud (section 1) [plus attempts] Possession of articles for use in frauds (section 6) Making or supplying articles for use in frauds (section 7)
Vagrancy Act 1824	Begging (section 3) Persistent begging (section 4)

Required Assessment

For those detainees who test positive for opiates and/or cocaine, sections 9 and 10 of the Drugs Act 2005 provide a power for the police to require them to attend an assessment with a drugs worker (see appendix two). Failure to attend, or to stay for the duration of the assessment, is a criminal offence, again punishable by imprisonment and/or a fine. Usually, this initial assessment will take place in the police custody suite during the period of detention but where this is not possible an appointment may be made for the assessment to be conducted at a later time.

At the conclusion of the initial assessment, the worker may decide that a further follow-up assessment is required and will make an appointment with the local CJIT. The same requirements to attend and stay for the duration of this assessment apply, along with the same penalties for failure to do so without good cause.

At court

Some of those tested on arrest will not be charged and so drop out of the criminal justice process at that point. Any continuing contact with a community drug-treatment service from this point on will be on a voluntary basis outside DIP. Those who are charged with an offence and taken to court may enter the next stage within DIP. Interventions at this point can be divided between pre- and post-sentence.

Pre-sentence: the Restriction on Bail

Some defendants who are charged and taken to court may be dealt with on their first appearance, for example if a guilty plea is entered and the appropriate sentence or disposal is straightforward. For these individuals, the post-sentence DIP arrangements described below may apply. For others, the courts will need to make a decision about whether to grant court bail or to remand in custody. Here, under powers introduced by section 19 of the Criminal Justice Act 2003 (amending the Bail Act 1976), where a defendant has tested positive on arrest, the court must take this into account in considering bail (see appendix three). More specifically, section 19 introduces for these defendants a reversal of the usual presumption in favour of bail, unless they agree to attend an assessment and participate in any recommended follow-up treatment. If they do agree, this then becomes a condition of their bail.

The purpose of the Restriction on Bail is to reduce the problem of offending on bail by ensuring that those defendants who have been identified as drug-using offenders are either channelled into community treatment (if bail is granted) or else remanded in custody. It also tests out whether they are likely to comply with a post-sentence treatment requirement, with this compliance information feeding into sentencing decisions.

Post-sentence: the Drug Rehabilitation Requirement

As already mentioned, the DTTO, a flagship of the criminal justice turn in the late 1990s, was restyled as the DRR under sections 209–211 in the Criminal Justice Act 2003, with the new arrangements coming into force for offences committed from April 2005 onwards. The DRR is one of 12 requirements that can be attached to a basic community sentence (other requirements include curfews, unpaid work, and residence restrictions). The requirement can be applied where the court is satisfied that an offender is drug dependent or has a propensity to misuse drugs and would benefit from treatment.

It includes both treatment and regular testing and the offender's progress is subject to periodic review by the court.

Strictly speaking, and for reasons that we explore further in chapter three, the DRR lies outside the DIP. The management of offenders on DRRs is the responsibility of probation rather than of CJITs. As we will see in later chapters, this poses some challenges for local practice in terms of providing a co-ordinated response to this group.

In prison

Many drug-using offenders end up in prison at some point. Here, their first point of contact should be with a worker from the CARAT service, mentioned above, who should carry out an assessment, offer relevant advice, and make referrals to other provision (see May, 2005). What other provision is available varies across prisons but includes clinical services (detoxification and maintenance prescribing), drug-free wings and rehabilitation programmes of various kinds (including therapeutic communities, 12-step programmes, and cognitive behavioural therapy). On release from prison, drug-using offenders should be contacted by CJITs or probation (if released on licence) to ensure 'continuity of care' post-release and, in particular, to address the serious problem for heroin users of the heightened risk of overdosing at this point (Farrell and Marsden, 2005). The Integrated Drug Treatment System (IDTS) was introduced in selected prisons in 2006 with the aim of enhancing and better integrating drug treatment and case management within prisons.

The picture then is of considerable expansion of drug-related provision within prisons since 1999, but building on a very low base indeed. An important review chaired by Lord Patel found that considerable shortcomings still exist (Patel, 2010), notably in terms of addressing the challenge of connecting what happens in prisons with what happens in the community. The prison end of the system remains problematic from a policy and practice perspective.

Our research study

The main study on which this book is based was carried out over the course of two and a half years between 2007 and 2009. Its general objective was to examine a specific area of British crime policy in order to explore how broader transitions in governance have played out in a particular field. Our research design was based on the principle that to address these concerns required a micro-macro study. To see the 'big picture' more richly and in a more nuanced way, we needed to see how it was constituted in interactions in practice on the ground, as well as how it was described in the 'blueprints' of government, such as policy documents. Accordingly, we designed a multi-level mixed-methods study.

The first main strand of the study looked at national policymaking. We collected a range of national policy documentation for analysis, including government strategies and action plans, parliamentary proceedings and reports, government press releases, policy guidance, and circulars. We also carried out nearly 30 interviews with senior individuals involved in, or knowledgeable about, policy-making in this area, for example officials in the Home Office and Department of Health, ministerial advisers, and national drug policy campaigners.

The second main strand involved in-depth case studies of practice in three local sites: site A, a city in the Midlands; site B, a mixed area in northern England, containing a mix of small towns and more rural parts; and site C, a large city in northern England. In each of these three sites, we analysed operational data, interviewed service managers and practitioners from a range of agencies (eg drug treatment, police, probation, magistrates), interviewed drug users, and conducted sustained *in situ* observations (in police stations, magistrates' courts, and treatment agencies). Our focus in these local sites was primarily on activities and practice in the community rather than within prisons, although we touched on certain prison-related issues, notably in terms of what has been called 'throughcare and aftercare', that is transitions into and out of prison. The rationale for this focus was largely on two pragmatic grounds. First, the main thrust of the policy developments in this area concerned the police, the courts, and probation, rather than the Prison Service. Our interest in policy inevitably pulled us away from looking too closely at prisons. Second, the issues for prisons and prisoners are sufficiently distinctive and complex that they merit, indeed require, a dedicated research study.

In total, we carried out over 220 interviews (including 77 with drug users), coded and analysed over 150 documents, and did nearly 80 hours of observation in criminal justice and drug-treatment sites. This wealth of empirical material is drawn on throughout this book. In addition, the book is also informed more generally by the first author's earlier involvement in the evaluations of the piloting of the Restriction on Bail provision (see Hucklesby et al, 2005, 2007) and of drug testing (see Mallender et al, 2002), as well as his work in the 1990s on drugs and criminal justice (see Dorn et al, 1994; Baker et al, 1994; Seddon, 1996; Dorn and Seddon, 1996).

Outline of the book

The rest of this book is organized as follows. In chapter two, we set out our theoretical framework for the book, which makes up the intellectual fabric for the whole. The framework aims to provide a set of tools for explaining why the criminal justice turn emerged in British drug policy at this time and why it has taken on the particular forms that it has. In chapter three, we examine the origins and development of this new direction in policy at the national level, through an analysis of policy documentation and of interviews we conducted with senior policy actors in the field. In chapters four, five, and six, we move on to look at how this policy turn has shaped practice on the ground, drawing primarily on our three local sites. Each of these three chapters focuses on a particular aspect of practice: chapter four on drug testing; chapter five on how coercion or criminal justice leverage works; and chapter six on how drug workers manage information and knowledge. Chapter seven then considers the impact of the criminal justice turn. We define 'impact' here in a broad sense. Lastly, chapter eight brings together the central arguments of the book and revisits the question of what this all tells us about the nature of social control and of the governance of security in the early twenty-first century.

2

Risk, Security, and the Criminal Justice Turn

[The Drug Interventions Programme] aims to break the destructive cycle of drugs, offending and prison […] It provides an opportunity for everyone to win: drug-misusing offenders get help through treatment and support, communities suffer less crime and the taxpayer saves money as criminal justice costs are reduced.

[Home Office, 2006a]

It's a nice simplistic thing, the government loves black-and-white things. It's the drugs causes the crime, so we force them to have treatment and all the crime will go away. So we've had DIP for how many years now, about five, and we've got more people in prison than we've ever had before, proportionately more than any country in Europe. So that's obviously doing really well!

[Senior manager, voluntary sector drug agency]

Introduction

In the previous chapter, we outlined the contours of the transformation that has taken place in British drug policy—in a nutshell, the 'criminal justice turn'. While commentators either oppose (Stimson, 2000) or support (Hough, 2001) the broad thrust of this transformation, little attention has been paid to providing explanatory accounts of why it has happened. A contribution by Duke (2006) is largely descriptive rather than explanatory. Probably the main substantial effort to date has been by Stevens (2007, 2011a) who develops an account that emphasizes the role of politics and ideology in policy-making in the drugs and crime field, concluding that the claims that underpin the criminal justice turn serve the interests of 'powerful groups'. While this is insightful up to a point, in our view, it too ultimately fails as an explanation. This is partly because of a certain vagueness about exactly who these 'powerful groups' are and precisely how they pursue their interests through policy-making. But also, and in common with many sociological explanations, Stevens tends to imply that policy can be directly deduced from these 'interests of the powerful', whereas we suggest that in fact it is possible to imagine a number of rather different programmes that might be deemed to serve that purpose. We need to be able to say something about why *this* particular programme emerged at *this* specific time. Our task then in this chapter is to provide the tools for developing an explanation that can better articulate this relationship between the general and the particular.

We pose the question in this form: why has the drug–crime link come in recent decades to be the principal lens through which the drug problem is viewed? This chapter attempts to set out a framework for answering this by situating this transformation in the drug field in the context of wider social change (Mugford, 1993) and shifts in social control over the last 30 or 40 years. The latter terrain has perhaps been most significantly explored by David Garland (2001) in *The Culture of Control* and we draw on his account here, as well as those of some of his critics, notably Loader and Sparks (2004). But, as we have already suggested, the 'big picture' of social change provides only part of an explanation.

A useful starting point is to think about some of the explanatory possibilities, in the broadest terms. It could be, for example, that the nature of the drug problem has changed in recent decades and that the criminal justice turn is explicable largely as a response to this new situation. Alternatively, we might understand the shift in drug policy as primarily related to wider transformations in social control strategies, largely unrelated to any change in the drug situation. This raises the thorny question of the relationship between problems 'in the real', problematizations, and policy responses. A sequence derived from Garland (2001) offers quite a helpful way of thinking about this. Broad patterns of social change often have an impact on the nature of existing 'problems' as well as throwing up new ones. They generate 'new risks, insecurities and opportunities' (Garland, 2004: 171). The same social transformations, then, also shape the ways in which these 'real' changes to the problem landscape are understood and 'imagined', leading to new 'problematizations' that pose novel 'policy predicaments'. Responses to these predicaments are, in turn, also moulded by this bigger picture of social change.

This sequence implies that we will need to explore two broad sets of questions. First, how has social change reshaped the nature of the threats seen to constitute the 'drug problem'? Secondly, how have these new challenges been adapted to? We need to investigate policy change as a package of governmental adaptations both to a new construction of the 'drug problem' and the new politics of drug control to which this construction has given rise (Garland, 2001: xi). In other words, we attempt to show that what may appear to be a puzzling turn taken by contemporary British drug policy can be understood in the wider context of the social, economic, cultural, and political forces that have shaped its emergence. As will become clear, and following Loader and Sparks (2004), we will place a rather stronger emphasis on the realm of the 'political' than Garland does.

The main body of this chapter is structured then as follows. We begin by describing how the structural, cultural, and political transformations of the last three decades—in short, the transition to neo-liberalism—have profoundly reshaped the nature of what is described as the 'drug problem' in Britain. In crude summary, more drugs are being consumed by wider groups of people and what are perceived as drug-related problems have also escalated (although the latter are still primarily concentrated in a very small minority of users). We then argue that this refigured drug experience has led to a new 'problematization'—drugs are both 'everywhere' and deeply problematic—which has presented a new drug policy predicament. The criminal justice turn is, in part, an adaptation or response to this new predicament. The form that this adaptation has taken, with its focus on risk and security, has in turn itself been shaped and structured in part by the wider shift to neo-liberalism but, at the same time, has also been a product of *political* struggle.

The emergence of a new drug policy predicament

The drug situation in early twenty-first-century Britain would be almost unrecognizable to an observer from even 30 years ago. The 1980s and 1990s, in particular, saw dramatic changes, as charted by a series of studies (eg Pearson, 1987a; Parker et al, 1988, 1998a, 1998b). Pinpointing the beginnings of changes of this kind is always difficult but we can perhaps detect the early traces of these transformations as far back as the 1950s. Lyle (1953), for example, noted a sharp upturn in prosecutions for cannabis offences in London at the start of that decade. In an interesting account, he describes a police raid in April 1950 on Club 11 in Carnaby Street, which found among the 200 or so young patrons a drug haul that included cannabis, cocaine, morphine, and prepared opium. He goes on to catalogue other similar raids across the West End of London. We might perhaps understand what Lyle is describing here as the start of what would be seen today as a youth drug subculture, although at this stage it was very small indeed and almost entirely London-based.

It was in the first half of the 1960s that this nascent trend developed and accelerated in a significant way. The use of amphetamines under a variety of names—from 'pep pills' to 'purple hearts'—spread as part of youth music culture (Hebdige, 1975). Heroin and cocaine use also became more common during the course of the decade (Bewley, 1965, 1966; Spear, 1969). The total number of heroin addicts known to the Home Office increased from 68 in 1959 to 342 in 1964 and 2,240 in 1968, indicating a very rapid rate of expansion (Spear, 1969). In 1967, the first non-pharmaceutical illegally imported heroin (known as Chinese heroin) appeared in the West End of London. Arguably, then, the 1960s was the point at which Britain's 'slumbering encounter with drugs' (Pearson, 2001: 55) was shaken into life. Yet Pearson (2001) encourages us to put these developments in some perspective. Even by the end of the decade, the heroin scene, for example, was still very small in absolute numbers, largely confined to London and associated mainly with a bohemian underground community of musicians, students, and middle-class 'drop-outs'. It was, at most, a regional 'mini-epidemic'.

It would be a decade later that Britain's drug problem was truly transformed in scale, extent, and nature. Starting in 1979, but taking off properly in the first couple of years of the 1980s, cheap heroin from Iran, Pakistan, and Afghanistan suddenly became available in several towns and cities in northern England and Scotland that had no previous heroin history (Ditton and Speirits, 1981; Haw, 1985; Pearson et al, 1986; Parker et al, 1988; Fazey et al, 1990). In contrast to their predecessors, the new heroin users were mainly young and unemployed and came from the most deprived housing estates and neighbourhoods (Pearson, 1987b), often supporting their new habits through involvement in acquisitive crime and drug dealing (Parker and Newcombe, 1987). The heroin 'epidemic' quickly came to be seen as a major social problem at a national level. Indeed, some commentators saw it as evidence of the more general urban malaise induced in the former industrial heartlands of northern England by Thatcherite social and economic policy (Peck and Plant, 1986). The discovery at the end of 1985 of the high prevalence of HIV among injecting drug users (see Robertson, 2005) cemented the feeling that Britain was now in the grip of a major and grave drug problem. From this point on, it rose significantly up the political agenda, attracting increased government funding and more and more policy attention.

In the 1990s, the drug situation in Britain underwent further significant changes. New outbreaks of heroin further spread its geographical reach across the country (Parker et al, 1998b), while crack cocaine started to enter into the repertoire of some drug users (Brain et al, 1998). But perhaps the most significant transformation occurred in the area of the everyday experiences and encounters of young people with drugs. In a series of publications, Howard Parker and colleagues set out a challenging new set of claims (Measham et al, 1994; Parker et al, 1995, 1998a, 2002; Williams and Parker, 2001; Aldridge et al, 2011). Drawing on a longitudinal study of young people in the north-west of England, they argued that the availability of drugs and levels of experimentation significantly increased in the late twentieth century, to the point that certain kinds of 'sensible' recreational drug use, primarily but not solely cannabis smoking, have become commonplace rather than exceptional, cutting across social class, gender, and, to some degree, ethnic lines. Today's young people, they argued, are 'drugwise' to an unprecedented degree, with nearly half trying drugs at least once and many more having contact with drugs even if they themselves do not take them. They coined the term 'normalization' to describe this transformation.

The normalization thesis has been controversial in some quarters and remains contested (Shiner and Newburn, 1997, 1999; Blackman, 2007; Shiner, 2009). At the very least, however, Parker and his colleagues make a powerful case that drugs (or at least certain drugs) have become a more common part of young people's lives than before. As South (1999: 6) puts it, 'something profound has happened in relation to the place of drugs in everyday life since the mid-1980s', even if that 'something' might be better characterized by a term other than 'normalization'. Perhaps the most significant point, as Parker (2005a) observes, is that we can no longer really talk about young people's drug experiences in terms of pathology or 'deviance' as would have been the case in the 1960s, for example. The theme of 'exceptionality', which South (1999: 8–11) suggests has dominated drug policy discourses for a long time, no longer fits very well with young people's experiences in contemporary Britain.

So how might we understand these shifts in the drug situation in the wider context of social change during this period? There are two key dynamics that are critical here: globalization and consumption. One way to understand the transformed *availability* of drugs on the streets of Britain—from a tiny network of bohemian individuals in 1950s London to widespread availability across the entire country in the first decade of the twenty-first century—is in terms of broader globalizing processes. The extension and expansion of global flows and networks of people, money, and commodities has been viewed as one of the defining features of the late twentieth century. We should be cautious about overstating the novelty of globalization, as we can trace this back over a much longer history than we might imagine (see Held et al, 1999: 16–20). The economist Jeffrey Sachs (2000: 579) identifies the period from 1870 to 1914 as the first long phase of globalization, a period famously described by John Maynard Keynes as an 'extraordinary episode in the economic progress of man' (Keynes, 1920: 11). Indeed, there is even a case to be made that in the domain of trade the extent of globalization during that period outstripped what we see today (Thompson, 2000: 97–102). Nevertheless, many agree that globalizing processes have developed with a distinctive intensity and rapidity in recent decades (Bauman, 1998).

Globalization has had a profound impact on the transformed British drug situation that we have described. To take the example of the heroin 'epidemic' in the early 1980s, Pearson (1987b: 66) argues this was only possible because of the opening up of new supply routes from south-west Asia from 1979, which made brown smokeable heroin suddenly available in cheap and plentiful supply. In basic terms, the infrastructural developments that have facilitated the trading of *licit* goods in recent decades, namely the enormous improvements in transport and communications networks, have at the same time made it considerably easier to trade *illicit* ones (McGrew, 2000: 129). Opium grown in the fields of Afghanistan today ends up as heroin on the streets of cities right across the globe, from Paris to Cape Town, from London to Lagos. Similarly, coca produced in Columbia is consumed as cocaine or crack right around the world. The trading routes along which these drugs travel so speedily and efficiently are underpinned and facilitated by these infrastructural improvements (Friman, 2004). Today, the global drug trade has become a vast transnational business worth billions (Reuter and Greenfield, 2001; Kilmer and Pacula, 2009). A market of this size and scale obviously requires the ability to hold, transfer, and exchange money, both within and across nation-state borders. Furthermore, as an illegal and cash-intensive market, the ability to launder money—to hide its illicit source and make it appear legitimate in origin—is essential. The increased global flows of finance that have been another central characteristic of globalization have thus been equally essential to the transformation of the British drug situation. As a result of advances in communications and information technology, coupled with the liberalization of national and international financial controls, real-time near-instantaneous financial transactions are now possible 24 hours a day right across the world and at low cost (Held et al, 1999: 213–14).

We can situate then the significant reshaping of the British drug experience since the 1960s in the wider context of social change during this period, notably the extension and expansion of global flows of trade and finance. But this is not the whole story. Economies in many developed countries have also seen over the last few decades another fundamental shift: the transition from production to consumption. This has involved profound cultural as well as economic changes. In their important book setting out their normalization thesis, *Illegal Leisure*, Parker and his colleagues locate the new experience and place of drugs in the lives of young people that they describe in precisely this context of a new experience of adolescence and young adulthood in which consumption has achieved a cultural and economic centrality (Parker et al, 1998a: 21–31; see also: Miles, 1998, 2000; van Ree, 2002). The conspicuous consumption of commodities for the purpose of pleasure, including drugs and alcohol, has become part of how young people create and establish their identities (Miles, 2000; Jones, 2004). This, too, has had a globalizing dimension. Indeed, the homogenization of culture—symbolized in the worldwide pervasiveness and ubiquity of consumer brands like Coca-Cola and McDonalds—is perhaps central to popular understandings of what globalization means. As Held et al (1999: 327) put it, 'there is no historical equivalent of the global reach and volume of cultural traffic through contemporary telecommunication, broadcasting and transport infrastructures'. This 'cultural traffic' has served, in part, to create new sets of assumptions about leisure and standards of living.

The new primacy of consumption has not been restricted just to 'mainstream' youth either. As Jock Young (1999, 2002, 2003b) has argued in a series of contributions, those at the sharpest end of social exclusion, rather than rejecting this consumer culture, actually seem to embrace it with particular fervour. Consumption, and the accumulation of conspicuous indicators of consumption, can be seen as a way out of the 'ghetto'. Collison (1996: 431), for example, describes how the drug-using offenders in his study wanted to be 'super-consumers'. According to Young, there is, however, an anomic disjunction between this cultural inclusion in the consumer 'dream' and the structural exclusion of certain groups from opportunities to achieve it. Participation and engagement in the informal economy, in which drugs circulate alongside other goods and services, becomes a means for some to resolve this conflict. In this sense, the expansion in the global flow of consumer brands and symbols, from Nike trainers to Gucci watches, adds to the pressures in deprived localities to become involved in the informal economy and, consequently, in many cases with illegal drugs (Seddon, 2008a).

In this way, we can locate shifts in the British drug situation over the last 30 years in the context of wider social, economic, and cultural transformations during the period. What challenges though has this transformed drug experience posed for policy-makers? At the heart of the predicament is the perception that 'drugs' are now pervasive in society and particularly among young people from across the social class spectrum, becoming embedded in leisure activities involving youth from diverse backgrounds (Thornton, 1995; Measham et al, 2001). This is central to the idea of normalization. At the same time, serious drug problems have become interwoven with some apparently intractable social issues, such as high crime rates and neighbourhood deprivation. This presents a dangerous political cocktail, rooted partly in the undifferentiated way in which 'drugs' tends to be deployed as a signifier in policy discourse, covering everything from cannabis to crack cocaine. 'Drugs', as defined in this broad sense, are both everywhere *and* deeply problematic. This, in a nutshell, is the new drug policy predicament in late-modern Britain that has structured and constrained the 'policy horizon in which all decisions must be made' (Garland, 2001: 105).

We can see evidence for the political salience of this predicament throughout the last 30 years. Take, for instance, the heroin 'epidemic' in the 1980s, described above. This rapidly became the focus of significant mass media attention, not only in the popular press but also in broadsheet newspapers (see Stimson, 1987; MacGregor, 1989; Kohn, 1987: 119). At the same time, it was a focus for policy action as well. In 1984, a cross-departmental Ministerial Group on Drug Misuse was set up, chaired by Home Office minister David Mellor, which eventually produced the first ever national drug strategy in Britain, *Tackling Drug Misuse*. The previous year, the Central Funding Initiative (CFI) had been initiated, which provided around £17 million for local drug services between 1983 and 1989 (Mold and Berridge, 2007). The apparent 'normalization' of youth recreational drug use uncovered by Parker et al (1998a) and the emergence of a drug-oriented dance culture (Measham et al, 2001) provoked a new round of media attention from the late 1980s onwards (see Blackman, 2007), bringing the drug policy predicament further to the forefront of political concerns. The 1990s saw a raft of major policy developments, including two further national drug strategies—*Tackling Drugs Together* in 1995 and then *Tackling Drugs to Build a Better Britain* in 1998—as well as the establishment of local multi-agency Drug Action Team partnerships across the country. As we will see in chapter three, as Prime Minister between 1997 and 2007, Tony Blair took an extremely close interest in drug policy, at times driving it more strongly than any of the ostensibly responsible government departments. The policy predicament has certainly been keenly felt by policy-makers in the last three decades.

The new culture of drug control

So faced with this policy predicament, 'drugs' has risen sharply up the political and policy agenda, even attracting strong and sustained prime ministerial interest. But how exactly have policy-makers responded to this predicament and how can we understand these responses? As we will outline below, we suggest, adapting Garland (2001), that one way to understand them is as constituting the emergence of a new culture of drug control involving a 'reworked pattern of cognitive assumptions, normative commitments, and emotional sensibilities' (Garland, 2001: 175).

The rise of risk

The conventional narrative for analysts of British drug policy is that after a period of policy stagnation in the 1970s, the last three decades have seen two distinct phases (see Stimson, 2000): first, from the mid-1980s to the mid-1990s, a public health or 'harm reduction' approach, particularly focused on efforts to prevent the spread of HIV such as, for example, the development of needle-exchange schemes (ACMD, 1988); second, from the mid-1990s, an emphasis on crime and the development of drug interventions in the criminal justice system. Most recently, there have been some indications that under the coalition government formed in 2010, we may be entering a third phase in which drug policy is strongly shaped by welfare reform concerns, that is the desire to shift individuals off social security benefits and into employment, although it is too early to say whether this will turn out to be a sustained or significant development (see Wincup, 2011).

Contrary to this narrative, we will argue here that there is a strong continuity that runs through British drug policy from the 1980s to the present and that these two (or three) phases can be better understood as variations within the same basic policy paradigm. A first reason to doubt the standard account is a simple chronological one. We might note, for example, that the policy interest in drug-related crime can be traced back long before the election of New Labour in 1997. For instance, action research projects to establish referral schemes for drug users arrested and held in police stations began as early as 1986 (Dorn et al, 1990; Dorn, 1994), coinciding with the pioneering needle-exchange pilot projects of the mid-1980s. The influential Advisory Council on the Misuse of Drugs, an expert body set up to advise government, also produced three important reports on criminal justice in the first half of the 1990s (ACMD, 1991, 1994, 1996). It is hard, then, to sustain the conventional narrative. The criminal justice turn developed in parallel with the public health or harm reduction approach, rather than following it (Seddon et al, 2008).

So what alternative account might we construct? Using the lens of risk helps us here. There is a long history of viewing drug users as a threat or danger to society. Kohn's book *Dope Girls* provides an insightful account of how anxieties about race and gender in the early decades of the twentieth century became intertwined with new conceptions of drug users as sources of social threat (Kohn, 1992; Seddon, 2008b). But in the late 1960s, we start to see these conceptions mutate in a subtle but significant way as the idea of 'danger' (a characteristic of individuals) gives way to that of 'risk' (a set of factors applying across a population) (see Castel, 1991).

In our view, we can see the first signs of this new way of framing the drug problem in the mid-1960s. The second report of the Interdepartmental Committee on Drug Addiction, known as the second Brain Report after its chairman Sir Russell Brain, described addiction as a 'socially infectious disease' requiring monitoring, surveillance, and containment (Ministry of Health, 1965). This phrase looks both back to the past and forward to the future. Alluding to the idea of 'disease' harked back to Brain's predecessor, the Rolleston Report from the 1920s, which famously described addiction as a 'manifestation of disease and not as a mere form of vicious indulgence' (Ministry of Health, 1926). More importantly for our purposes here, the notion of a 'socially infectious disease' reframes the drug problem as a question of the management of risk. We argue that this has gone on to become the dominant way of thinking about the matter over the last 40 or so years. So we have seen the drug problem recast as a matter of risk factors—whether in relation to a metaphorical 'social disease' (as in the Brain formulation), a real disease (during the HIV scare in the 1980s), criminal victimization (in the criminal justice turn), or, most recently, welfare dependency and joblessness.

The emergence of this type of risk-oriented strategy became most pronounced in the early 1980s, notably in the policy known as harm reduction, in which preventing drug-related harms (eg overdose, contracting blood-borne viruses through sharing injecting equipment) came to be prioritized over preventing drug use itself. Illustrating this connection between the notions of risk and harm, in some of its earliest incarnations, the term 'risk reduction' was used interchangeably with 'harm reduction' (Newcombe, 1992: 2). Typically, this development has been viewed as a consequence of the discovery of the HIV threat in 1985. However, as Mold and Berridge (2007) observe, it is more accurate to say that its roots were in place a little before this. The CFI, mentioned above, which was announced in late 1982, provided for a proliferation of drug services of various kinds and marked a move away from the narrower medical model of the previous 60 years towards a more multi-disciplinary and social approach. It was in this context, and *before* the advent of concerns about HIV, that the risk-oriented harm reduction approach first developed: 'The multiplicity and diversity of institutional sites enabled the rapid development of a new discourse on drug problems, which came to be seen as "harm minimization"' (Stimson and Lart, 2005: 182). In viewing drug users as potential sources of harm, to be managed and controlled, we see the notion of risk becoming a key organizing principle in the field. It is notable that around the same time as Russell Newcombe's pioneering article on harm reduction in the drug field appeared in 1987, so too commentators more generally were making the first sightings of risk-based practices across diverse fields—the original German-language version of Ulrich Beck's landmark book *Risk Society* was published in 1986, for example, and a series of highly influential papers on risk appeared between 1986 and 1988 (Reichman, 1986; Simon, 1987, 1988). A short but insightful paper by Mugford (1993) was one of the few contributions at the time to see this connection between the emergence of harm reduction within drug policy and the wider 'rise of risk' within neo-liberal societies. Building on Mugford's early contribution, others, such as O'Malley (2004: 155–71), have also argued that there is a close affinity between the concepts of 'harm' and 'risk' in the government of drug users.

We can develop this a little further by looking more closely at this affinity. A key point is to understand the *distinctive* ways in which risk technologies are deployed. Dean (1999: 133–4) offers a useful summary of some of the particular characteristics of contemporary risk technologies:

[The] 'individualization of risk' is a key index of a retraction of the social-ized risk-management techniques associated with the welfare state and the emergence of new forms of governing in contemporary liberal-democratic states [...] The individualization of risk [...] is linked to a form of govern-ing that seeks to govern not through society but through the responsible and prudential choices and actions of individuals on behalf of themselves and those for whom they feel an emotional bond.

For Dean, neo-liberal risk technologies are no longer socialized and instead operate through individual choices. The goal of inter-ventions is to generate the conditions under which the behaviour of drug users is more likely to move in desired directions, by enabling and encouraging them to act prudentially. We can see here more clearly the affinity between harm reduction interventions (eg the provision of needle-exchange services) and the criminal justice interventions (eg making attendance at a drug treatment service a condition of bail). Both are based on a shared problematization (drug users as threats to the community), a shared conception of drug-using subjects (rational choice-makers), and a shared strategic response (urging, enjoining, and enabling responsible choice-making to reduce risk). We might note, too, the significance in this respect of the very name 'Tough Choices' given to the extension of the Drug Interventions Programme in 2005. More broadly, as Garland (2001: 198) observes, writing about crime control, to the extent that these strategies of 'responsibilization' rely on manipulating the costs and benefits associated with different choices, they have particular resonance with wider contemporary political understandings about citizen-subjects: 'Accounts that highlight rational choice and the responsiveness of offenders to rewards and disincentives chime with today's common sense and with the individualistic morality of our consumer culture.'

So the criminal justice turn can be understood as the latest iteration of a risk-oriented strategy traceable as far back as the 1960s but that emerged most strongly from the 1980s in response to the new policy predicament that we outlined earlier. This may be viewed as a provocative and controversial thesis by some. As we have argued above, it points towards a very strong conceptual or thematic consistency between harm reduction (seen by many as 'progressive' and welfare-oriented) and the criminal justice approach (seen by many as 'regressive' and punitive in orientation). But, in our view, locating developments in drug policy in this bigger picture of social change is a vital first step in our explanatory account, as it provides a vantage point from which we can see connections of this kind that otherwise remain hidden from our gaze.

The big picture, however, is obviously insufficient as a mode of explanation for policy. Simply to diagnose drug policy as becoming risk-oriented in response to a new policy predicament does not tell us on its own very much about the exact form it may take at any given moment, as Richard Sparks observes in relation to penal policy:

Even if it is true [...] that today major political arguments take place *on the terrain of risk*, it in no way follows that we can know in advance how those arguments will turn out, still less that they will turn out identically in different national-political settings [...] We can, for this reason, no more deduce the contemporary condition of the penal realm from a totalising idea such as the 'risk society' than we formerly could from an undifferentiated notion of 'capitalism', though both can be seen as crucial to its analysis.

[Sparks, 2001: 161–2, emphasis in original]

Looking at the big picture can only help us to unearth the underlying generative structure in which policy is based, rather than explaining its exact form. To do this, we suggest, requires consideration of the role and significance of *politics* and it is to this that we now turn.

The politics of drug control

The idea that the drug field is particularly susceptible to politicization and political manipulation has, of course, considerable resonance. Indeed, the criminal justice turn is viewed by many as one of the clearest examples of this, as politicians have sought to tighten the screw on problem drug users by ratcheting up coercive treatment measures for those going through the criminal justice system. The Drugs Act 2005, for example, which contained several criminal justice measures, was rushed through the parliamentary process immediately before the general election that year and was seen by some commentators at the time as the product of exactly this kind of political populism (eg Stevens, 2007). Indeed, the naming of the 'Tough Choices' project described in chapter one, consciously echoed the then British Prime Minister Tony Blair's famous (and profoundly 'political') pledge in the 1990s to be 'tough on crime, tough on the causes of crime' (see Garside, 2003).

But what does 'playing politics' actually mean in the context of drug policy? Drawing on the work of the great anthropologist Mary Douglas, Richard Sparks has argued that terms like 'politics' and 'populism' are generally deployed in policy analysis in 'decidedly thin and unilluminating' ways that are 'not themselves explanations' but rather 'are introduced when explanation fails' (Sparks, 2001: 172)—'wheeled in after other explanations are defeated', as Douglas (1992: 167) puts it. In other words, when a policy development appears not to make 'rational' sense, it is dismissed as the result of politicians 'playing to the gallery'. A more fruitful approach, Sparks argues, is to understand concepts of 'threat' and 'risk' as inherently political notions in which social anxieties and cultural preoccupations are embedded. So instances of 'politicization' are not only to be expected but also may tell us much about the organization and values of particular communities or societies.

This suggests some important lines of enquiry for us to follow. From this perspective, we would expect that the construction of particular aspects of the drug experience as 'threats' or 'risks' would be shaped by the prevailing cultural preoccupations of that time. Following Garland (2006), we see the 'cultural' as referring to a distinctive dimension of social relations that concerns attitudes, values, meanings, sensibilities, and so on. The politics of drug policy, in this sense, refers to the ways in which the policy-making process interacts with, reflects, and reproduces these wider cultural meanings.

So how can we understand the criminal justice turn in relation to this notion of cultural preoccupations? The idea of a risk-based response of course presupposes that a certain type or category of risk has been identified as requiring or deserving governmental attention. The question of risk identification or selection is therefore fundamental. A 'realist' view holds that risk selection is a neutral and rational process, involving an objective assessment of probabilities and of the scale of harms. It is from this perspective 'obvious' that we will be most concerned about the gravest risks and dangers we face. Cultural theories of risk, on the other hand, take a radically different view, claiming that in fact we actively 'choose the classes of dangerous events and harms that we worry about' (Hacking, 2003: 22). In their study of ecological and environmental dangers, Douglas and Wildavsky (1982) coined the concept of 'risk portfolios' to capture this notion that risk selection is an active, political, and cultural process. They argue that the portfolio of risks about which societies are concerned changes markedly over time and differs from place to place. In Douglas's (1992) view, this process of assembling the risk portfolio is a means through which communities or societies create boundaries between what is culturally acceptable and what is threatening. Douglas and Wildavsky argue that changing risk portfolios can therefore be partly understood in terms of shifts in social arrangements:

The choice of risks to worry about depends on the social forms selected. The choice of risks and the choice of how to live are taken together. Each form of social life has its own typical risk portfolio. Common values lead to common fears [...] Risk taking and risk aversion, shared confidence and shared fears, are part of the dialogue on how best to organize social relations.

[Douglas and Wildavsky, 1982: 8]

What then are these shared or common fears that have been shaping this new construction of the 'risk portfolio'? A series of important works by criminologists have suggested that in recent decades there has been a new cultural formation in which anxieties about crime and insecurity have risen to the fore. David Garland's (2001) *The Culture of Control* is perhaps the first and most influential account of this idea. Two more recent books, by Richard Ericson (2007) and Jonathan Simon (2007) respectively, offer further insights. Ericson argues that it is a distinctive feature of neo-liberalism to place the promise of security, in the sense of freedom for citizens from harms, at the heart of its governmental vision. The paradox of security, however, is the problem of uncertainty, that is, our limited ability to know what will happen in the future. In the face of this paradox, he argues, the tendency is towards more criminalization and the intensification of surveillance. In this view, the criminal justice turn in drug policy might be understood as connected with this broader 'neo-liberal search for security in the face of uncertainty as the basic condition of human knowledge' (Ericson, 2007: 30). Similarly, Simon (2007) argues that with the collapse in the late 1960s of the 'social model' of governing, we have moved in recent years increasingly towards a strategy of 'governing through crime', in which the exercise of power and authority across diverse fields is built around the category of crime and metaphors of crime. Again, from this perspective, the contemporary policy obsession with the drug–crime link is another example of this more general shift. Taken together, this criminological trilogy can help us to explain how anxieties about crime have led not only to the 'heating up' of penal policy but also to the 'criminalization' of social policy more broadly (Rodger, 2008). Viewed in this light, we can better understand the politics of drug policy, not in terms of populism or 'playing to the gallery', but rather as embodying and relaying these contemporary cultural preoccupations with crime and insecurity.

Ericson's foregrounding of the idea of security points us towards some further ways of understanding the politics of drug policy. In the international relations literature, and particularly the work of the Copenhagen School (see Buzan et al, 1998), the idea of securitization refers to the process by which a matter comes to be defined as 'an existential threat, requiring emergency measures and justifying actions outside the normal bounds of political procedure' (Buzan et al, 1998: 24). The emphasis here is on securitization as a political intervention that is achieved through 'speech-acts'. Setting aside its state-centrism, this offers a useful framework for thinking about the emergence and development of the criminal justice turn. The political and discursive construction of certain types of drug users as criminal predators (as discussed by Stevens, 2007) has been used to justify measures that would otherwise lie outside the bounds of normal politics—for example, reversing the standard presumption in favour of bail for defendants who have tested positive for opiates or cocaine, as in the Restriction on Bail provision (Hucklesby et al, 2007). It can be understood, in other words, as an outcome of a securitization process that is fundamentally *political* in nature.

Our appropriation of this idea of securitization might seem to some readers to be stretching its conceptual bounds to breaking point. The Copenhagen School, after all, is really concerned with notions of national security, hence their emphasis on 'existential threats' to the state. Olaf Corry (2012), for example, argues that the type of risk-security logic we explore in this book involves a move to a 'second-order security politics' that is better described by the neologism 'riskification' than simply as a new form of securitization. In terms of analytical precision, Corry is no doubt right to makes this distinction. Nevertheless, in our view, rigidly holding to it may obscure some significant links between these two modes of security politics. In an interesting piece, Richard Sparks (2006) argues that there are important connections between 'states of emergency' and more 'ordinary anxieties' that are critical to any analysis of the 'politics of insecurity' in the early twenty-first century. He suggests that in an increasingly networked and globally interconnected world, distinctions between, on the one hand, national territory and threats to the state and, on the other, threats to local communities or individuals, may be becoming much less clear. As a result, these different levels of threat increasingly come together to create for individual citizens the type of 'ambient fear' that Bauman (1998, 2007) and others (Beck, 2009) see as characteristic of the contemporary social world. In this sense, widening the scope of the concept of 'securitization' may be a helpful way of developing our understanding of the politics of social policy-making, in general, and drug policy-making in particular.

As Valverde (2007, 2011) notes, the connection between these two levels of threat can also be found in Foucault's much earlier discussion of the concept of security in his 1978 lecture course at the Collège de France, published in English as *Security, Territory, Population* (Foucault, 2007). The English word 'security' does not exactly correspond with the French word '*sécurité*', which refers to the 'future-oriented management of risks' (Valverde, 2007: 172). The area of national security, in the sense of the defence of the sovereign, is covered in French by the word *sûreté*. In this light, we might understand the politics of the criminal justice turn in British drug policy as a project of *sécurité* animated by a wider and more diffuse set of anxieties, including, but by no means restricted to, concerns about *sûreté*. To put it another way, the politics of drug control in recent decades has been articulated in relation to this wider nexus between risk and security that has been viewed by many criminological (and other) commentators as a distinctive feature of politics and government over the last 30 or so years.

It is for this reason that we cannot properly understand the political dimension of recent drug policy-making by seeing it in conventional terms of populism or politicians 'playing to the gallery'. Rather, the contemporary politics of drug control has to be set in the context of this more general cultural preoccupation with risk and security. Focusing on the criminal justice turn in recent British drug policy offers us a specific substantive case study of the ways in which this new politics of insecurity is shaping social policy in new directions.

Policy actors

Any discussion of the politics of policy-making, however the idea of politics is theorized or understood, inevitably raises the question of the role of individual policy actors—speech-acts, after all, require a speaker. We argue here that the micro-environments of policy-making are not merely reducible to the playing out of larger structural or cultural forces. Rather, they constitute a significant sphere of action in their own right, which needs to be described and accounted for. It follows that an explanatory account of policy change will need to attempt to generate detailed descriptions of the roles of individuals in the making of policy. This resonates with more conventional historical scholarship, which has often sought to remind us of the significance of individual actors in bringing about change. For these scholars, to explain change over time requires us to investigate the role of specific actors in making decisions and taking action. A similar, albeit less prominent, strand can also be found within the sociological literature. A good example here is Paul Rock's series of micro-sociological studies of criminal justice policy-making (eg Rock, 1995, 1996).

Applied to our study of the criminal justice turn in drug policy, this implies we need to build up a detailed picture of how key actors developed ideas, formulated policies, garnered consensus, managed disagreement, made decisions, and took action. This involves a form of historical inquiry that Loader and Sparks (2004: 12) describe as 'historical recovery'. This type of investigation would draw on two main types of empirical material: analysis of documents (reports, memos, minutes of meetings, strategy documents, action plans, emails, etc) and interviews with policy actors (politicians, civil servants, political advisers, campaigners, policy researchers, etc). To take the example of the 'Tough Choices' initiative, and specifically the question of how it acquired that name, we would seek to uncover, for instance, who first coined the name, what they meant it to convey, what their immediate colleagues thought of it, whether there were any alternatives suggested, how the 'Tough Choices' name prevailed, and so on. This is, in other words, a fairly conventional type of contemporary history, which attempts to piece together the narrative of who did what, when, and where.

But this is not the end of the story. Loader and Sparks (2004), drawing on the work of Quentin Skinner (Skinner, 2002; Tully, 1988), suggest that we can and should aim to go beyond descriptive accounts of the micro-processes of policy-making. Indeed, this is self-evidently essential if we are to *explain* rather than just *describe*. The central insight that Loader and Sparks (2004) take from Skinner is that we should attempt to understand not only what policy actors are saying but also what they are doing in saying it. Skinner's approach to the analysis of politics is founded on the Wittgensteinian notion that 'words are deeds'. He argues that to grasp fully the meaning and significance of political utterances and discourse requires us to pay attention to their character as forms of social action rather than simply as forms of communication. In other words, in our study of policy-making we need to try to uncover something of the motivations and intentions of the range of actors involved in influencing and shaping policy. According to Skinner, this can only be done by looking at the social and political context in which these actors engage in the various negotiations, compromises, and struggles out of which policy is made. Picking up our 'Tough Choices' example again, we would be interested in exploring how different actors interpreted the possibilities and limits presented by the 'political and institutional settings they find themselves operating in' (Loader and Sparks, 2004: 13) and how, as a result, they encoded/decoded keywords like 'tough', 'choices', 'responsibility', 'opportunity', and so on in particular ways. For actors operating within the Home Office, for example, the word 'tough' would no doubt have a distinctive 'meaning-in-use' (Loader and Sparks, 2004: 13), which would not necessarily be the same for actors based in other institutional settings, such as the Department of Health or a national drug treatment provider. It is only through a detailed empirical study of the micro-processes of the making of recent drug policy, drawing on a combination of oral historical enquiry and analysis of documentation, that we can develop this kind of nuanced and fully contextualized understanding of the criminal justice turn.

An integrated explanatory account

The discussion so far has suggested a number of dimensions that our explanatory account needs to encompass. We can think of this framework as having three domains or axes or levels.

(1) There is what is best described as a *macro or structural level*. This refers to the attempt to locate drug policy developments in the wider context of structural shifts in society. So, we have argued that we can understand the criminal justice turn partly as a manifestation of the transition to neo-liberalism and its distinctive risk-based forms of governance.

(2) There is also a *cultural or political* dimension. It is here that we can attempt to understand the politics of drug policy and public discourse about it, both of which have long been recognized as vital parts of the story. We argued that this political dimension should be viewed as referring to how the policy-making process reflects and is shaped by wider cultural concerns, preoccupations, and anxieties.

(3) There is also a more *contingent or micro* dimension. This concerns the role that individual actors play in shaping policy decisions and action. This should offer more than simply a narrative account of 'who did what, when, and where' in the policy-making process (although that descriptive or narrative element is important and interesting in its own right). It should also seek to generate a contextualized account of the motivations and intentions of individual actors involved in influencing or making policy (see Loader and Sparks, 2004: 11–13).

We described these three areas above with deliberate imprecision as domains, axes, or levels. Which of these terms we choose is of some significance. The term 'levels' implies a hierarchical relationship of some kind; 'axes' suggests a set of intersecting relationships operating across different dimensions; while 'domains' carries the idea of relatively autonomous fields in the same plane. The critical question all this points to is this: how can we conceptualize the interplay or relationships between these three aspects of our explanatory framework? This is a complex question. Sociologically minded readers will have noticed that it is a version of one of the thorniest questions within sociology concerning the theory of action: what is the relationship between structure, culture, and agency? We do not claim to have a definitive answer here, although our inclination is to think of structure and culture as setting the boundaries or parameters within which policy actors operate (and for this reason, we slightly favour the term 'axes'), although the relationship is more complex and recursive than that suggests, as we indicate below. David Garland (1990: 128) points to the crux of the matter:

Structures do not work all by themselves, somehow managing to control all the outcomes by automatic means. Instead, it is a matter of decision-making agents [...] who consciously perceive the bounds of political possibility and adjust their actions within them, sometimes struggling to change the rules of the game, more often making compromises with the constraints which they face. This argument suggests that structures are made effective—or are made to change—through the medium of human action and the specific struggles and outcomes which such action will always involve.

In other words, the three areas of our explanatory framework are not entirely separate but are, in fact, interlinked and mutually constitutive. This chimes with Giddens' (1984) well-known theory of structuration in which he argues that structure and agency are two sides of the same coin, rather than separate spheres. In a similar vein, Loader and Sparks (2004) argue for a nuanced reading of the interplay between these domains in which neither the role of individuals nor the realm of culture are reduced to being seen as merely 'epiphenomenal to the master patterns of structural change' (2004: 16). They position the concepts of 'politics' and 'political culture' at the heart of their account of this complex interplay.

We argue that it is here that Garland's (2001: 175) emphasis on culture is significant. Recall his claim, referred to earlier, that it is the shifting 'cognitive assumptions', 'normative commitments', and 'emotional sensibilities' that provide a guide to the emergence of the new 'culture of control'. He goes on to argue that it is this reworked cultural pattern that helps us to understand how this transformation has occurred, as it has become 'inscribed in the field, motivating the actions of crime control agencies, giving new purpose and meaning to their practices, and altering the practical effects and symbolic significance of their conduct' (2001: 175). This, in other words, provides a means by which we can integrate our three different axes of inquiry. From this perspective, if we understand policy-making as a form of 'situated problem-solving action' (Garland, 2004: 171) in response to policy predicaments that are socially structured but politically framed, then the idea of culture, in Garland's sense, becomes a key mediating mechanism between the three axes in our theoretical framework. It is for this reason that we find it useful to consider the criminal justice turn as representing the emergence of a new *culture* of drug control.

Cultures of practice

This new culture—and its pattern of new assumptions, sensibilities, and values—flows not only through the national policy space in the way we have described but also, of course, shapes the everyday practices of, and interactions between, actors operating 'on the ground' at the intersection of the drug treatment and criminal justice systems. These actors include police officers, civilians working in police custody suites, drug workers, defence solicitors, prosecutors, magistrates, court clerks, court legal advisers, district judges, probation officers, and many others. Here, the picture becomes yet more complex—this new cultural formation is filtered through and mediated by the very different organizational cultures of the various agencies in which these actors are based. This makes for a rich but highly variegated and 'messy' picture at the level of operations. This is of interest in itself, and arguably much of the literature on the sociology of punishment and social control fails to engage at this level (see Lippert and Stenson, 2010), but our interest in understanding this level goes further than this. To varying degrees, what happens in practice 'on the ground' can feed back up to policy-makers and have an influence, however modest, on policy development. This is particularly the case where a policy programme is new and evolving, as with the criminal justice turn. We certainly observed this dynamic relationship when doing the local fieldwork on which chapters four, five, and six draw.

Conclusions

The theoretical framework set out in this chapter provides the underpinnings and structure for the rest of the book. Its purpose is to give us the intellectual tools to make sense of this transformation in British drug policy, to explain its emergence and its subsequent development and implementation in practice. In the next chapter we begin this explanatory task by looking at the origin and evolution of this policy development at the level of national policy-making. We explore this through the detailed analysis of both policy documentation and interviews with key policy actors in this field, bringing together documentary and oral historical enquiry. We attempt to explore the situated motivations of these actors in the manner described above, tracing how the evolution of the criminal justice turn in recent British drug policy can be understood as a (socially structured and culturally shaped) process of problem-solving action in the face of the new (socially structured and politically constructed) drug policy predicament that we described at the beginning of this chapter.

The present chapter has also served as an argument for a particular type of historical sociology. As will be evident by now, we find David Garland's (2001, 2004) work very persuasive and helpful here but we have sought to build on and develop his approach, notably by drawing on the insightful critical commentary on *The Culture of Control* by Loader and Sparks (2004). The rest of the book provides readers with a test case on which they can assess and evaluate the explanatory power and usefulness of our theoretical framework. We begin this process in the chapter that now follows.

3

The Politics of Drug Policy-Making

The concept of drug-related crime has been influential because it is tactically and structurally useful to powerful groups in discursive struggle.

[Stevens, 2007: 77]

Less politics would be good as well I think. A bit like the Bank of England, they took it out of the government's remit [...] Why not move drug policy to a group like that? 'We didn't decide, they decided.' I like that idea.

[Senior manager, voluntary sector drug agency]

Introduction

In this chapter, we attempt the difficult task of recovering and reconstructing the emergence of the criminal justice turn within drug policy at national level. We do this in small part in a rather old-fashioned spirit of conventional narrative history, borne out of the desire to document for the historical record how a significant moment of public policy came to pass, in the manner perhaps of Elton's (1967) famous defence of traditional historical studies, *The Practice of History*. But as we set out in the previous chapter, our principal frame for this historical account is much more ambitious, as we seek to locate this policy development in the wider context of social change at the turn of the twenty-first century.

To recap briefly, we attempt in this chapter to trace how the criminal justice turn can be understood as a (socially structured and culturally shaped) process of problem-solving action in the face of a new (socially structured and politically constructed) drug policy predicament. We explore this by focusing in particular on the motivations and intentions of the range of actors involved in influencing and shaping policy, as a way of piecing together this emerging new or reworked cultural pattern of 'cognitive assumptions', 'normative commitments' and 'emotional sensibilities' (Garland, 2001: 175).

We described in chapter two this sequence derived from Garland (2001) of new problems and problematizations posing new challenges to which policy actors respond. As we will see, in the messy reality of policy change, it is not quite so easy to separate out as clearly as this these steps in the sequence. The process is more iterative and dynamic. Accordingly, in our exposition in the main body of this chapter, we try to capture this more complex picture by proceeding more or less chronologically.

Early responses to the heroin 'epidemic': the 1980s

As we described in the previous chapter, the heroin 'epidemic' in the 1980s was a landmark in Britain's drug experience. It transformed the scale and nature of the drug problem and placed it as a significant matter of public and political concern. This new drug situation had a direct impact on the work of many practitioners, including, as we will see, several who went on to become key national policy actors later on. As rates of drug use among the population going through the criminal justice system rose dramatically, so criminal justice agencies at different points of the process found themselves dealing with unfamiliar matters. At the same time, specialist drug services and generic health/welfare providers also started to find themselves having more and more engagements with the criminal justice system. One of the very earliest examples of this was experienced by Lifeline, a drugs charity in the north-west of England. Lifeline had established an Induction Programme in Manchester in 1977 designed to prepare people for residential rehabilitation (usually in a therapeutic community) (see Yates, 1979; Strang and Yates, 1982). But by the early 1980s, this had become, *de facto*, a court bail assessment programme, as so many of the clients were involved in the criminal justice system, attracting funding from the Home Office (Yates, personal communication). In this sense, it was one of the forerunners for the type of criminal justice interventions that were to flourish in the following decades, even though it had not initially been designed for that purpose. It is significant, too, that at that time Lifeline was part of NACRO, the national offender rehabilitation charity. In interview, Roger Howard, then an assistant director at NACRO and later, as we will see, a key figure in the

British drug policy field, recalled the Lifeline work in the early 1980s, describing it as 'well ahead of its time'.

There was a marked shift felt by the criminal justice system, as well. At the front end of the process, the police were seeing more and more heroin users brought into custody suites. A local initiative that was to have a lasting impact on national drug policy began to take shape in 1984 in Southwark in South London. In July that year, in response to the impact of the heroin epidemic that had hit the area particularly hard in the previous few years (see Burr, 1987), a multi-agency Working Party on Drugs Misuse was set up to assess the scale and nature of the drug problem in Southwark and to make strategic and practical recommendations for responding to it. One of the 12 projects eventually recommended by the Working Party in early 1986 was a 'police referral scheme' (Southwark ARPP Monitoring Group, 1991: 4). Jud Barker, co-ordinator at the time of the Southwark Working Party, described in interview where the idea came from:

That's an interesting story how that happened [...] And it came from, it was inspired by an episode of *Hill Street Blues* [...] It's a really wonderful story [...] there's this episode, cop walks in with a junkie and he says, 'You can go to that desk and get help or you can come to my desk and I'm gonna book you,' and that seemed like such a neat idea.

The initial proposal for a referral scheme foundered, but the idea was revived in 1987 and a small-scale interim trial run of the scheme operated from late 1987 until the beginning of 1989. This then turned into what became the very well-known Southwark Arrest Referral Pilot Project, which began operation in January 1989 as a pilot action-research project funded by the Home Office (Southwark ARPP Monitoring Group, 1991). The basic operational model involved all arrestees being given a 'help card', which included the phone number of a dedicated drug worker based in the local Community Drug Team (Barker, 1992). The idea of police referral was also being explored in some other areas in the late 1980s. From around 1986, for example, Nicholas Dorn and colleagues based at the drug information charity ISDD (now DrugScope) were involved in a series of action-research projects in different locations (Dorn et al, 1990; Dorn, 1994). But, as we will see, the Southwark scheme provided a particularly significant catalyst to the next phase of policy development in the 1990s, although it experienced some considerable implementation difficulties during its pilot phase in 1989 and 1990 (see Barker, 1992), from low take-up rates to more 'cultural' problems of inter-agency working, as Jud Barker recalled in interview:

The infamous Carter Street Police Station, which is now closed down. There was a DI [Detective Inspector] there and he said, 'Oh, those cards. We got your box of cards, we're getting rid of them, we're giving them to everybody', cos we were just trying to get the police to just give them the cards, you know. And he said, 'You wanna see how?' and he took a box of them and dropped them out the window.

The heroin 'epidemic' also raised new challenges for the probation service, as Mike Trace, an important figure in subsequent policy development, remembered: 'Mid-80s I was working in the UK in general probation hostels work. I was running a couple of probation hostels in North London and gradually became aware that everybody living there was a heroin addict.' Similarly, Paul Hayes, later Chief Executive of the National Treatment Agency and, as we will see, a central figure in the criminal justice turn, described in interview his early experiences as a probation officer in London:

It's a bit difficult to pinpoint exactly when it was but when I first started working as a probation officer in Tower Hamlets in '77, you could count drug users on the fingers of one hand which is difficult to imagine now looking back on it. And the concentration was among middle-class dropouts and leftover hippies rather than mainstream working-class people who were the bread and butter of the [probation] business, as they still are. And then gradually, well I say gradually, it changed fairly dramatically really [...] Where it became for me real meat and drink of the work, was when I became a senior probation officer and moved to Southwark, initially to Peckham and then to Bermondsey. And the North Southwark area was one of the places, along with Liverpool and Manchester and Glasgow, where the epidemic hit earliest, so all of a sudden there was a normalization of heroin use, exclusively heroin use then [...] amongst white working-class criminals. [...] So that was how it first impacted on me, from being something that was exotic to quite quickly becoming normal business.

In response to it becoming 'normal business' for probation officers, in 1988 the Demonstration Unit in the Inner London Probation Service (ILPS) was tasked with examining the issue and Paul Hayes was given the lead in developing a service-wide response to working with drug-using offenders. As we will see, the drugs-focused work of the Demonstration Unit proved to be highly significant to later national developments. Its initial work primarily involved trying to determine the scope and scale of the problem in inner

London, through a survey of the client caseload (ILPS, 1989; Boother, 1991). As Nino Maddalena, then a probation officer in London and later a key figure in both the Home Office and the NTA, suggested in interview, this was an important move:

> There was a kind of watershed I think around [...] the Demonstration Unit that Inner London Probation Service had [...] This was kind of the late 80s and it really began to look at probation caseloads and began to uncover the level of drug misuse of probation clients in a way that I think had been either swept under the carpet a bit or probation officers weren't sufficiently knowledgeable about that they weren't asking their clients the right questions. And what emerged from the Demonstration Unit work was quite fundamental certainly for Inner London Probation.

Based on the work of the Demonstration Unit, in May 1990, the Chief Probation Officer of ILPS issued a policy circular that addressed, *inter alia*, the thorny question of how to respond to client disclosure of illegal drug-taking:

> The provision of information and services would not constitute collusion with offending, but would be a realistic and flexible attempt to engage and hold offenders in dealing with their criminality and drug misuse so that the service we offered was effective rather than cosmetic.
>
> [ILPS, 1990]

This question of disclosure became one that needed to be addressed at national level. By then Paul Hayes had taken on the national policy lead on drugs and he recalled the challenges involved in shifting the position:

> We needed a policy shift that made it clear that disclosing you had a drug problem didn't mean you'd be breached or you'd be prosecuted [...] Well there was an entire process of tightening central control and a firming up of the management processes within probation to narrow the individual capacity of probation officers to act. So that meant that by the time we faced this dilemma it was something that the service had to own as a policy shift rather than allowing individual practitioners to find their own way to it. So we were actually stymied for about 12 months in what we could do, trying to get them to own this policy. And in the end, we tried to get the DPP [Director of Public Prosecutions] to agree that it would be alright not to prosecute people and the DPP said 'that's a very interesting dilemma'. In the end we got the Home Secretary to sign it off and basically the way in which we did it was we, we couldn't have done it without the growing concern about HIV which meant that in many ways across government all bets were off. And all sorts of things that hadn't been able to be contemplated suddenly were contemplated.

The reference here to HIV is significant as it reinforces the point we argued in chapter two that the emergence of the criminal justice turn is rooted in a broader shift since the late 1960s towards seeing (certain types of) drug users as threats or sources of risk. Managing these risks—the *sécurité* project (Valverde, 2011: 10)—started to become an increasingly prominent governmental objective in the 1980s as the problem itself expanded and became more salient politically.

We also see clearly here how the public health and criminal justice agendas not only share the same roots but also developed in tandem. As Paul Hayes suggests above, without the HIV threat, this crucial step in the probation response to drug-using offenders would not have happened at this point. Indeed, a number of interviewees observed that these early criminal justice developments were often built on financial resources from the health sector:

What drove the first expansion in the mid 80s was concern about AIDS and HIV and the transmission by injecting use, that was the sole reason.

[Russell Webster]

What was happening in the 80s was […] the other side of the coin from what's happened in the 90s, in that all the money was on the HIV side. So when we identified there was a clear link between drug use and crime and a group of people who weren't accessing treatment and they needed the treatment for their health needs but also they needed access to harm reduction services, we were able to tap in to the health money. That was the stuff that was around at the time to deliver criminal justice services, just as actually in the last ten years it's been the other way round.

[Paul Hayes]

We should not overstate this, of course. While anxieties about the spread of HIV may have been critical, perhaps even central, to these early developments of the criminal justice agenda, they were not the sole driver. We note, for example, as we described above, that the initial Working Party that eventually led to the Southwark arrest referral scheme was first convened in the summer of 1984, while the first evidence of a connection between injecting drug use and HIV did not emerge until late 1985 (Robertson, 2005). As we know from Angela Burr's (1987) research, in Southwark concerns about heroin-related crime were paramount during this period, although no doubt HIV subsequently provided an additional impetus to the development of the pilot during 1986 and 1987. Underlining the significance of the crime side of the issue, the eventual national funding source for the Southwark pilot was the Home Office.

What we see then in the late 1980s is a set of related anxieties or insecurities about health and crime bubbling up in those local areas most affected by the heroin outbreaks and driving efforts to respond in new ways to the new drug problems presented. The development of the court side of Lifeline's Induction Programme in Manchester, the work of ILPS' Demonstration Unit in London and the Southwark pilot police scheme can all be understood in this light. In this chapter, we have, of course, selected initiatives that led to later developments of the criminal justice agenda, but there were other innovative responses that emerged at this time, notably needle-exchange schemes (Stimson et al, 1988 ; McDermott, 2005). While these are not part of our story in this book, it is significant that these too were mostly framed around the notion of drug users as sources of risk. Indeed, as we have already noted, 'harm reduction', the umbrella term for these more health-focused initiatives, was often called 'risk reduction' in its early days (Newcombe, 1992: 2). A further point to note about this early phase of criminal justice developments is the involvement in some of these initiatives of several individuals who, as we will see later in this chapter, were to become key policy actors—notably Paul Hayes and Roger Howard, but also Nino Maddalena and Jud Barker.

Building on local initiatives: the early 1990s

As we have seen, the second half of the 1980s saw a range of local initiatives pop up in response to new local problems. We have argued that they shared in common a risk-based frame for perceiving and responding to these new insecurities, a way of thinking that in the drug field can be traced back to the late 1960s and that can be located in the wider context of the emergence of risk-based forms of governance within neo-liberalism.

Moving into the 1990s, in broad terms, the early part of the decade saw some of these local initiatives picked up by central government and extended more widely across the country. The Home Office Drugs Prevention Initiative (DPI), the first phase of which ran from 1990 to 1995, was crucial here, notably in developments at the police stage. As Charlie Lloyd, then based in the DPI, noted in interview 'arrest referral became a big thing for the Drugs Prevention Initiative'. Under the auspices of the DPI, the Southwark arrest referral project expanded to surrounding London boroughs (Greenwich, Lewisham, Lambeth, and Wandsworth) to become a south London scheme. The DPI also contributed funding to schemes elsewhere in the country. As Paul Hayes observed in interview, this marked the beginning of a shift from local innovation to a more centralized standardization:

You've got arrest referral which gets picked up by the Home Office after its organic growth, picked up by the Home Office, bit of structure put on it so it's not as variable as it was, becomes face-to-face everywhere rather than handed-out cards.

An important part of the role of the DPI in its first phase was to help develop the evidence base for locally based prevention work, including arrest referral initiatives (see Turnbull et al, 1995). The second phase of the DPI, which ran from 1995 to 1999, focused further on developing the criminal justice work by investing in what it called 'demonstration projects'. One of these was the south London scheme that had developed from the original Southwark pilot. Others included schemes in Derby and Salford. An official in the Home Office at the time described in interview the rationale for phase two:

I think at the end of that first phase, the view that the Home Office ministers took was that the concept is a valid one, demand reduction. What we now needed was a period, which is why we went into DPI phase two, where we had some structured learning going on. So if we know the concept is valid, what works and what works best? What kind of approaches are more promising? [...] There were some demonstration projects, as they were called, looking at whether arrest referral was a valid route to go down.

Evaluations of these demonstration projects were conducted by Professor Mike Hough and his research unit and the published reports became influential documents (see Edmunds et al, 1998, 1999). Even more influential was a literature review that Hough conducted, published as *Problem Drug Use and Criminal Justice: A Review of the Literature* under the auspices of the DPI (Hough, 1996). Hough had been in a senior position in the Home Office Research & Planning Unit and had initiated work by researcher Joy Mott on the drug–crime link at the beginning of the 1990s (Mott, 1991). He left the Home Office in 1994 to take up a Chair in Social Policy at South Bank University, which, as he recalled in interview, turned out to be the start of a significant involvement in the development of the criminal justice agenda, beginning with this review:

One of the first big jobs I did when I left was that literature review on the evidence about tackling links between drugs and crime [...] Charlie Lloyd [...] asked me to do that literature review when I was fairly fresh at South Bank and I did it working quite closely with him and Jud Barker.

Another event at around the time Hough arrived at South Bank University proved even more momentous and would have a lasting impact. At the beginning of 1994, Tony Blair, then Shadow Home Secretary, published a piece of work conducted with Greater Manchester Police, which estimated that heroin users were responsible for half of all property crime. Putting to one side the dubious provenance and accuracy of this estimate (see Baker et al, 1994; Dorn et al, 1994; Stevens, 2008), this was significant in several respects. First, it marked the public debut of Blair's personal interest in drug policy. As we will see, this would continue throughout his time in frontline politics up until 2007, when he stood down as Prime Minister. Second, it advanced the primacy of 'drug driven' crime as one of the central threats or risks posed by the drug problem. Third, it ratcheted up the political 'heat' on the drugs issue. This was the beginning of a broader strategic attempt by Blair and colleagues to reposition the Labour Party as the 'party of law and order'. His strategy—encapsulated in the slogan 'tough on crime, tough on the causes of crime', first coined in 1993—was to outflank his political opponents by being prepared to match (or exceed) them in terms of promoting punitive policies, while at the same time pursuing more conventionally left-leaning strategies to tackle the causes of crime. As we will see, the notion of 'tough'-ness would prove to be significant in the realm of drug policy.

This marks quite a significant juncture, in terms of understanding the politics of drug policy-making during this period. We see here two strands of thinking that became intertwined in the development of the criminal justice agenda. First, there is the notion that using the criminal justice system to find drug-using offenders provided an opportunity to give them help and support that they might otherwise not receive—what we might term a welfarist strategy. Note, for example, this observation by Mike Hough in interview: 'I think that the people who were involved at the time all thought that it was a good liberal humane thing to do, rather than a "tough" way of tackling drug problems.' Second, there is a more punitive strand that sees 'cracking down' on certain types of drug users as a way of addressing societal anxieties about crime and security. In quite an important sense, this dual character to drug policy is nothing new. As one of us has previously argued (Seddon, 2007b), drawing on Garland (1985), this liaison between punitive and welfarist mentalities is embedded in the origins of the British drug control system in the early twentieth century. But, as we will see, it provided a distinctive dynamic to the unfolding of the criminal justice agenda at the turn of the twenty-first century.

Developments during this period in probation work with drug-using offenders followed a similar trajectory to those at the police station, as local innovations were taken up and spread more widely across the country. Interestingly, one of these innovations was sparked initially by the Home Office DPI, which, as we have seen, was so central to the development of arrest referral in the early 1990s. Under phase one of the DPI, a small probation project in West Glamorgan in Wales was funded. The Drug and Alcohol Related Offenders Project (DAROP) was a screening, assessment, and referral service for probation clients, involving close working between drug agencies and probation (Raynor and Honess, 1998). As was noted in the foreword to the published final evaluation report (Raynor and Honess, 1998: i), the experiences of establishing DAROP would prove to be relevant to the implementation of the then recently proposed DTTO pilots, to which we will return later in this chapter.

Perhaps more significant than DAROP was the work of the ILPS Demonstration Unit we described earlier. This was influential on an important report published in 1991 by the Advisory Council on the Misuse of Drugs (ACMD) on the role of probation in responding to drug use (ACMD, 1991). In the same year, and following on from the work of the ACMD, a new sentencing power for the courts was created under Schedule 1A(6) to the Criminal Justice Act 1991, which allowed for a requirement for treatment for drug or alcohol dependence to be made part of a probation order. The 1A(6) orders proved to have a variable impact in practice for a variety of reasons (Hayes, 1992; Lee, 1993, 1994; Rumgay, 1994; Lee and Mainwaring, 1995; HMIP, 1997) but set an important marker for subsequent court-sentencing powers, as Nino Maddalena, then a probation officer in London, observed in interview:

They were seen as a useful tool [...] And obviously I guess it was the precursor to DTTOs. All it meant was that you could genuinely have treatment written in to your probation order and have real sanctions for someone who was subject to one of those 1A(6) requirements. You had some sort of control and some sort of way of trying to impose treatment in that respect. But there were issues with them, there were always problems that you needed to have a named treatment provider you know qualified treatment provider and they were therefore a bit hit and miss in terms of their effectiveness and [...] whereas they might have been quite widely used in the London area that certainly wasn't across the board in probation services nationally.

The orders also set the template for a distinctive way of conceptualizing drug-using offenders as rational choice-makers, a form of subjectivity that has underpinned the criminal justice turn, as we have already noted in chapters one and two (see also Seddon, 2011). An article by Paul Hayes published in the *Probation Journal* in 1992, which discussed the then new 1A(6) orders, contained this striking passage:

Current understanding of drug/alcohol misuse emphasizes the user's continuing ability to make choices. Users are no longer seen as out of control, but as able to remain in control of their behaviour so as to, for example, decide which drugs to purchase and at what price, to take decisions about safer sex and safer drug use; to be capable of being in employment, and to be able to care appropriately for their children. In this context, it becomes increasingly difficult to sustain the idea that, despite being able to exercise responsibility over these areas of their lives, drug/alcohol misusers are not capable of exercising choice and, therefore, of being responsible for their offending [...] [H]olding drug/alcohol misusers culpable for their offending [...] also offers probation officers the opportunity to persuade courts that drug/alcohol misusers are as capable of change and of being empowered to exercise rational choice about their future behaviour as other offenders.

[Hayes, 1992: 83–4]

We see here one of the architects of the criminal justice agenda explicitly building a model for these interventions based on notions of 'choice' and 'responsibility'. This is a considerable conceptual move as 'addiction' up to this point had always been defined by terms such as 'loss of control', which implied that addicts were *not* responsible for their behaviour. Indeed, this is rooted in the origins of the addiction concept in the late eighteenth century (Levine, 1978; Seddon, 2010a: 16–34). He also makes clear the connection between choices about offending and choices in other areas, including health. This underlines our argument about the shared foundation for health-oriented harm reduction and the criminal justice agenda within drug policy.

To conceive of drug-using offenders in this way as more or less 'free' choice-makers, and to seek to govern them through those choices, also resonates strongly with wider neo-liberal control practices, as dissected by governmentality scholars, notably Nikolas Rose (1999, 2000). This is an important point. The 'big picture' of social change—the transition to neo-liberalism—not only throws up new predicaments and problems but also shapes how they are responded to, both in policy or political terms and at the level of the particular mechanisms and tools that are deployed to govern human conduct.

Other important national players in the field were also involved in developing the drugs agenda for probation in the wake of the 1991 Act. The Standing Conference on Drug Abuse (SCODA), at the time the umbrella membership organization for drug services in England and Wales, initiated a criminal justice project in 1992. Two development workers were employed by SCODA to work with Middlesex Area Probation Service to raise the profile of drug users as a distinct group within their caseload, through a combination of facilitating discussion groups, running training sessions, and advising on policy and protocols (for an account of the development project, see Dorn and Lee, 1995). This then led to the publication of a guide to partnership working between probation and drug services (Hart and Webster, 1994), which was disseminated nationally to SCODA members and more widely.

The SCODA initiative was funded mainly by several charitable trusts, as well as a smaller contribution from the Home Office. It is a good example of this coming together of different political drivers. SCODA's interest in criminal justice was almost entirely as a new means to bring funding into the drug service sector in order to help more drug users. In this sense, it was recognizing a 'business opportunity' for the sector, as Mike Trace observed:

By the mid-90s, you had the beginnings of a criminal justice profession [in the drug field]. And SCODA had a criminal justice forum which I think I chaired for a while. It was quite a vibrant group, dotted around the country, people doing creative things. All based around similar models.

At the same time, the financial and other support that SCODA was able to mobilize for the initiative was boosted, to a significant extent, by the anxieties concerning the perceived problem of drug-related crime. The drug field, and bodies like SCODA, were able to capitalize on these anxieties by making the case for drug treatment as part of the solution to these apparently growing insecurities.

As a further indication of the growing prominence of the criminal justice agenda, by the mid-90s, Roger Howard, formerly an assistant director at the offender-focused charity NACRO, had become SCODA's Chief Executive.

We have seen, then, that the first half of the 1990s saw early local innovations that had arisen in response to new local drug problems in the 1980s being taken up centrally and extended more broadly across the country. Arrest referral schemes in police stations and initiatives involving the work of the probation service in the courts were the two principal areas in which this happened. The political dynamic for this involved the coalescing of two quite different ways of thinking about the problem: first, that criminal justice work provided a means of extending the reach of drug agencies to help this new client group; second, that criminal justice work provided a mechanism for tackling drug-driven crime and making communities feel safer.

The other main policy development at this time appears on the face of it to be rather different, although, as we will see, this turns out not to be quite so clearly the case. In the Criminal Justice and Public Order Act 1994 a new power was introduced for the mandatory drug testing of prisoners. This had initially been announced in October 1993 by the then Home Secretary Michael Howard in what became known as his 'prison works' speech, which marked a clear attempt to move penal policy in a more punitive direction. After the legislation was passed, a programme of urine testing was piloted in 1995, with the pilot then rolled out nationally in 1996 (Edgar and O'Donnell, 1998; Singleton et al, 2005).

Several aspects of this are significant for our account here. At a general level, as Downes and Morgan (2007) observe, Howard's 'prison works' speech marked the beginning of a lengthy political contest up until 1997 in which the two main parties, Conservative and Labour, tried to position themselves as the 'toughest' on crime and punishment. We have already noted Blair's first response from the Labour side, coining the 'tough on crime…' soundbite and producing estimates with Greater Manchester Police of the scale of heroin-related crime. This is important as we can see how the distinctive political context of the mid-1990s strongly shaped this phase of the development of the criminal justice agenda in drug policy.

But although the political intent was to 'get tough' on drugs in prisons, the introduction of mandatory drug testing also had a quite unexpected and paradoxical side effect. Mike Trace, then working for the Parole Release Scheme (PRS), a charity providing support for prisoners with drug problems, recalled how Howard's initiative ironically had a positive impact for the work of PRS and similar organizations:

The prison service institutionally and the politicians were not comfortable [...] [with] the idea that there were thousands and thousands of prisoners who had a history of drug problems but who were also using inside [...] You had the odd governor who was up for it, you'd have the odd sort of policy person who wanted to explore it but by and large institutionally it was 'there is no problem, this is just the NGOs kicking up'. That changed with Michael Howard. He didn't intend to change it that way but basically he came along and did a classic leadership Home Secretary thing and said 'I'm going to sweep away all this nonsense, of course there's a drug problem in the prisons and my instinct is to stamp it out by urine testing and catching and punishing people'. So that actually did us a lot of good [...] because first of all it scotched straightaway the argument that there wasn't a problem and second of all got all the health agencies saying if you're gonna urine test everybody you've got to have services for them.

This paradoxical side effect highlights the tight liaison between the welfarist and punitive poles within the politics of drug policy-making at this time. Even what on the face of it appears to be such an unequivocally punitive move cannot escape the influence of the welfarist impulse. It is the twin dynamic that we need to understand in order to grasp this political dimension properly. Indeed, for some of the policy actors that we interviewed, the rhetoric of 'toughness' and 'prison works' provided an added impetus for developing initiatives like arrest referral, on the basis that they represented a more palatable community-based alternative (from a welfarist perspective) to the prison-focused 'Howard agenda', as Mike Hough observed:

My thinking was that it was a constructive thing to do and much better than the alternative which was to go for massive imprisonment. I was approaching it as a liberal criminologist rather than as a rather illiberal drugs researcher. The drugs researchers probably thought that I was horribly illiberal but they didn't have Michael Howard sitting on their shoulder saying 'prison works'.

Arguably, though, to frame these two political impulses as 'alternatives' was to misread them as representing a dualism rather than a duality, to borrow from Giddens. Ironically, Tony Blair's two-part 'tough on crime, tough on the causes of crime' soundbite suggested a surer and more instinctive grasp of this point. The coupling of these two strands can perhaps be best understood as occurring under the sign of 'public safety', that is as a response to anxieties about crime and security, a point nicely captured by drug policy consultant Peter McDermott in interview:

In the days when you have old ladies waiting on two years for their hip replacement, you know, how can you justify people saying we're not going to have any longer than two weeks waiting time for drugs treatment when people have got to wait for two years to have their hip replaced, you know. People who have worked hard all their lives and, you know, tried to be decent, respectable, hardworking members of society, and those people see it as a slap in the face, I guess. So the criminal justice agenda justifies that spend which probably couldn't be justified any other way I think.

By revealing the scale of the drug problem within prisons, the introduction of testing also had a destabilizing effect on the issue of prison security, as it highlighted the failure to prevent drugs from entering prisons. Prison security was a toxic issue at this time for the Conservative government. A series of lapses and breaches in 1994 and 1995, including the escape of category A prisoners from Whitemoor and Parkhurst prisons, proved highly embarrassing politically for a Home Secretary who had sought to stake a claim to 'tough' leadership on criminal justice matters. The mandatory testing programme formed part of a security-focused prison drug strategy published in 1995 (Prison Service, 1995), which emphasized control measures on supply and demand, rather than treatment (see Seddon, 1996). However, the national roll-out of the testing programme in 1996 raised a serious political difficulty for this prioritization of security, as the ongoing testing data repeatedly pointed to a fundamental security failure—the inability to stop an illegal commodity from entering prisons.

To summarize, the first half of the 1990s was a significant period in the development of the criminal justice turn. Local initiatives that had emerged in the 1980s in response to new drug problems were taken up and extended across the country through a combination of new central funding mechanisms and new legislation. As we have seen, these developments involved the assembly of some of the core components of the reworked cultural pattern of drug control that we are concerned with in this book, notably the notion of the drug-using offender as a rational choice-maker.

Nationalizing the criminal justice agenda: the New Labour years

The previous two sections should have clearly established by this point that it is a myopic reading of this history to view the criminal justice agenda as a New Labour invention. Indeed, in many respects, it could even be argued that the New Labour period from 1997 to 2010 was simply one of the later stages within a much longer story, rather than the heart of that story. Nevertheless, as will become apparent, the speed of change and the level of policy ambition increased significantly after 1997. And with this shifting up of gears, the balance of political forces or drivers appeared to shift somewhat as well.

The centrepiece of the New Labour government's first programme in this area was the Drug Treatment and Testing Order (DTTO), which had in fact appeared in their manifesto for the 1997 general election. As we have seen, the DTTO had several antecedents from the beginning of the decade but the specific genesis of the idea could be traced back to 1994. Many of our interviewees identified one particular individual as the most important figure here:

A bloke called Justin Russell, it was Justin's bright idea [...] Justin had been to the States, he'd looked at drug courts, he concluded that drug courts wasn't the way forward in an English context because of the style of the courts, the attitude of the judiciary and various other reasons.

[Paul Hayes]

Russell had had a brief spell at the Home Office at the beginning of the decade, where he had contact with people like Charlie Lloyd and Joy Mott, and he had then taken up a post at the Mental Health Foundation (MHF) managing the Foundation's grants programme on drugs, alcohol, and learning disabilities. Interestingly, one of the projects funded under this programme was the Parole Release Scheme run by Mike Trace that we have already mentioned. While still at MHF, Russell took a Harkness Fellowship in the United States, focusing on drug interventions in the criminal justice system. On his return to the United Kingdom in mid-1994 and armed with his Fellowship report *Substance Abuse and Crime (Some Lessons from America)* (Russell, 1994), he recalled in interview that he had an immediate interest in trying to use his research to influence British policy: 'I think I sent Liz Lloyd, at [Tony] Blair's office, my Harkness report when I came back from America, and she wrote back saying "That's very interesting."' In late 1994, in response to a public advert, Russell applied for and was appointed to a Home Affairs advisory post for the Labour Party and it was from here that his influence grew. He became the *de facto* adviser to Jack Straw who was the Shadow Home Secretary in the run-up to the general election in 1997. A junior colleague of Straw's, George Howarth, was given the task of co-ordinating an informal advisory committee to work up pre-election ideas on drugs and crime and this small committee drew in some of the key policy actors who had been operating in the field over the previous 10 years. Mike Hough described his own involvement with this group:

I seem to remember being involved in two or three meetings with Ruth Allen and Justin Russell and Roger Howard and Paul Hayes and possibly Mike Trace just discussing how things like DTTOs might work. And I think it was, obviously the drug court idea from the States was significant and Ruth Allen, who was working for Labour then, was trying to develop a policy. I think that they were clearly pre-election casting around for how they might shape some sort of sentencing option. Then clearly after the election they were fine-tuning by consulting with people like Paul Hayes, Roger and myself.

Justin Russell described in interview how the DTTO concept derived from his study Fellowship in the United States, illustrating nicely how this transatlantic influence actually happened:

It was, basically, drawing directly on my Harkness experience, I said, 'If you were going to construct a new form of intervention for drug-involved offenders, based on American good practice, what would it look like?'. And acknowledging the fact that we can't completely replicate the American drug court experience [...] what might it look like? You know, and then the DTTO drew on that. So it involved what I thought were the key elements. So it had to be at least three months. Testing was an integral part, testing whether people were going along with it and keeping all sides of the deal honest and, actually, regular review was the other really key innovation, which was one of the big lessons I picked up from America actually. Both the symbolic and the practical importance of bringing someone back before a court to have their performance reviewed and to talk about how they progressed, which was a completely, actually, it was completely unique, hadn't ever been done before in the British system, for any sort of sentence, so that was a big change actually.

The DTTO was piloted in three sites for a period of 18 months, from late 1998 to early 2000, with one of the pilot sites led by Paul Hayes in his capacity as a senior probation manager in London. The pilot experienced some implementation difficulties (see Turnbull et al, 2000) but the DTTO was rolled out nationally in October 2000. Despite some (more or less) critical assessments about its efficacy in the next few years (eg Fowler, 2002; Hough et al, 2003; HMIP, 2003; NAO, 2004; Turner, 2004), the DTTO continued as a central plank of the criminal justice agenda until its restyling in 2005 as the Drug Rehabilitation Requirement (DRR). At around the same time as the DTTO pilot, a significant additional investment from the Home Office of £20 million over three years was put into arrest referral schemes, as part of a wider initiative, the Crime Reduction Programme. Home Office Circular 41/1999 specified the ambitious objective of ensuring that all police custody suites had a scheme in place by 2002.

By this point, then, interventions at both the police and proba-tion stages had become well developed nationally from their ori-gins 15 years earlier as locally driven experimental initiatives. The third main plank of policy was an attempt to improve drug-related provision within prisons. As we described in chapter one, in 1999 the CARAT service was introduced across the entire prison estate, with the aim of ensuring a more consistent response to drug-using prisoners. Although this largely failed to grasp what was arguably the key challenge here—providing support to prison-leavers—the CARAT initiative at least demonstrated the political will to 'do something' at the prison end of the system in a way that would have been unthinkable just 10 years earlier when, as we discussed earlier in this chapter, even the presence of drugs in prison would have been largely denied by government agencies.

From around 2001, the momentum for the criminal justice agenda gathered pace. One critical development was the establishment of the National Treatment Agency (NTA) in that year, with Paul Hayes as its Chief Executive. The NTA was set up as a cross-departmental special health authority and charged with the goal of improving the accessibility and quality of treatment across England. The impetus for establishing the NTA was led by two key actors: Justin Russell (as adviser to the Home Secretary, Jack Straw) and Mike Trace (as dep-uty drugs czar). Russell described the rationale in these terms:

I think it was the frustration, it was this ongoing turf war between us [Home Office] and the Department of Health, about how treatment money should be spent, prioritised, how we should performance manage the treatment providers really. Make sure they were actually delivering what they were meant to. Just something that raised the game of the whole system and in my mind very much influenced by the success of the Youth Justice Board at the time, which seemed to have made a real difference in driving forward a reform agenda and really raising the game of youth justice teams locally [...] And I think it was also, in some ways, a way of getting round Department of Health and having an independent body that would validate our belief that offenders should be being prioritised for treatment.

This binding together of the health and crime agendas was highlighted by Mike Trace as critical to the case for the NTA and to its eventual purpose:

The defining reason for setting up the NTA was that it was never correct to call drug treatment entirely a health issue, very relevant to today's debates, because you'll never get enough money spent on it. The fact is that this government, and a UK government whether Labour or Conservative, would not invest anywhere near the money they're putting in to drug treatment at the moment if it didn't reduce crime. So if you just put it entirely as a public health issue, which is probably broadly more correct in terms of ethics and human rights, you wouldn't have anywhere near the budgets you have now. So my whole reason for inventing the NTA was that you have to square that circle. You had to have something that was a health budget line and a health policy line but was trusted by the Home Office to reduce crime [...] So that was the real drive for me and that's where Justin Russell really started to get involved. He'd been floating round the issue for years before that but Justin was the big ally to win the political battles to get the NTA off the ground, so I was very grateful to him.

In the same year, another important development began to emerge. Funded by the Home Office, a pilot programme of drug testing was introduced, first in three sites, with an additional six added later on (see Mallender et al, 2002; Matrix & Nacro, 2004; Deaton, 2004; Seddon, 2005). Initially, the drug-testing pilot was led by Nino Maddalena in the Home Office but he then took up the new position of Criminal Justice Manager at the NTA, continuing his central involvement in the area. The testing pilot covered the span of the criminal system but its most significant component was the introduction of testing in police custody suites as a means of identifying drug-using offenders at their point of first entry into the criminal justice system. During the pilot, this was restricted to detainees who had been charged, primarily because of concerns about proportionality under the European Convention of Human Rights, as Nino Maddalena recalled:

And I certainly remember in the very early days sitting around in the Home Office with all these learned legal types, human rights experts and Liberty all shaking their heads 'we'll never get this past the lawyers, it's a clear breach of human rights blah blah blah'. Well somehow or other they did get it past.

Drug testing had been championed by Justin Russell who during 2001 moved from the Home Office to become a special adviser on home affairs to the Prime Minister. As we will see, Blair's influence and interest in the drug policy field reached a high point at this time, lasting until well after the 2005 general election. This also coincided with a shift in the balance of the political drivers for the criminal justice agenda, with the overriding 'public safety' mission being increasingly inflected with punitive and control discourses rather than welfarist ones.

As the drug-testing pilot developed, discussions within government began to take place in the second half of 2002 about a more ambitious development with the aim of bringing together the various interventions that had developed independently over time into a single system. Initially called the Criminal Justice Interventions Programme (CJIP) but soon renamed the Drug Interventions Programme (DIP), this idea of enhancing the co-ordination of the different drug-focused activity in a systemic way rapidly became central to the policy agenda. Paul Hayes, by now heading the NTA, described the basic concept:

What we put to the PM [Prime Minister] was that for a relatively modest investment, instead of growing arrest referral or DTTOs or whatever, if you made a relatively modest investment in knitting it all together you actually get a hell of a lot more value. And he bought that and then he basically said [to ministers] 'work it up'.

Hayes' 'relatively modest investment' ended up being a substantial amount of money. Indeed, the opening up of the public coffers after the 2001 election was a critical condition for this development, as Nino Maddalena argued in interview:

The big catalyst for DIP was the spending review 2002, where suddenly there appeared to be an almost bottomless pit of money that was available for this agenda [...] Suddenly you had all this money and the kind of things that I would talk about in much more of an abstract way with other colleagues—wouldn't it make much more sense to have a much more co-ordinated more integrated approach to all of this because the big problem was the silo thinking—[…] Suddenly with all this money available it seemed like we could actually pull all this together, do the almost unthinkable and get police, probation and prisons working together.

At the beginning of 2003, as local areas were gearing up to start delivering this co-ordinated system by setting up local Criminal Justice Intervention Teams (CJITs), a senior and experienced civil servant, Peter Wheelhouse, was brought in to head the programme at national level. Wheelhouse immediately became a key actor in the policy field and would remain so for the next five years that he held this post.

The local CJITs and the CJIP/DIP initiative took some time to bed in and implementation in the first years was slow and difficult, as several interviewees involved recalled:

Getting it off the ground was incredibly difficult. Getting Drug Action Teams to take it on board, to understand the concept, to buy into the concept and I think we all thought for the first six months to a year 'this is gonna go badly wrong' cos nothing seemed to happen. We didn't have a very well developed performance management system at the time so it was not as easy to see the activity levels but it all seemed to get very quickly bogged down in terms of local barriers, local problems trying to get DATs on board, to get them to implement and deliver. It all happened very slowly and I think we all felt 'man, this probably isn't gonna happen'.

[Nino Maddalena]

I took the job at the end of January 2003 and it was supposed to go live in April 2003. It was a massive boulder to get moving and that required a lot of energy and a lot of calling in of previous experiences.

[Peter Wheelhouse]

After this difficult first year, and driven to a great extent by the Prime Minister, the next phase of development began to unfold, motivated by a view that a more radical and extensive use of the coercive potential of the criminal justice system was both possible and desirable:

I think there was a feeling after a while that things were starting to go well and that we might, and although we thought we were being really ambitious at the start of the 2003, we might actually have not been ambitious enough.

[Peter Wheelhouse]

The first stage of this was the piloting of the Restriction on Bail provision between 2004 and 2006, which we described in chapter one (see Hucklesby et al, 2005, 2007). To recap briefly, this was an intervention designed to use the leverage of court decisions about bail/remand to channel defendants identified as drug users into treatment. The second stage, was the 'Tough Choices' project, implemented in 2006, which consisted of a package of measures contained in the Drugs Act 2005: the move to Testing on Arrest (which had previously been after charge only), the introduction of the Required Assessment and the national roll-out of the Restriction on Bail.

The use of the name 'Tough Choices' was indicative of the prime ministerial desire to ratchet up the coercive dimension of the criminal justice agenda. By emphasizing to such an extent this side of the twin political dynamic we have discussed throughout this chapter, some tensions came to the surface. Nino Maddalena, at this point heading the NTA's criminal justice work, described his own reaction to it:

I don't know who came up with it but it was the Home Office that proposed it—I very much objected to it. In the first Tough Choices national programme board I very strongly recommended that we didn't use it. Simply because it just seemed a little bit crass. It just seemed unnecessarily provocative really. Kind of telling people 'you've got this tough choice'. I dunno, it just seemed unnecessary. I couldn't even see why we had to have [a separate project name], I couldn't see why it couldn't just be part of the emerging DIP programme.

The political dimension of the name was very clearly grasped by many of the policy actors we interviewed. Paul Hayes, for example, observed:

Part of the dynamic of all of this is an uneasy negotiation between those of us who have to do it on the ground and sell it to clinicians […] and an impulse from number 10 to make it as punitive as possible and as controlling as possible […] because it plays well politically. So the more you can talk about 'gripping' offenders, which was the Prime Minister's favourite word, and offering them a 'tough choice' of prison or treatment, then there is a tendency to want to emphasise the bits of it that play well to the Daily Mail audience.

[Paul Hayes]

Peter Wheelhouse recalled a more prosaic origin for the project name:

I can trace the name back to a member of my team […] The project needed a name and at one staff meeting we were talking about, you know, 'This is just about putting more choices in front of people' and somebody said, 'Well why don't you call the project, why don't we just call it Tough Choices?' And the Tough Choices thing was just intended originally to be our internal sort of project name and it's one of those things that then just suddenly was picked up. And I can't remember who it was picked up by. I always tend to blame No 10 for these things but it may not have been them. But it got into the parlance and Tough Choices became the accepted name for the whole package. It wasn't a bad name. It did what it said on the tin, you know. And so that's how the sort of Tough Choices name emerged. As in all these things people tend to think there must be some really clever reason behind it. It wasn't. It was just, you know, it just sort of happened.

We see here the importance of understanding the politics of drug policy-making from a cultural perspective. While all these actors clearly had a shared understanding of the template for the overarching policy project—using the criminal justice system to identify, target, and channel drug-driven offenders into treatment in order to reduce crime—nevertheless, the 'meaning-in-use' of terms like 'tough' varied considerably. For the Prime Minister and his advisers, like Justin Russell, it perhaps resonated in three distinct ways: as consistent with a longstanding approach to issues of crime and disorder ('tough on crime…'); as signalling a determination to address public anxieties about security and safety; as likely to generate desired headlines in certain popular newspapers. For many actors in the Home Office, the word 'tough' would have been largely unremarkable, as control and coercion are core elements of policing and criminal justice—hence Peter Wheelhouse's understated account of the project name as merely descriptive ('it did what it said on the tin'). For actors in the health sector, like the NTA, the term would fit much less comfortably with their cultural milieu, which partly explains Nino Maddalena's aversion to it despite his otherwise seemingly unequivocal support for the criminal justice agenda.

The other element of the name, 'choices', was equally significant. Here, we can see the thread that we have argued runs through British drug policy right back at least as far as the 1980s: drug users understood as rational, calculating choice-makers. Drug policy, then, aims to set in place mechanisms that can mobilize and enrol the self-regulating capacities of autonomous individuals in ways that are aligned with governmental objectives (see also Seddon, 2011). This same view of the drug-using subject underpins interventions as diverse as the needle-exchange schemes pioneered in the late 1980s and the Restriction on Bail provision piloted 20 years later.

It is evident now that the implementation of 'Tough Choices' in 2006 and 2007 largely marked the high point of this New Labour phase of the criminal justice agenda, in the sense that there were no

significant 'new' initiatives after this. The only other major development, the initiation of the Integrated Drug Treatment System
(IDTS) in prisons, which we described in chapter one, also started
in 2006. And so it is here that we end our account of this period of
national policy-making.

Conclusions

In this chapter, we have attempted to reconstruct the emergence of
the criminal justice turn in British drug policy. Inevitably, this recon-
struction has been partial and incomplete and no doubt at times
inaccurate. Nevertheless, through this process of historical recovery, we have tried to set out an *explanatory* account of this policy
development, rather than a purely descriptive one. We have sought
to go beyond, on the one hand, explanations that see policy change
only through the lens of wider social change (as a manifestation of
the 'risk society', for example) and, on the other, accounts that look
solely at the role of individual policy actors in driving policy (in our
case, for example, Justin Russell or Paul Hayes). Drawing on, and
extending, Garland's (2001) idea of policy development as a form
of problem-solving action, we have tried to tease out the interplay
between the macro and micro levels.

In the next three chapters, we shift down to the local level and
look at how the criminal justice agenda in drug policy was implemented in three local areas. Our purpose here is to move from
examining the 'reworked cultural pattern' of national policy—the
new culture of drug control—to a consideration of how this new
culture shapes the array of interactions and interventions that make
up the sphere described usually as 'practice'. Chapter four begins
this trilogy of 'practice' chapters by investigating what happens in
police stations, focusing in particular on how drug testing and
assessment processes operate as initial risk-filtering devices.

4

Police Custody: A Risk-Filtering Machine

[Drug] tests are data in a flow of information for assessing risk [...] Information revealed by drug tests can be folded into the decision-making algorithms of the system.

[Feeley and Simon, 1994: 179]

I think [drug testing]'s a breach of human rights, the same as everything else the police do. But then they're the police, aren't they. They can get away with doing what they want.

[Site B, service user, B3SU4]

Introduction

This chapter is the first of three in which we shift down to the local level to look at the implementation of drug policy in three local areas. As we described in chapter one, we carried out a mix of quali-tative and quantitative research in three locations: site A, a city in the Midlands; site B, an area in northern England, containing a mix of small towns and more rural parts; site C, a large city in northern England. Across the three sites, we conducted 105 interviews with managers and practitioners in the various agencies involved in delivering interventions (police, drug treatment, probation, magis-trates, etc) and 77 interviews with drug users in contact with the criminal justice system. We also carried out 62 hours of formal observation in police custody suites and magistrates' courts and spent 16 hours shadowing and observing drug workers in the com-munity and in treatment bases. In addition, we spent many hours informally observing practice in different locations and points in the system. We draw on these data in this trilogy of chapters in order to explore how the new culture of drug control that we examined in chapters two and three has shaped the assemblage of interactions and interventions that make up the realm of practice. Examination of this realm is vital. Governmental blueprints are rarely, if ever, directly or straightforwardly translated into practice. Indeed, policy implementation is typically a messy business, in which 'plans' and 'practice' often mutate through an interactive process of mutual feedback. In this sense, it becomes essential to look at both areas together. As O'Malley (2004: 26) puts it, 'such "failures" to translate the blueprints of rule into practice are part of the genealogies of new technologies and rationalities'.

To recap, the new or reworked cultural pattern of drug control that we are examining in this book is based on a problematization of the drug–crime link as a threat to public safety or security. Specifically, 'drug-motivated' crime (that is, heroin and crack users stealing to 'feed their habit') is constructed as a significant driver of local crime rates and therefore as a major source of insecurities within communities. The 'drug-motivated' offender (who uses heroin/crack and is heavily involved in acquisitive crime) is to be targeted as a source of risk to the security of local neighbourhoods. Interventions with these 'high-risk' individuals are focused on addressing the factors which most heighten the security risks they pose, primarily heavy use of (relatively) expensive drugs.

In this way, we can conceptualize the suite of drug interventions in the criminal justice system as a co-ordinated mechanism for the administration of risk, aligned with the overall goal of enhancing security. We should say a little here about exactly how we are using the term 'risk', as it has been the subject of a dizzying range of approaches across the social sciences (for useful collections, see: O'Malley, 1998, 2006; Mythen and Walklate, 2006; Zinn, 2008). Our own understanding of risk is that it is a *governmental* or practical concept that is made up in order to govern specific problems. It is a complex and malleable category that can take on many different forms, depending on the problem-solving task to which it is being put to work (see O'Malley, 2004: 1–28). One of its key characteristics, present in all its varieties and variations, is that it is concerned with the aggregate or population level. As Jonathan Simon (1987: 67) put it in his pioneering article on the 'emergence of a risk society', risk consists of a 'set of techniques for aggregating people, representing them as locations on a population distribution, and treating people on the basis of this distribution'. This moves the focus away from a concern with dangerous individuals towards one focused on risks distributed across a population, as Castel (1991: 281) observed in a classic essay in the landmark collection *The Foucault Effect*: 'New strategies dissolve the notion of a *subject* or a concrete individual, and put in its place a combinatory of *factors*, the factors of risk.' Hence, individuals are 'no longer pertinent as the objective, but simply as the instrument, relay, or condition for obtaining something at the level of the population' (Foucault, 2007: 42). In the present study, the instruments or relays are the drug-using offenders, while the objective is the reduction of local crime rates and enhanced feelings of safety or security within neighbourhoods.

In this trilogy of chapters, we use this idea of a risk-management model as a way of framing our analysis of drug interventions in the criminal justice system. Our ethos of investigation in these chapters is critical but largely non-normative. We are not so concerned with questions about the ethics of these interventions and practices. Rather, our interest is in generating a concrete analysis of this specific 'security project' and its logic, scope, and techniques (see Valverde, 2011). This, we suggest, provides a much better basis or foundation for those who wish to develop normative arguments about what should be done. It is difficult to make claims about what *ought* to happen before what actually *is* happening is properly understood. The present chapter focuses on the start of the process by looking at what goes on in police stations. It is here that much of the risk identification, targeting, and filtering takes place. Indeed, we argue that the best way of understanding this zone of action is to conceptualize the drug-testing and assessment processes in the police station as elements of a risk-filtering machine. The two main sections of the chapter examine these two stages of filtering in some detail, drawing primarily on material from our research in the three local sites. The conclusion to the chapter brings together this analysis and returns to a consideration of exactly what is meant by this term 'risk'. It should be noted that our fieldwork was conducted after the move to testing on arrest rather than after charge and so it is Test on Arrest practices that we examine here (for a discussion of Testing on Charge, see: Mallender et al, 2002; Deaton, 2004; Matrix and Nacro, 2004).

Drug testing

The point of arrest and subsequent detention in police custody marks the entry of individuals into the criminal justice process. Within the logic of a risk-management model, this population of entrants to police custody needs to be sifted to locate the high-risk drug-motivated offenders that are the focus of concern. There are two factors that might readily identify this risk group: their alleged offence type (income-generating property crime) and their drug use (frequent use of heroin and/or crack). These are brought together through the mechanism of the set of 'trigger offences', via a two-step process. The first step is that if a detainee is arrested for one of these offences, that 'triggers' the requirement for a drug test to be conducted. The list of 'trigger offences' is summarized in Table 1.1, in chapter one, and is also reproduced in appendix one. The initial version was contained in Schedule 6 to the Criminal Justice and Court Services Act 2000 and has subsequently been amended by legislative orders. In essence, the list includes acquisitive offences, like theft and robbery, plus possession/supply offences relating to Class A drugs only. The second step is the drug test, which detects the presence of opiates and cocaine in the body. Individuals selected through these two steps are then deemed to constitute the target risk group, as acquisitive offenders who use heroin and/or crack. Let us now explore these two steps in more detail.

Step one: trigger offences

There were mixed views from police and DIP staff we interviewed in the three sites about the appropriateness of trigger offences. Some suggested that all arrestees should be drug tested, regardless of alleged offence. This implies a preference for making the net as wide as possible at this stage. Within a risk-management logic, this makes some sense, provided that filtering mechanisms further on in the process are efficient and effective. Other interviewees recommended a more modest widening of the net by adding further crimes to the list of trigger offences, for example violent or public order offences, or prostitution. Many recognized that all suggestions for widening the net would raise resource issues. Partly for this reason, several interviewees maintained that the current trigger offences were appropriate and constituted the bulk of crime types connected to heroin/crack use. Some interviewees questioned whether simple possession offences should be a trigger offence since not all users of heroin or cocaine are necessarily involved in acquisitive crime. Indeed, in all three sites, it was clear that testing was picking up a number of users of powder cocaine who were, by and large, not involved in income-generating crime.

As an initial net, the trigger-offence mechanism is clearly likely to work reasonably effectively. All those arrested for acquisitive (or supply/possession) offences could potentially be drug-motivated offenders and therefore are appropriate targets for testing. But, of course, at the same time, it is also possible that individuals arrested for other types of offences could be part of the target group. For example, a person who is a regular shoplifter, stealing to get money to buy heroin, could nevertheless be arrested on occasion for other kinds of offence, such as criminal damage. To address this gap, the legislation provides that an individual who has been arrested for a non-trigger offence and brought to the police station, may be required to be tested on the authority of an officer of at least the rank of inspector. This discretionary power, usually termed 'inspectors' discretion' or authority, can be used where the officer believes there may be a connection between their drug use and their alleged offence.

In all three of our local sites, inspectors' discretion or authority was rarely used. For example, in site B, between 3 and 6 per cent of tests were authorized under this discretionary power, compared to a national target of 10 per cent. During our fieldwork, we observed various drives to increase the use of inspectors' discretion. In site C, there was an initiative to test arrestees brought to the police station for public order offences over the weekend between 8pm and 4am. In site B, DIP workers covering the police cells were encouraged to request tests to be carried out for people arrested for non-trigger offences where the arrestee was known or believed to be a drug user. In May 2009, there was a national call from the Home Office to increase the use of inspectors' discretion for violent offences. We can view these various initiatives as attempts to widen the testing net. They also, of course, potentially represented an opportunity for specific and easily identifiable groups to be targeted. Some interviewees expressed concern that this type of targeting could be used punitively or in a discriminatory way. A custody sergeant in site C doubted the legality of this:

Mmm. Inspector's Discretion. At the end of the day, you've got to have some sort of evidence. You can't just do it but they were asking us to do it for all public order offences and my view on it, and I spoke to the boss about it, you can't do it. You can't just say, 'right, I tell you what, what we're going to do now is carte blanche we're going to test everyone.' You can't. Unless they actually bring a law in saying that that's going to happen. You can't just make that decision locally. You're breaching a person's human rights more than likely and you're breaching the powers that we have to do it. And if something happens or they get injured or an officer gets injured, then you've got all the complications of that. So we can't actually do it. There's got to be some sort of evidence.

[Site C, police staff interviewee (C3PS1)]

We return to this question of legality in the conclusion to the chapter but simply note here that this custody sergeant reminds us that however powerful the risk-management logic may be here, the demands of the justice system ultimately perhaps trump all. In the police station, officers are constrained not only by the legal powers they have available but also by the need to follow due process in the production and processing of evidence.

Step two: the testing process

The second step of this initial risk-filtering process is the administration of the drug test. This has become a routine procedure in police custody suites. During our fieldwork period, for example, the monthly average numbers of tests carried out were 410 in site A, 310 in site B, and 550 in site C. In site A, there were three custody suites in which testing was conducted, compared to just one in site B. In site C, there were five custody suites but two of these were designated for holding people arrested for serious offences.

The level of police efficiency in terms of testing detainees arrested for trigger offences was very high. The national standard was for 95 per cent of those arrested for trigger offences to be tested. In all three sites, this target was generally exceeded. Among the small number of arrestees who were not tested, some could not be because of mental health or other health reasons. This group would usually be tested during a later period of detention. The number who were simply 'missed' was very low indeed. In site A, for example, they often tested around 99 per cent of appropriate arrestees. As we will see, the police were able to embed the testing procedure very effectively in their standard checking-in routines and processes.

The timing of the testing within the custody process could vary, depending on the situation. It usually occurred when an arrestee was initially being processed in the custody suite and before they were interviewed by police officers. After creating the custody record, the custody sergeant would inform the arrestee of the requirement for the test and its purpose. From our own observations, as well as comments from some police staff interviewees, it was evident that the official wording provided by the Home Office to be read out at this point could be difficult for some arrestees to comprehend. In recognition of this, in site A arrestees were asked if they had been 'spit tested' before and if they would agree to be tested again. If they did, then the formal wording was read to them. The level of arrestee engagement with this part of the process was often minimal: 'I just read it out and at the end of it, they often just stand there staring at me, and I say, "Well, are you going to answer?" and they go, "Whatever, yes"' (Site A, police staff interviewee (A3PS1)). Although it was usual to conduct the test at this initial stage, this was dependent upon the demeanour of the arrestee and the custody suite workload. If a person was drunk or aggressive they may not have been drug tested for several hours or until the next day. If they were arrested during the night or there were several people arrested and brought into the custody suite at the same time the order of the procedures could change. For example, it was possible an arrestee could be interviewed before being drug tested. In site C, arrestees detained overnight were normally not tested until the following morning.

The test was conducted in each site in a specific room set aside for the purpose. In site A, for example, we observed tests taking place in a small doorless room within the custody suite where arrestees were fingerprinted, photographed, and drug tested. Those who had not been arrested before would also provide a DNA sample there. Drug testing had clearly become embedded within the police custody routine for processing detainees.

The test itself involves placing a 'stick' in the mouth and a swab on the end absorbs a saliva sample. It has to be kept in the mouth until enough saliva has been collected, which is indicated by it turning blue. We observed that detainees were generally asked to sit on a stool with their heads tilted forward to speed this process up, although it could still on occasion take up to 10 minutes for the full sample to be collected. While this was happening, detainees would typically be asked a range of questions about their shoe size, height, drug use, and whether they were on any medication. Once it has turned blue, the swab at the end is snapped off and placed in a tube, which is then inserted into a hand-held reader. The reader detects the presence of opiates and cocaine only. It does not distinguish heroin from other opiates, nor crack cocaine from cocaine powder. A result is produced within a couple of minutes. The detainee is then asked to sign a test result report slip and is offered a copy.

In our observations, detention officers generally appeared friendly and made some attempts to build a rapport with the person they were testing. Usually, the process was conducted smoothly without any difficulties but on occasion we witnessed deviations from 'textbook' procedure that had the potential to undermine the integrity of the sample. For example, in one observation in site C, where a female arrested for shoplifting was being tested, she was requested to remove it from her mouth to see if it had turned blue yet. In doing so, she dropped it on the floor, picked it up and then had it taken from her hands by the detention officer. Despite this, it was still used as a sample, rather than a fresh one being taken.

Most arrestees appeared to find the testing procedure fairly unremarkable, particularly those who had been through it before. Even 'first-timers' seemed to view it as simply an element within their processing through custody, far outweighed in significance by the arrest event itself, as this arrestee described in interview:

From when I got arrested and they found the stuff [cocaine] in the car, I was in a state […] I wasn't bothered if they were testing me or not at the time. So it was one of those things that it came to the point that I was thinking 'it doesn't matter what happens from now'.

[Site A, service user interviewee (A3SU1)]

Some arrestees even viewed drug testing as a positive initiative, either because it was seen as likely to lead to quicker access to treatment or, more prosaically, as it provided them with an opportunity to leave their custody cell for a while. A small minority held very negative views about testing, seeing it as an infringement of human rights and as a coercive practice. It was very rare, however, for individuals to refuse to be tested. Data from site A, for example, showed that only 1.4 per cent either refused or had their test aborted. This very low level of refusals or 'failures' has been a consistent finding since the first piloting of drug testing (see Mallender et al, 2002), no doubt partly because refusal is itself a criminal offence carrying a punishment of a fine or up to three months' imprisonment. Nevertheless, we argue that this is still a striking level of compliance, given that custody suites can at times be places of conflict and disagreement between police staff and detainees, as this extract from observation notes in the custody suite in site C illustrates:

There was a loud noise and I could hear a woman screaming 'don't hit me, don't fucking hit me, get your fucking boot off my leg'. I got up to have a look and as I did so the Inspector came racing through shouting 'the fucking bitch, the scumbag, the fucking dirty bitch'. She had spat in his face, just missing his mouth, hitting him just below his bottom lip.

Our observations suggested that while such high points of conflict were relatively unusual, there was an underlying lack of empathy, bordering on contempt, for drug users expressed by many police staff and officers, particularly among those without specific DIP responsibilities or roles. Again, in site C, we experienced that it was common to hear drug users openly referred to in our presence as 'scrotes', 'scum bags', 'smack heads', and 'druggies'. An example of this was when two officers were talking to a member of the research team about the custody suite getting busier with three separate arrests in the city centre expected to be brought in at around mid-day. One said, 'you see, it starts getting busier now that the fucking scrotes finally start getting out of bed', to which the other replied, 'yeah, the smack heads'll just about be rising at this time'.

In this type of context, we might expect then that it would be more of a battle to secure compliance with the testing process. Many of the arrestees we interviewed explained that they believed that if they complied they would be treated fairly and processed relatively quickly. The desire to get out of the police station as soon as possible in order to buy drugs was often cited as a significant motivation here. The converse belief was also prevalent, namely, that if they did not co-operate, they might be treated less favourably: 'I think if you're alright with them and don't give them no headaches, they're alright with you. But if you're stroppy and sarcastic and horrible with them, I mean they could make your life hard as well' (Site C, service user interviewee (C3SU1)).

It has been a repeated finding since the original piloting of drug testing that the accuracy of the test results has been called into question by many arrestees (see Seddon, 2005). Across each of our three local sites some service users expressed this concern. They recalled occasions when they had taken drugs recently before being tested but the result was negative:

They [the police] could tell cos I was gouching [drowsy]. My eyes and that was all over the place [...] He fingerprinted me, did a test, and he was like that, 'It's negative.' I was like that, 'Well it can't be cos I'm on something now. I'm out my face and I can't even be interviewed I'm that out my face.' He's like that, 'Well, you're negative, so, I don't know. We'll have to put you back in the cell.'

[Site B, service user interviewee (B3SU6)]

Some service users recalled repeatedly testing negative, despite having consumed opiates and/or cocaine:

I went out with me mate one night robbing ages ago and we got caught out on the job and I supped 80ml of methadone on the way to the job. You know, I had it in me pocket, cos I always take methadone out with me just in case. And I thought I'll drink it on the way. And it come up negative, next morning in the police station it were negative. Right, this time I went down it were negative, the time before that it were negative. When I got this DRR [Drug Rehabilitation Requirement], I got this DRR before I went to prison and I were negative then. When I got sent down for the, this were Bank Holiday Monday, last August Bank Holiday I were negative then as well. So they're not accurate. It were only a day before I'd used. I got nicked on the Sunday night, I'd used on the Saturday, crack and heroin and it were negative.

[Site B, service user interviewee (B3SU7)]

During one of our observations at site A we witnessed an arrestee dispute a test result. She had been reported by a member of the public for using drugs in a vehicle and was arrested for possession. Her drug consumption was very recent. Prior to the test being administered, she admitted to using heroin and crack cocaine. However, the test result was positive only for cocaine and negative for opiates. The following extract from our observation notes records the immediate responses to this:

She [the arrestee] looked at me quizzically and said 'Bloody hell, that stuff must have been crap! That's done me head in!' The detention officer said 'It depends when you've taken them. If we tested you in 10 minutes they might show up. It's the machine. It could be very weak or strong and it won't show. Do you want your copy [of the test result report slip]?' She said: 'Yes, please. I'll frame that! That's never happened before. It shows you how shit the gear is in [Site A]. But, I've not had that much cos I've stopped injecting cos I got a clot so I've been smoking it on the foil and not that much cos I don't like the taste.'

These types of explanations for unexpected negative results—the quality of drugs and the threshold set on the testing equipment— were commonly given. In site B, during our fieldwork a temporary 'dramatic decrease' in the number of positive results for opiates was linked by police staff to a downturn in the purity of heroin locally. Police staff in site B were aware that some arrestees who did not test positive were giving positive urine tests at probation. This is because the oral test used in the police station is a *screening* test only, as explained on the website of the testing equipment manufacturer, Concateno:

One of the key concepts within drug testing is the application of a cut-off level. This is the decision point which segregates a test result as being either positive or negative. The cut-off for a test is given as a defined drug concentration. For drug screening tests, a cut-off is chosen that will minimise the number of false positive results. It is important to note that a negative sample doesn't mean that it is drug free; it might contain a drug at a concentration that is lower than the defined cut off.

[Concateno website, accessed 21 June 2011]

Within the logic of a risk-management model, minimizing false positives at this initial stage is in fact undesirable. The net at the entry point to the system needs to be sufficiently wide as to minimize false negatives. From this perspective, false positives are relatively unproblematic as they can be identified and filtered out at later stages, for example by a face-to-face assessment with a drug worker. False negatives, on the other hand, potentially mean that high-risk individuals are missed. Here, though, perhaps we again see the boundaries of how far risk logic can be pursued within a legal system in which there is always the central requirement to deliver justice and to meet the demands of due process.

According to policy guidance, negative testers should still be given the opportunity to see a drug worker if they wish and it was reported across all sites that on occasions this did indeed happen. However, it was rare for arrestees to make such requests and, even when they did, drug workers were not always able to see them because of their workload and the need to prioritize those with positive results: 'Because they're not testing positive in the cells, they're not really on our radar in DIP. We're looking at the positive testers' (Site B, DIP staff interviewee (B3DS1)). Arrest referral schemes prior to DIP had often involved cold-calling all arrestees in custody and offering support and advice related to drug use. Some DIP staff were aware they were missing an opportunity to give advice to negative testers:

So we probably do miss some but because they don't come in and test positive we don't get to see them. Because the emphasis is seeing these test on arrest people that have tested positive and by the time you've done all the paperwork there's not time to go to the cells because you might have somebody else in, you know, that has tested positive and they're a priority so they have to be seen. We do sometimes get people that will ask to see a drug worker who don't test positive, but we'll go and see them willingly yeah, but we don't actually go, be proactive go round the cells and talk to everybody.

[Site A, DIP staff interviewee (A3DS1)]

Some arrestees were also aware that a negative test result could divert them away from 'help': 'A few times I've been drug tested and I've come up negative, so they didn't give me no help. You know what I mean? So I go to prison, I'm fucking nearly dying' (Site A, service user interviewee (A3SU2)).

The two-step process as risk filter

Drug testing operates at the entry point to the criminal justice system as a mechanism for identifying the target high-risk group of drug-driven offenders. Two sets of risk factors are operationalized for this purpose: (alleged) offence type (mainly acquisitive offences) and drugs consumed (opiates and/or cocaine). The presence of the first risk factor triggers the drug test that then detects whether or not the second risk factor is present. The identified group then carries a risk marker (the positive test result) as they progress through the criminal justice system. As we will see in chapter five, this marker is central to decision-making by the criminal courts, both at the pre-trial and sentencing stages.

In our fieldwork in the three local sites, we identified a number of points at which the risk-filtering mechanism could potentially become inefficient or even fail. Perhaps the most significant of these was the level of false negatives. This opened up a space through which some of the target risk group could escape. Other points of inefficiency worked in the other direction by widening the net so far that too many arrestees who were not actually part of the target group were receiving the risk marker of the positive test. One of the most significant forms of this 'over-netting' was a consequence of the inability of the testing equipment to distinguish between crack cocaine and cocaine powder. Many interviewees suggested that this had led to 'recreational' cocaine users who were not generally acquisitive offenders being caught by the DIP net. Indeed, so significant was this trend that in site C a new cocaine-focused intervention was created to provide a pathway for this group in the treatment system and similar initiatives were under consideration in the other two sites.

Nevertheless, despite these problems, overall, testing in police custody appeared to operate reasonably well as a way of sifting the population at this entry point. It was certainly a process that the police proved capable of implementing in a consistent and effective way, by building it into custody routines and procedures. Rates of positive tests varied a little over time and between sites but generally hovered around 40 per cent. This is worth remembering, as it means that well over half of those tested are filtered out at this point for receiving a negative test result. This, we suggest, is best understood as filtering (purposive evidence-based selection) rather than attrition (undesired and inadvertent loss).

The two-step mechanism also has the potential to be recalibrated. As we have already discussed, the list of trigger offences can be, and indeed has been, amended or added to. The drug types detected by the testing equipment could also be changed or extended, although this has not happened to date. In this way, the mechanism has an inbuilt flexibility and adaptability. It could be called into service for a number of different 'security projects'.

Required Assessments

An immediate consequence of an arrestee testing positive while in police custody is that they are required to attend an *initial* assessment carried out by a drug worker and, potentially, a second *follow-up* assessment as well. The introduction of these two types of Required Assessment in sections 9 and 10 respectively of the Drugs Act 2005 (see appendix two) marked, in effect, an attempt to create a mandatory arrest referral service. One of the central failings of the earlier voluntary schemes had been the vertiginously steep drop-out rates after initial contacts in the police station (Sondhi et al, 2002). As part of the 'Tough Choices' package, it also represented a stepping up of the coercive dimension of the policy, with failure to attend a Required Assessment being made a criminal offence punishable either by a fine (up to £2,500) or a short period of imprisonment (up to three months).

Given the desire to minimize drop-out at this point, considerable resources were devoted in all three sites to being able to provide, as far as possible, 'on-the-spot' access to a drug worker for an assessment. In site A, the majority of initial assessments were undertaken at the custody suite. There were three custody suites where DIP workers were available for initial assessments. At the busiest custody suite they were available between the hours of 8am and 10pm. Two shifts of workers operated during this time. In site B, workers were on site for a similar period. It had been considered whether to provide

24-hour cover at all of the custody suites for initial assessments; however, because the number of arrestees being tested out of hours was relatively small it was not considered cost-effective in sites A and B. If an arrestee tested positive out of hours an initial assessment appointment was arranged at the local drug service premises generally within 10 days of their arrest. It was recognized that the chances of breaching this appointment and being lost to the DIP process were clearly greater than if an appointment was possible at the custody suites.

In site A, after an arrestee tested positive a detention officer involved in processing the arrestee returned them to the custody desk where they were informed by the custody sergeant of the requirement to attend an initial assessment. Once the requirement was made, the police contacted the Specific Point of Contact (SPOC) worker who arranged for a DIP worker to do the assessment. A DIP worker would then check their computer systems to see if the arrestee was already known to them or on their caseload. Their history would also be checked on the probation databases, which provided a picture of drug use, offending history, and any related risks. If the client was already on the caseload they would receive a shorter assessment. Clients who were new to the CJIT received the full Drug Interventions Record (DIR) assessment up to section 8 in the form. This covers personal details, health, drug use, and social needs (housing, employment, etc).

In site B, DIP workers operated in police custody suites from 8am to 8pm on weekdays and 8am to 3.30pm over the weekend. If an arrestee tested positive outside these hours, they were given an appointment to return to the custody suite for their Required Assessment at 11am either the next day or the day after that (to ensure they had at least 24 hours' advance notice). The 12-hour weekday coverage was split into two shifts. At the beginning of each shift, the workers checked the drug test books and a tray containing RA1 forms (which give formal notice to an arrestee that having tested positive they must undergo a mandatory assessment). Checks were also made at the custody desk, where the custody folder included information on all detainees who had been in custody. Police staff marked a 'T' next to all those arrested for trigger offences. A board next to the custody desk recorded the names of those currently held in cells and whether they had been tested or needed to be tested. Those with positive tests who were still in the cells were prioritized by workers for an assessment. Any who had been detained overnight and who had been given an appointment to return but who were still being held would also be visited and offered the chance to have their assessment before they left custody. Drug workers were able to access the case management database to check whether a detainee was already known to the DIP team.

Different arrangements were in place in site C. A team of drug workers provided 24-hour cover to the five custody suites from a central base in the city centre. The agreement in place was for a member of that team to attend at the relevant custody suite to carry out the assessment within one hour of receiving the call from a custody officer informing them of a positive result. The 24-hour cover was provided through a three-shift rota: an early shift from 7.30am to 3.30pm; a late shift from 2pm to 10pm; and a night shift from 10pm to 7.30am. For the night shift only, workers were based at home and available on a 'call-out' system.

The provision in site C of 'round-the-clock' cover, coupled with a one-hour response time, was clearly an attempt to minimize attrition at this point. It did mean, however, that unlike in the other two sites, the DIP team did not have a permanent presence in the custody suites. It also, of course, was an expensive model for the Required Assessment. In interviews with staff from several agencies, concerns were expressed as to whether resourcing 24/7 cover was an appropriate way of spending the local DIP budget.

It's a very, very expensive service to run 24 hours a day in my opinion, very expensive […] I don't think it's necessary. […] Do you honestly think that people should be doing DIRs at 3 and 4 o'clock in the morning? Do you honestly think you're going to get accurate information off somebody who's just been arrested at that time in the morning? […] That is a lot of hours in a week that you could be doing something a lot more constructive.

[Site C, DIP staff interviewee (C3DS5)]

The initial assessments in all three sites were brief, lasting between 10 and 20 minutes, the shorter assessments tending to be for individuals already on the DIP caseload. In site A, the assessment usually began with a statement about confidentiality issues to elicit consent from the arrestee to sharing information with other agencies. During the assessment, the workers usually also gave relevant advice and information, for example concerning safer injecting practices and this was seen as vital:

That person's got a waiting period between their initial assessment and their follow-up assessment appointment. You can't leave it four or five

days before giving somebody advice or information that might be potentially life saving, you know. So, everybody would give that information.

[Site A, DIP staff interviewee (A3DS2)]

Arrestees were also provided with information about relevant
services that they could access themselves before a follow-up assessment and a freephone number for further advice. At the end of the
assessment, a decision was made about whether a follow-up assessment was required and, if it was, the purpose would be explained.
From interviews and observations, we noted that this general
process did not appear to differ greatly between the three sites.
In site B, a particular effort was made by DIP workers to make the
process feel less like one of information extraction and more like a
'helping' one. The assessment questions tended not to be read out
directly or in strict sequence. Part of the tension here is that the DIR
is a monitoring and research form which is meant to be completed
alongside a 'standard' assessment, as Home Office operational
guidance makes clear: 'The DIR is not an assessment tool but rather
a record which, for monitoring and research and continuity of care
purposes, gathers information which the worker will have obtained
while carrying out the assessment' (Home Office, 2009: 13). Yet,
from our fieldwork it appeared that most of the time, the content of
the DIR almost entirely drove the assessment. A DIP worker in site
A recognized this tension and the difficulty it presented:

I don't want them to feel that I'm just there to gather information from
them. I want them to feel that I'm interested, because I am interested, that's
why I'm here doing the job […] Otherwise, I think if you just ask the questions and record the information, you're not really giving anything back to
the person that you're interviewing. And it's important that you do because
it's kind of the intervention, isn't it? That you can give some harm minimi-
sation advice and let them know that if they do want to engage with CJIT
that there is more to it than just sitting in a room and being told to give lots
of information that is useless if it's not utilised.

[Site A, DIP staff interviewee (A3DS2)]

The need, however, at busy periods in the custody suite to process
people quickly did tend to make the assessment appear at times
more as information-extraction than as a therapeutically oriented
assessment. In an observation in site C, for example, we saw a
young male, arrested for shoplifting and testing positive for opiates
and cocaine, undergo an assessment that lasted barely 10 minutes
from start to finish, even though he was a 'new' contact, not known

to the DIP team and not in touch with any treatment services. It was evident from observing his physical demeanour that he was extremely uneasy and agitated throughout the assessment, yet it still proceeded at breakneck pace.

In interviews with arrestees, it was clear that there were mixed experiences and feelings about the initial assessment. For many, the opportunity to leave their cell and talk to somebody different was welcome. Some also welcomed the advice and information they were given and viewed the assessment as likely to act as a fast track into treatment. Others were less positive, feeling that a period of detention at the police station was not conducive to a helpful inter-action with a drug worker, as this drug user in site B recalled of his own recent experience in custody:

It's at the wrong time. They're trying to assess you. You're not interested, you know, they'll come in and 'Oh, I just want a chat with you,' and you're in your cell dying. It's, like, 'I don't want to chat, you know' […] I just wanted to get out of there. My main concern was to please get bail so I can commit more crime, get more drugs, if I'm honest.

[Site B, service user interviewee (B3SU8)]

On the other hand, some drug workers expressed the view that it was precisely for this reason that the police station was potentially such an important site for intervention. A point of crisis could be a spur to reflection on the part of the detainee and an opportunity for engagement with a drug service. Indeed, this notion of the crisis point of arrest as a window of opportunity has been a theme throughout the development of arrest referral, going back to the pioneering projects of the 1980s (see chapter three).

The decision at the end of the initial assessment as to whether a follow-up appointment was required marks a second stage of risk filtering, after the testing process. Across all three sites, this filtering was a discretionary matter for the DIP worker doing the assess-ment, although there were some 'rules of thumb' to guide this deci-sion. In site A, those already on the DIP caseload, subject to a DRR or receiving treatment would generally not be required to attend a follow-up. Nor would those considered to be 'non-problematic' drug users. In site B, DIP workers had similar discretion but some reflected in interview that they found it difficult to make decisions about further intervention for 'non-problematic' drug users and it is here, of course, that the filtering operates. These workers observed how 'recreational' cocaine powder users were less likely to want to 'sign up' to DIP because they perceived themselves as different to other drug users. They often claimed their drug use was recreational and not a problem. In these cases, DIP workers stated they would inform the individual that they did not expect to see them in the custody suite again and if they did they would challenge them about their 'recreational' drug use. It was also acknowledged in site B that there was not much they could offer this client group in terms of treatment and therefore discretion was used where appropriate to filter them out of DIP. However, there was a perception among some DIP staff that this form of drug use could lead to serious personal and social consequences:

I mean, you know, a lot of them they'll say they're recreational users, and you'll actually dig a bit deeper, and it's like they're using every single weekend, and they're using, like, hundreds of pounds, and it's causing them loads of problems […] They just think of it as a recreational drug, you know, and it's not necessarily, especially if they're getting arrested all the time […] I mean, like I said, it's not necessarily a dependent drug habit. But it is problematic, isn't it? You know what I mean? It's causing them to be arrested, and it's causing them to get into debt, and it's causing them relationship problems, and that kind of thing.

[Site B, DIP staff interviewee (B3DS4)]

In site C, a broadly similar approach to the follow-up assessment was followed. Certainly, those people who were already properly engaged with treatment would not be required to attend the second assessment: 'If they're stable in treatment, attending regularly, we wouldn't give them the follow up, purely because they're coming anyway and it's just another thing that we didn't really need to sort of impose on them' (Site C, drug treatment worker (C3TS5)). In all three sites, the follow-up assessments took place at local drug service bases in the community. In site C, for example, there were five different locations where they could take place and an appointment would generally be made at the base nearest to the individual's home address. It was suggested by many workers that a fuller assessment at this stage was much easier to do, away from the pressured and tense setting of the police custody suite. While the information gathered during the initial assessment would often be revisited, the main focus of the second assessment was on identifying whether the individual required further intervention and, if so, planning what this should involve. It was stated in interviews that follow-up assessments tended to last between 15 and 30 minutes.

As most initial assessments took place in the police station, as we have already discussed, the question of enforcement rarely arose. For follow-up assessments, however, this was a more significant matter. In site C, after considerable teething problems, they developed a workable enforcement system, albeit one that relied as much on persuasion as actual enforcement and which could be quite protracted. An individual who missed their appointment would be given until the end of that day to attend. If they failed to do so, the police would be notified and would send out a letter that day that stated they had seven days to attend at the drug service or else a warrant for their arrest would be issued. Receipt of this letter was sufficient for many to make contact with the drug service. If the seven-day period elapsed, the process of issuing an arrest warrant could take up to a further seven days. Executing warrants once issued was a hit-and-miss affair, partly because of the size of the city. If an individual happened to be stopped or arrested for another alleged offence, the warrant would come to light as it would be flagged up on the Police National Computer (PNC). On occasion, the police would proactively attempt to execute a number of warrants on a single day in order to clear some of the backlog, but it was not unusual for a warrant to remain outstanding for some time.

In the other two sites, the breach process operated much more swiftly. In site B, for example, a missed appointment would be immediately chased, with workers checking whether the individual had been rearrested and sometimes even making a visit to their home address. If by the end of the day, they had still not been contacted and had not attended at the drug service, the breach file would be immediately compiled and the breach circulated by the police and flagged on the PNC. The local Divisional Intelligence Office would also be contacted and an officer might attempt to find and arrest them. This speedy processing of breach cases was viewed as critical to the effectiveness of the Required Assessment. In site A, the breach process could begin as soon as 30 minutes after the missed appointment. A DIP worker would provide a statement to the police informing them of the failure to attend. The police would check whether the individual was in custody or hospital and, if not, circulate information on the PNC. This processing of breach cases was stated to be an important part of police work within DIP:

We get quite a few breaches as well. The chaotic life that people lead, or some people lead, around their drug misuse means that, for whatever reason, they quite regularly don't turn up and quite a lot of our time is taken up by producing files to get these people arrested and put before the court.

[Site A, Police staff interviewee (A3PS3)]

In terms of the effectiveness of the Required Assessment process, we can certainly say that a very high proportion of those carrying the risk marker (a positive test result) ended up seeing a drug worker at least once. The attrition at the point of the initial assessment was minimal. In site C, for instance, it was not untypical for monthly attendance rates at initial assessments to be as high as 98 or 99 per cent. This was a significant development compared to the voluntary arrest referral schemes. What is less clear is what benefits flowed from this. We consider the difficult question of evaluating impact in chapter seven. Here, we confine ourselves to the observation that a 10- or 15-minute interaction between a drug worker and an arrestee, with the primary goal of basic information collection, is unlikely on its own to yield benefits, whether viewed in terms of public health or crime reduction. The critical question is whether it opens up a pathway into treatment. This is a matter we pick up in chapters five and seven.

Conclusions

We have argued in this chapter that the drug-testing and assessment processes operating in police custody suites function as a risk-filtering machine at the entry point to the criminal justice system. This could be presented visually as a risk funnel. Figure 4.1 presents the first few layers of this.

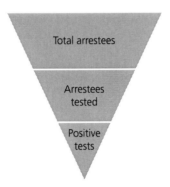

Figure 4.1 Risk funnel

We can understand then this stage as a risk funnel but, as we noted earlier, risk is not a monolithic or unified concept. So what idea of risk is at play here? Several points are worth making. Perhaps the most obvious is that risk in this context is a *governmental* concept, that is, it is a way of 'ordering reality [...] a way of representing events so they might be made governable in particular ways, with particular techniques, and for particular goals' (Dean, 1999: 131). In this sense, the associated subject, the 'drug-motivated offender', is an invented governmental category rather than a label descriptive of reality. We observe, in passing, that viewed in this light the extensive literature that seeks to uncover the 'real' nature of the drug–crime link arguably misses the point. The 'drug-driven' or 'drug-motivated' offender is a classification that is made up in order that the behaviour of a small sub-group of offenders can be governed in a certain way, for certain ends.

A key distinction that O'Malley (2004) emphasizes is between risk and uncertainty. While the former is conventionally associated with statistical calculation of aggregate futures, the latter tends to be understood as involving less precise assessments of the future that are non-statistical and may be about single events. O'Malley (2004: 18–21), however, refuses any clear-cut or rigid binary, suggesting that the two concepts represent end points or poles on a continuum, rather than defining types. At one point in his discussion, he goes further and speculates that their relation may be even more complex than this, operating across multiple axes that cannot be captured on a single continuum. The risk-selection practices that we have described taking place in police custody suites are obviously not numericized calculations but they involve more than mere professional intuition or judgement. Indeed, the trigger-offence mechanism is based on what could be termed a 'statistical' association between income-generating acquisitive crime and dependent use of heroin and crack (see Bennett et al, 2008). Clearly, then, we are talking about a hybrid or blend of risk and uncertainty, rather than one or the other.

This hybrid can be understood as a configuration of particular forms of risk and uncertainty, brought together in the technology of the trigger-offence mechanism. Again, following O'Malley (2004: 21–4), we can identify some of the elements within this configuration. The dominant element is 'epidemiological' or 'actuarial' risk, in which the goal is to identify and intervene with individuals in the risk category in order to reduce the level of harms for the population. Secondary elements include 'clinical' risk (concerned with risks to the targeted individual) and 'diagnostic' uncertainty (relating to expert assessments of individual futures). We have, then, an assemblage or ensemble of elements that is not fixed and may vary.

A recent and original paper by Klima et al (2011), drawing on legal theory, points to a further way of thinking about the relation between risk and uncertainty. Building on work by the legal scholar Elizabeth Fisher (2007) on risk decision-making, they argue that the concept of justiciability (legal determination of fitness for specific policy purposes) provides a meta-narrative against which different configurations of risk/uncertainty can be positioned and their utility or appropriateness assessed. This suggests an interesting way of evaluating the trigger-offence mechanism as a risk/uncertainty technology. Using this lens, we can take another look at the two steps of the mechanism.

The first step, the set of trigger offences, was constructed to reflect the types of offences connected with problematic heroin and crack use. The evidence base here was primarily the NEW-ADAM research on arrestees conducted by Trevor Bennett and colleagues (eg Bennett, 2000), as well as earlier studies from the 1980s (eg Parker and Newcombe, 1987). In the run-up to the original launch of the drug-testing pilots in July 2001, this evidence-based approach was described in presentations by Home Office officials as one of the ways in which any potential legal difficulties with the European Convention on Human Rights could be avoided. In other words, it was felt likely to provide sufficient protection against any legal challenge on the basis that it showed that testing was a proportionate, evidence-based, and targeted response to the problem of drug-motivated crime. Calls to widen the set of trigger offences, or even to test all arrestees, look much less robust or suitable as a way of filtering the population from this perspective of justiciability.

The second step, the test itself, was constructed on a similar basis. As the research evidence indicated that heroin and crack were the two drug types most strongly associated with acquisitive offending, the test was designed to detect these two substances only. Again, this was to ensure that in the face of any legal challenge, testing could be defended as a proportionate response. The scope for error in the test was accommodated by providing a means for arrestees to dispute test results (either on the basis that they were incorrect or because licit medication may have caused the positive result).

All disputed tests were sent for a confirmatory laboratory test for a definitive result.

Viewed in this way, the drug test was an appropriate tool for executing the policy objective and one that could stand up to legal challenge. The concept of justiciability helps us here to see how the fitness for purpose of this technology is not particularly related to the basis for the assessments of the future (risk calculations based on science/statistics or uncertain judgements drawing on professional expertise) but rather to how well these assessments can withstand a legal evaluation.

In the next chapter, we move forward to the next stage in the process. We examine how the leverage of the criminal justice process is used to attempt to channel targeted individuals into treatment. We focus on decision-making in the criminal courts and how the risk marker generated in police custody goes on to influence court decisions both pre-trial (the Restriction on Bail) and at the sentencing stage (the Drug Rehabilitation Requirement). We will argue that while activity at the police station can be seen as the operation of a risk-filtering machine, at the court stage the focus shifts to the management of these identified risks.

5

Criminal Courts: A Risk-Management System

When they [the public] don't abide with the laws of the land, then we [the police] are there to coerce because we say that's bad for society. What you're doing is bad for society. If you're burgling somebody's house, or you're committing a fraud, or whatever you're doing in terms of criminality, that's no good to society […] And if that's to do with drugs misuse, then we're going to coerce you to get better. And it's pure management.

[Site A, police staff interviewee (A3PS4)]

The risks are significant. The risk of more criminality, the risk of the spread of BBVs [blood-borne viruses], and it's the whole harm reduction agenda. Risk to themselves and harm to the community. So let's try and keep them engaged in treatment.

[Site A, Regional staff (A2RS2)]

Introduction

In the previous chapter, we began our task of exploring how the criminal justice turn in drug policy has been implemented in practice in three local sites. There, we focused on the entry point to the process and set out a case for understanding the drug-testing and assessment processes in the police station as elements in a risk-filtering machine. In this chapter, we move on to a consideration of two interventions at the court stage that share the goal of directing drug-using offenders into treatment services: the Restriction on Bail provision (RoB) and the Drug Rehabilitation Requirement (DRR). The RoB operates at the pre-trial and pre-sentence stage and attempts to direct targeted defendants towards treatment by making the granting of bail conditional on entering and engaging with it. The DRR is a requirement that is attached to a community sentence and that also seeks to engage offenders in treatment, through a combination of regular urine testing and court reviews.

In the next two sections of this chapter, we will describe how these two interventions operated in our three local sites.

At the heart of our argument in this chapter is that these court interventions can be most fruitfully viewed as part of a risk-management system. We explore this idea at some length in the third section that follows. But, before we proceed, we wish to say a little more here about the concept of risk management. Just as risk is not a single or monolithic category, so the notion of *managing* risk requires some elaboration. To talk of the management or administration of risk implies, at a basic level, efforts to reduce the likelihood of threats occurring and/or to mitigate the impact of harms that do occur. Taking these types of risk management in reverse, the mitigation of impact can be achieved in many ways but one of the most significant is through what O'Malley (2004: 21) calls an insurance model (see also: Reichman, 1986; Simon, 1987; Ewald, 1991). This involves 'risk spreading', where the impact of harms is distributed across time (through the payment of regular premiums) and across populations (through the creation of risk pools) (O'Malley, 2004: 21). As Jonathan Simon (1987: 63) put it in a pioneering paper, the insurance model is essentially a 'systematic way of organizing experience to provide for future contingencies'. This model of risk management typically involves the monetization of harms (O'Malley, 2004: 22).

The other main type of risk management, which we might call preventive, is concerned with minimizing the chance of harms or threats occurring in the first place. This operates by identifying risk factors, that is factors associated with a higher likelihood of the threat being realized, and then seeking to reduce or eliminate them. The assessment of 'likelihood' may in some instances be statistical or probabilistic, while in others it may be more centred on expert judgements or assessment. Often, it may involve a hybrid of these different forms of calculation. A further dimension along which the preventive mode can vary concerns the strategic position of individuals. What O'Malley (2004: 22) calls 'clinical' models seek to intervene with specific individuals in order to reduce harms that they may experience. This contrasts with models, variously termed 'epidemiological' or 'actuarial', which also act on individuals but only as members of risk groups, with the overarching purpose of reducing harms at the level of the population.

In broad terms, then, we see the court interventions that we are examining in this chapter as largely preventive forms of risk management. As we discussed in the previous chapter, being arrested for a 'trigger' offence and testing positive for opiates/ cocaine are identified as risk factors for involvement in drug-motivated acquisitive offending. The interventions seek to address what is viewed as the main driver for this behaviour, heavy use of heroin or crack, by engaging targeted individuals in treatment. For some agencies, this may be seen more as a 'clinical' model, aiming to help individuals, but clearly the main thrust of the strategy is on reducing harms associated with crime victimization for the wider population. Indeed, as we saw in chapter three, many key national policy actors explicitly defined the project in terms of potential community safety gains. In this way, it can be understood as fundamentally a security project.

At another level, and stretching things only a little, we might view these interventions in a certain sense as also involving a form of risk spreading. By spending public money drawn from general taxation on this system of targeted drug interventions, we are in effect pooling our collective resources in order to distribute the harms created by drug-driven crime. This, of course, resembles the model of risk management most associated with twentieth-century welfare states and their efforts to provide social security (see Simon, 1987: 66–7). This, in turn, points us towards an alternative sense in which we might view this as a security project. For Simon (1987), these twin strategies of aggregation and security represent two faces of the same risk-based logic.

Let us now turn to examining the details of this particular security project, by looking at how these court-based interventions functioned in practice in the three local sites. We will describe operations at the pre-trial and sentencing stages, respectively, before considering how they can be understood as constituting a risk-management system.

Pre-trial: the Restriction on Bail

After detention in the police station, the next stage for defendants who are charged with an offence is to appear in court. Aside from those cases that are dealt with in their entirety on first appearance (eg if a guilty plea is entered and the sentence/disposal is straightforward), the courts usually have to make a decision about bail. In other words, during each period between court hearings, the court must decide whether a defendant should be allowed to remain in the community (remanded on bail) or should be held in prison (remanded in custody). Under the Bail Act 1976, there is a general presumption in favour of bail (on the basis that all defendants are still legally innocent at this point), rebuttable on various grounds (likely failure to return to court, risk of offending on bail, potential to interfere with witnesses). In making the bail decision, the court also takes into account the seriousness of the alleged offence, the defendant's previous bail record, previous convictions, and so on (for further details on the operation of court bail, see: Hucklesby, 1994, 1996, 1997, 2009).

Section 19 of the Criminal Justice Act 2003 amended the Bail Act to introduce the Restriction on Bail provision (RoB) (see appendix three). In effect, this reverses the usual presumption in favour of bail for defendants who have tested positive in police custody, *unless* they agree to attend treatment and then engage in any recommended provision. If they agree, their engagement with treatment then becomes a condition of their bail. The RoB was piloted in three areas between 2004 and 2006 (see Hucklesby et al, 2005, 2007) and then rolled out nationally in 2006 as part of the 'Tough Choices' project.

Clearly, we can view the basic concept of RoB from within the logic of the risk-management model we have outlined. Defendants who are charged and arrive in court carrying with them a particular risk marker (a positive drug test) are only granted bail and allowed to remain in the community on the condition that they engage with drug treatment (which is conceived as an intervention designed to reduce their risk of offending). From this perspective, it is a key component within the overarching security project that we have been discussing. How, though, did it actually operate in the three sites we looked at?

Tracking positive testers

In site A, the RoB team was based in the court building and consisted of two drug workers and an administrator. A major task for the team was to track all positive testers who appeared in court. They were provided with a list of these testers by the police and recorded the expected date of court appearance for each one in a diary, which was checked on a daily basis. On average, the team would have around 20 cases to track each day, across 18 courtrooms. In each of those courtrooms, the RoB team would provide the legal adviser and the Crown Prosecution Service (CPS) lawyer with a copy of the drug test result and would leave a form with the court usher to record the outcome of the hearing. At the end of each session, before lunch and at the close of the afternoon, they would collect the completed forms. This system was developed because the team obviously did not have the capacity to cover or be present in all the courtrooms. On occasion, a team member would sit and observe cases in one of the busier rooms. Magistrates would sometimes take advantage of their presence to solicit information or just to alert the defendant to the identity of the worker they would need to go and see after the hearing. A team member could also be requested by telephone to attend to provide information. Defendants who were made subject to RoB would be instructed by the magistrate to go to the team office in the court building for assessment and to make an appointment with the treatment service. At the end of each day, the team would attempt to reconcile the record of outcomes in each courtroom with the list of those who had attended their office.

This way of working had been developed over time to provide an effective system for ensuring that attrition at this stage was minimized. The complexity of processes, however, made this extremely challenging, as this member of the CJIT in site A described:

We've had lots of people who have been on RoB for over a year, some people get RoB in the morning, they're adjourned for a fast delivery report for the afternoon, they come to you and they're only on RoB over lunch time. You know? I mean the, the systems have got to be flexible enough to cope with that and of course people don't have one offence going through the courts at a time, they might have half a dozen things. Each one they've tested positive for, some they've been assessed in the cells, some they haven't, some they've gone to court for, some they've been bailed back, some the police have dropped the charge and you've got to make sense of all that. And everybody's got their own paperwork and of course every positive test will have had an initial assessment, possibly a further assessment and often people come to you and you'll have a stack of paper like that. And you try to figure out exactly what's happened and there's somebody, an admin worker, who's trying to sort out from the Required Assessment side, whether people should be breached or not and you're trying to, you know, just have a system that will keep tabs on all of this.

[Site A, DIP staff interviewee (A3DS6)]

The daily workload for the team was also quite unpredictable. Defendants did not always turn up at court. On one day of our observations in court, only one out of the seven listed to appear there actually arrived in the courtroom where we were observing. Other cases may not appear in court as they have been cautioned at the police station, although the RoB team would not always be informed of this.

In site B, similar systems and arrangements were in place. Two workers were allocated to cover the two courts in the area. They had access to the court diary, which provided details of positive testers due to appear. Using this information, they would inform legal advisers and CPS lawyers prior to hearings about any defendants who might be eligible for RoB. They would also, at this point, make it clear to the legal adviser whether they considered a defendant to be 'appropriate' or suitable for RoB. One category generally judged as 'unsuitable' was those assessed as 'recreational' cocaine powder users. During hearings, workers sat in the courtroom when available and would respond to queries from magistrates.

After a RoB was applied, the magistrate would inform the defendant that they were required to report to the court worker before leaving the building. The worker would arrange an appointment for them at the community drug service. They would then be required to sign for the appointment and would be given details of the appointment date/time and directions of how to get there.

Arrangements in site C were also similar, with two core members of the court team. A daily email would be sent by the police to the team with the list of defendants with positive tests due to appear that day. A worker would cross-check against the Test on Arrest and probation databases to find out if any appointments were already set up. Where possible, the team would attempt to speak informally to eligible defendants prior to their hearing, either in the cells at court if they had been held there, or else outside the courtroom. Again, as in the other sites, workers would sit in court for some hearings and respond to requests for information but were not able to cover all hearings. Defendants made subject to a RoB would be required to go to the RoB office in the court building before leaving, where they would be given details of their treatment appointment.

Breaching and enforcement

A key element of the RoB was how it was enforced. In principle, failures to attend treatment appointments or to engage properly with treatment constituted a breach of a bail condition, which is an offence under the Bail Act 1976. Enforcement practice in the three local sites varied. Generally, courts neither requested nor received progress reports or updates on defendants with a RoB. It was assumed that if a defendant had not been breached that they were complying with the requirement. Failures to attend, whether at the RoB office immediately after the hearing or at treatment appointments in the community, were usually responded to quite swiftly in all three sites. In site A, for instance, this would normally be done the next day, while in sites B and C the process could be started within hours. The basic process involved informing the police and sending them a witness statement (containing details of the missed appointment). The police would check the individual was not being held in custody or in hospital and then issue an arrest warrant, updating the PNC at the same time. Exactly how long it would take then for them to be arrested obviously varied from hours to weeks.

A source of some controversy in all sites concerned the response of the courts to failures to comply with the RoB. It was often the case that defendants who had been breached would nevertheless be made subject to RoB again and that this process on occasions could be repeated multiple times within a particular bail period. This practice of 're-RoB-ing' caused considerable concern for CJIT (and other) staff as it appeared to run counter to the basic model of the requirement, as expressed by a regional representative of the National Treatment Agency: 'Restrictions on Bail was one of those things that came and said, you know, "Actually, you've got a choice here between being banged up [in prison] and going into treatment. Which do you prefer?"' (Site A, Regional staff (A2RS2)). Having this message drummed into them by national and regional Home Office and NTA officials, some workers were then dismayed by the apparent readiness of magistrates to put people back on a RoB after a breach, as this CJIT case manager in site B observed:

It can be pretty disheartening for [the CJIT team] when it's just the same old same old coming round again. And it's then how do you break that cycle? Without help from external agencies, it's very hard to do […] It makes a mockery of what we're trying to do, where you've got this coercive nature, where we're saying 'Engage with us or face the consequences'.

[Site B, DIP staff interviewee (B3DS5)]

It was suggested by some interviewees, and was also evident from our observations in court, that this issue was partly a consequence of the way in which RoB was applied. Rather than defendants being offered a clear choice between custody or treatment, the actual practice in the courtroom was different:

> One of the things that tees me off no end is that Restrictions on Bail appear to me to be a complete waste of time because they're actually imposed in a very routine way. I mean nobody in court ever says, 'Actually we're going to remand you in custody but we're willing to release you on bail subject to restrictions given you've committed one of these notifiable [trigger] offences'. It's never put in those terms, it's 'We're going to remand you on bail, go and see the CJIT worker after court.' And that's the extent to which the court says it's significant. And then the person doesn't turn up and they go back to court and they get another RoB, and it just becomes a nonsense.
>
> [Site A, DIP staff interviewee (A3DS7)]

In other words, the 'tough choice' between prison and treatment was not being explicitly offered in the way that many thought it was going to be:

> I thought they were going to be given the option when this Restrictions on Bail started. For example, 'We could remand you or you could go on Restrictions on Bail. Which would you prefer?', but it's not like that. It's not like that. If they're going to give a person bail and they have tested positive they will automatically be given Restrictions on Bail.
>
> [Site A, DIP staff interviewee, (A3DS8)]

This is a significant point that we return to later. In some respects, it is perhaps not surprising that the application of RoB appeared to be 'automatic' for eligible defendants, rather than a 'tough choice' offered to them, as other bail conditions (curfews, residence requirements, etc) do not require the consent of defendants. In interviews, magistrates also expressed an awareness of the problem of prison overcrowding and that a decision to remand in custody was not to be taken lightly. They suggested it was particularly difficult to remand a person in custody where their index offence was relatively minor, as it was not felt to be a proportionate response. Given the prevalence of shoplifting among this population, we would not expect then that custodial remands would be used that often, even where a defendant was in breach of RoB. In other words, there is a point of tension here between the demands of justice on the one hand, and those of control strategies on the other.

Sentencing: the Drug Rehabilitation Requirement

For those defendants found guilty, the next stage at court is sentencing. Where a custodial sentence is not deemed necessary or appropriate, a community sentence may be considered. The framework for community orders was revamped under sections 209–211 in the Criminal Justice Act 2003, with the new arrangements coming into force for offences committed from April 2005 onwards. The DRR, replacing the earlier Drug Treatment and Testing Order (DTTO), is one of 12 requirements that can be attached to a generic community sentence (other requirements include curfews, unpaid work, and residence restrictions). A DRR can be applied where the court is satisfied that an offender is drug dependent or has a propensity to misuse drugs and would benefit from treatment. It includes both treatment and regular testing and the offender's progress is also subject to periodic review by the court.

In our three local sites, we investigated the whole process of applying and implementing DRRs. In broad terms, practice was quite similar across the sites. If magistrates were considering attaching a DRR to a community sentence, the hearing would usually be adjourned for probation to prepare a report setting out their recommendation. A full pre-sentence report (PSR) would involve a detailed face-to-face assessment being carried out with the offender. This would consider any previous history on DRRs/DTTOs/RoB, treatment history, levels of drug use, and motivation. During this period, which could last several weeks, the offender would still be on remand and, assuming it had been imposed, would remain on RoB. In site B, on occasion a fast delivery report would be requested instead of a full PSR and this would usually be provided on the same day. Across all three sites, it appeared that probation recommendations about the suitability of an offender for a DRR tended to be followed by magistrates.

As part of a community sentence, DRRs are managed by probation teams. As we noted in chapter one, the funding stream was entirely separate from the DIP budget and so it was not delivered by the CJIT. In site A, a multi-disciplinary Substance Misuse Team, made up of offender managers, probation service officers, and drug workers, provided all elements of the requirement. The model in site B was slightly different with a probation team working closely with a specialist DRR team in a drug treatment service, the latter providing the clinical components of treatment, such as, prescribing of opiate substitutes. Aside from specialist drug treatment, the other central part of the DRR was the provision of set hours of contact each week, to be filled with a range of activities. The number of hours varied, depending on how intensive the requirement was, but could be as much as 15 hours per week. Activities included counselling, advice (on housing, debt, benefits, etc), computer classes, and so on. An offender in site B gave a good flavour of what could be on offer:

There's someone for my debt problem, there's someone for my anxiety and I've got a housing support worker. She comes to see me, makes sure I'm paying me bills. She shows me the rent that's being paid and makes sure I go shopping. There's counsellors you can speak to for depression and things like that. There's activities that you can do, I find massage and acupuncture are very good. And Boxercise that I go to sometimes, just to take your anger out.

[Site B, service user interviewee (B3SU8)]

This high level of structure was intended to occupy the time of offenders in a constructive way and this appeared to be beneficial for some. For others, the number of appointments each week proved very difficult to manage and in some cases led to the order being breached. In recognition of this, strategies were developed to help offenders keep track of their schedule. In site B, for example, offenders were provided with a diary sheet containing all their appointments for the week, which they were required to sign. They were also given a local bus pass. If progress was judged to be positive, the number of weekly contact hours could be reduced after the first 16 weeks.

Interviews with offenders suggested some variability both between and within sites in the *quality* of contacts with key workers, who were meant to co-ordinate the different components of the sentence. Some described weekly appointments that appeared to amount to little more than a brief 'hello' and 'how are you?' (see also Best et al, 2010). Indeed, in one site, we observed 'contacts' that consisted of a worker standing outside smoking enquiring about the well-being of their clients as they came in to the building to collect their methadone. But other key workers were clearly very highly valued:

She's really good because she's got a passion for it and it comes through and it shows that she cares. And when you see someone caring that much you actually start thinking about that person and it becomes, like, 'I wonder what she'll think if I mess up,' and it becomes another element, another chain of thought in that process that helps you, like, make the right decision.

[Site B, service user interviewee (B3SU9)]

Supervision and testing

The supervision of the DRR involved two core elements: contact with the probation team and urine testing. In site A, for example, an offender would be required to meet a member of the probation Substance Misuse Team at least twice a week, on top of the activity appointments we have already described. The purpose of these meetings was to address offending behaviour, help organize the schedule of activities, and check on general progress. Typically, offenders in all three sites were required to attend for drug testing twice a week, at least for the first 16 weeks of the order. This frequency could be reduced after this but often was kept the same. Offenders who admitted drug use could sign a form to confirm this, instead of undergoing the test. Probation officers felt that that even if an individual was consistently producing negative tests, it was helpful to continue with twice-weekly tests in order to provide evidence for the court of sustained behavioural change. A weakness of the urine testing mechanism was felt to be that it offered only a binary positive/negative result and gave no indication of amounts used. This meant that an individual could make significant reductions in their drug use, in terms of frequency and/or quantity, but this would not be reflected in the test, which would remain positive. If a probation officer believed an offender's claims to be cutting down, they might include that in a review report:

I'll probably make the comment that we're unable to evidence reduced drug use through drug testing because the drug tests are for the presence of the drug not for the quantity. But I might put something like, 'however, their presentation suggests that their disclosures are accurate.' By that I could mean that maybe they're looking in clearly an improved health, maybe they've gained a bit of weight, they're attending, they're not drug-affected when they come to appointments.

[Site A, probation staff interviewee (A3PR1)]

We see here the bringing together of a range of types of information—test results, verbal statements, professional judgement—as part of the monitoring and surveillance of these 'risky' individuals. This is critical to the operation of the DRR as part of a risk-management system (see Ericson, 1994). We explore the significance of knowledge production further in chapter six.

Court review

In addition to supervision by the DRR team, however that is structured, a central element of the Requirement is regular review by the courts. These review hearings have been viewed as critical to the effectiveness of these types of community sentence since the first piloting of the DTTO in 1998, although the evidence base for their usefulness is mixed (see Festinger et al, 2002; Marlowe et al, 2005; McSweeney et al, 2008).

The basic model for the reviews was broadly consistent across our three sites. Review hearings typically took place roughly every six weeks. The DRR team would prepare a review report for the court, setting out the offender's progress, including test results and any non-attendance at appointments. The hearing would usually involve several magistrates (in site B, a 'panel'), with legal advisers and probation staff also in attendance, the latter typically giving an oral summary of the review report at the start of the hearing. Magistrates would usually praise the offender if their progress was good. Where this was not the case, they would question the offender to try to find out why they were, for example, missing appointments and to remind them of the importance of complying with the order. Probation staff could also be questioned about their role and how they were addressing any identified issues or needs. At the end of the hearing, the offender would be given targets to achieve before the next review hearing, for example to continue getting negative test results or to start attending a particular activity. Hearings could last up to 15 minutes.

There were attempts in each site to ensure that there was continuity across hearings, with an offender being seen by the same magistrates at the next hearing, although this was not always possible. In site B, they operated a panel system to try to achieve this. Magistrates in that site reported in interviews that this review panel work was among the most rewarding that they did, precisely because of this continuity, which gave them a rare opportunity to follow a case over time. Nevertheless, across all three sites, some magistrates observed that at times they felt powerless to help during hearings when issues were raised on which they had no means of intervening. One described the role as being 'their critical friend', while another emphasized the importance of striking the right balance between interrogation, supportiveness, and encouragement:

You really can be very inquisitorial, very direct with people in a supportive way and tell them when things are not going well and support them [...] And the trick is to try and not be patronising. These are people that sometimes have had a rough deal and it's very easy to get into finger wagging.

[Site A, magistrate (A3MG1)]

Not all offenders felt this balance was very well achieved and had quite a negative view of their interactions with magistrates at the review hearings:

You have a court review every month to see how you're getting on and they're talking down to you and talking about your drug problem and you're just thinking they're from a different era anyway. They're so detached from my life and my world. You [the magistrates] haven't got a clue so for you to pass judgment on me when you don't understand anything. It were just like that. They were just ticking boxes, 'oh, so what've you done? Oh you've been engaged in this, oh very good, very good.' Just ticking a box. You're just thinking, you're just going through the motions but I think obviously they feel like they're doing some good.

[Site B, service user interviewee (B3SU9)]

Interestingly, we observed one of this offender's review hearings and he gave a good impression of being polite, engaged, and responsive to the magistrates' questions, despite the views about the process that he expressed in interview. This illustrates quite nicely the difficulties in bridging this type of gulf of understanding. As we will see later in this chapter, the notion of social distance is of some theoretical significance, as well.

Breaching and enforcement

It was intended that breach proceedings should be initiated if an offender missed two consecutive appointments (without a good reason) or failed to take a drug test or behaved in an unacceptable way with a probation officer. Neither positive drug tests nor committing another offence were grounds for breach. In practice, in all three sites the DRR team often treated offenders more flexibly and leniently. Generally, they would not breach immediately after a couple of failures to attend: 'We try really hard not to breach people and to get them to comply with the order. But if they're not then, in terms of credibility we have to take the orders back to court' (Site B, probation officer (B3PR1)). In this way, there was considerable discretion exercised at this decision point. We return to this question of flexibility in the next section. Here, we simply note that some CJIT staff observed that probation practice for DRRs differed from their own in relation to RAs or RoB, where swift enforcement action in response to non-compliance was viewed as critical to their success. There was some concern that this inconsistency, made possible by the structural separation of DRRs from DIP, could be confusing for individuals progressing through the system who might have failures to attend appointments treated quite differently at one stage of the process compared to at another.

Once the decision to initiate formal breach proceedings was taken, the breach case would come to court. The court has the power to revoke the DRR and resentence or to continue the DRR with an option to vary its requirements (eg to increase weekly contact time or frequency of testing). It was evident that it was unusual in all three sites for a first breach to lead to a revocation. Even a second breach would not necessarily do so. In site B, magistrates explicitly indicated in interview that it would usually be at a third breach that they would consider revocation and resentence, possibly imposing a custodial sentence. This was stated as a pragmatic position in recognition of the difficulties many offenders found in the early weeks of a DRR in adjusting to the demands of the order: 'Cos they've had such chaotic lifestyles, they can't seem to get this idea they've got an appointment, they've got to get there on time, they've got to have their urine test on time' (Site B, magistrate (B3MG1)).

Risk management: a regulation perspective

How then can we understand these interventions at the court stage as elements of a risk-management system? The first point to note is that although, as we discussed in chapter four, the police station is a key site for risk identification and targeting, it is also clear that further risk filtering takes place at the court stage. Individuals who carry the risk marker of a positive test can nevertheless be diverted away from drug interventions when they reach court for being at either end of the continuum of risk. A defendant, for example, charged with a very serious offence is likely to be remanded in custody rather than have a RoB imposed, as they will be considered to pose too high a risk to be left in the community. If convicted, such an offender would probably also receive a custodial sentence rather than a community order with a DRR. At the other end of the continuum, we have the example described earlier from site B of CJIT workers recommending that 'recreational' powder cocaine users were not suitable for RoB as they posed a low risk in relation to drug-driven crime.

This risk filtering is also an ongoing dynamic process. Successful compliance with a RoB, for instance, was viewed as evidence supporting the appropriateness of imposing a DRR post-conviction. Conversely, an individual who was breached while on a RoB might be assessed as unsuitable for a DRR, on the basis that they had demonstrated an inability to engage properly with treatment. In other words, the monitoring of compliance with an intervention at the remand stage could feed into decision-making further along the criminal justice process. Similarly, the management of a DRR that we have described—through urine testing, supervision, and court reviews—folds this risk information into decision-making processes about revocation and resentencing, including the potential option of confinement of an individual offender in prison. In these ways, offenders are either kept in, or diverted out of, the system of drug interventions as they progress through the criminal justice process. In other words, the risk funnel that we described in chapter four continues to operate at the court stage.

These filtering processes are important, of course, but represent only part of the picture. Recalling our discussion in the introduction to this chapter, we can also consider how these interventions operate as a preventive model of risk management. The basic outline of the operational model can be simply stated: directing targeted individuals into drug treatment and keeping them engaged with it. Its overarching purpose is to improve security and safety in communities by reducing the likelihood of these individuals committing drug-driven crime. We can separate out, then, three components of the model:

(1) identification of risk targets;
(2) direction of those targets into treatment;
(3) engagement and retention of targets within treatment.

The first component was discussed in some detail in chapter four, focusing on the police station as a site for this identification of risk targets. We have also observed in this chapter how some risk filtering occurs at the court stage as well. What about the second and third components? We will argue here these are most usefully conceptualized as a regulation problem and we examine them in the rest of this section by drawing on empirical and theoretical resources from the interdisciplinary field of regulation studies.

First, then, what exactly do we mean by 'regulation' in this context? For John Braithwaite (2008: 1), the idea of 'steering the flow of events' best captures the sheer breadth of the notion of regulation and its potential for application across very diverse domains. A more detailed definition is offered by Julia Black:

Regulation is the sustained and focused attempt to alter the behaviour of others according to defined standards or purposes with the intention of producing a broadly identified outcome or outcomes, which may involve mechanisms of standard-setting, information-gathering and behaviour modification.

[Black, 2002: 26]

It is immediately clear that we can quite readily map our criminal justice drug interventions onto much of Black's definition, as they can be described as a 'sustained and focused attempt to alter the behaviour of others', 'with the intention of producing a broadly identified outcome', involving mechanisms of 'information-gathering and behaviour modification'. What light then can the regulation literature shine on the risk-management system we have described?

Our starting point here is in fact a Foucauldian insight rather than a regulatory one. In a lecture given at Dartmouth College in 1980, Foucault (1993: 203–4) made this observation about power:

We must not understand the exercise of power as pure violence or strict coercion. Power consists in complex relations: these relations involve a set of rational techniques, and the efficiency of those techniques is due to a subtle integration of coercion-technologies and self-technologies.

We take these two terms (coercion-technologies and self-technologies) to mean, respectively, techniques that use force, violence, or threats to govern conduct and techniques that seek to enrol the self-regulating capacities of individuals by aligning them with governmental object-ives. The analytical significance of Foucault's observation for our pur-poses is that it suggests that talk of 'coerced' or 'quasi-compulsory' or 'mandated' treatment through the criminal justice system potentially blinds us to the 'subtle integration' of these two types of techniques of power and, in particular, to the importance of self-technologies.

If we look at the two court interventions we have examined in this chapter, the RoB and the DRR, they share a similar structure as regulatory interventions that integrate these two kinds of technolo-gies. Risk targets (identified by drug tests and assessments) are offered the opportunity to engage with drug treatment. Those who accept have this engagement monitored, with sanctions threatened should they fail to comply. Those who reject the offer potentially face an alternative disposal (typically imprisonment). We can see then that both operate within a framework of incentives and sanctions that is structured to maximize treatment engagement. Costs and benefits associated with different choices are manipulated in order to shape behaviour. The aim is to structure the cost–benefit distribution so that choosing treatment becomes the best way to 'maximize utility', to use economists' language (see Becker, 1968, 1976). From this perspective, it is irrelevant whether an individual has impaired or attenuated faculties of reason as a result of their addiction, *provided* that they are still to some degree 'sensitive to changes in the balance of profit and loss' (Lemke, 2001: 199). It is also evident that the goal of this type of control strategy is not to change what Dilts (2008: 87) calls the 'deep subjectivity' of individuals. Rather, as Foucault (2008: 260) put it in his famous discussion of American neo-liberalism during his 1979 course of lectures at the Collège de France: 'Action is brought to bear on the rules of the game rather than on the players […] [T]here is an environmental type of intervention instead of the internal subjugation of individuals.'

Action to alter the 'rules of the game' for a particular purpose is, of course, the core of what is meant by regulation and what is studied by regulation scholars. One major area of debate here has been about the appropriate balance between rewards and punishments. Two highly experienced drugs researchers that we interviewed argued that this was one aspect of these criminal justice interventions that was misjudged:

This seems to be the perfect area for contingency management work, yet, the first mistake is that all the contingencies are negative, so they're all punitive contingencies […] reward contingencies work much, much better. They also just aren't attuned to a population who are low in motivation for treatment, where you really do need a proper twelve-week window to build a therapeutic alliance and develop any kind of working relationship that would allow you to start making progress.

[David Best, drugs researcher]

Maybe we should actually incentivise them to go into treatment rather than 'stick' them. So you wonder whether it wouldn't be a much better idea, even if they test positive, you say, 'You don't have to go in, but here's a voucher, and if you go in and you stay in for 12 weeks, you can cash that.'

[Howard Parker, drugs researcher]

An important contribution by Braithwaite (2002) argues that despite this intuitive view that rewards work better than punishments in motivating human behaviour, this is in fact only true in certain contexts. In broad terms, he suggest that rewards are most useful in markets, where they will tend to motivate efficiency through competition as market actors compete for new business. But when it comes to many regulatory contexts, he argues that rewards work much less well. Part of the reason for this is that they are conducive to what has been variously termed 'creative compliance' or 'regulatory ritualism'. This refers to the phenomenon of regulatees focusing narrowly on satisfying the letter of regulatory standards in order to get the reward, while losing sight of the broader outcomes for which those standards are proxy measures. To take Howard Parker's example, we can quite easily imagine that if vouchers of sufficient value were offered for staying in treatment, some individuals would focus on meeting whatever attendance requirements were set for qualification for the reward, with much less interest in the actual goal of purposeful engagement with treatment.

Even without rewards, this problem of people gaming the system by subverting regulatory incentives was repeatedly identified in our research. In site A, for example, several CJIT staff referred to some defendants on RoB 'working the system' or 'finding their place in the dance' as one rather nicely put it. It was claimed that some defendants came to know, for instance, what types of excuses for missing appointments were most likely to be deemed acceptable. One offender in site B on a DRR reported that on the day we interviewed him, he had just had his first 'proper' negative urine test. Asked to clarify this, he explained: 'People bring other people's piss in, don't they. It's just one of those things, isn't it […] That's my first real negative that' (Site B, service user interviewee (B3SU10)). A probation officer asserted that this was impossible, as although they did not directly observe offenders in the toilet when they were providing samples, they would nevertheless usually be sufficiently near to be able to hear a bottle or jar being opened. Whether or not this was the case, our research in general suggested that calculative game-playing was not an uncommon tactic adopted by individuals in response to efforts to control or direct their behaviour.

But why does gaming occur? According to regulation scholars, the key to answering this question revolves around understanding how people *respond* to regulation. Drawing on Brehm and Brehm's (1981) theory of psychological reactance, it is suggested in the regulation literature that 'intentions to control are reacted to as attempts to limit our freedom, which leads us to reassert that freedom by acting contrary to the direction of control' (Braithwaite, 2002: 17). This reassertion is the 'reactance effect', while the 'control effect' refers to the extent to which we wish to act in accordance with the desired direction of control. The net impact of regulation is thus the control effect minus the reactance effect. Reactance effects are greatest when control threatens to impinge on something we value very highly and lowest when it concerns something we care little about. Direct and visible efforts to control, whether through rewards or punishment, may also in some contexts tend to increase the reactance effect, as they undermine intrinsic motivation to comply and encourage game-playing or even defiance. They suggest to a regulatee that they are not trusted by a regulator to 'do the right thing' unless they are either bribed or threatened. This is why rewards work much better in markets—the impersonal hand of the market will not be viewed in the same way as communicating this negative information about the regulatee's identity (Braithwaite, 2002: 19).

We saw repeated evidence of reactance effects in our research. Some defendants and offenders worked against measures like the RoB and DRR precisely because they resented the imposition on their freedom that they represented. This defendant in site B described his feelings towards the RoB:

I felt a bit pissed off for fucking having to go back to court just for missing an appointment […] They should make it voluntary. They shouldn't make you do something cos a lot of lads will just say, 'they aren't going to make me do fuck all'. If they're ready to get their self sorted, they'll come themselves, won't they. Do you know what I mean? They'll come. They should just ask them, 'Do you want an appointment with us? Do you want us to get your [methadone] script sorted?'. Most people will say, 'yeah', and they'll come to it. It's when you get told to do something. I don't like getting told to do something.

[Site B, service user interviewee (B3SU10)]

Building on this concept of reactance, Valerie Braithwaite and colleagues have developed motivational posture theory to help explain why regulatees have variable responses to regulatory strategies (see Braithwaite, V. 1995, 2003, 2009; Braithwaite et al, 2007). Much of her empirical work was conducted in the area of tax compliance but the theory has been applied and tested in other domains. The essence of the theory centres on the concept of social distance:

Motivational postures are the social signals that individuals send to authority, to others, and to themselves to communicate preferred social distance from that authority. Motivational postures are conglomerates of beliefs, attitudes, preferences, interests, and feelings that together communicate the

degree to which an individual accepts the agenda of the regulator, in principle, and endorses the way in which the regulator functions and carries out
duties on a daily basis.

[Braithwaite et al, 2007: 138]

Crucially, these different motivational postures help explain differential engagement, co-operation, and compliance with regulators. Five postures have been identified: *commitment*, *capitulation*,
resistance, *disengagement*, and *game-playing*. We have already discussed game-playing and so focus here, briefly, on the first four.

Commitment and *capitulation* are associated with higher levels
of compliance, the former reflecting a positive belief in the moral
authority and desirability of the regulator, the latter a more resigned
deference to its legitimacy. We saw some evidence for both postures
in our research. Some interviewees clearly felt that DIP was a positive initiative that could provide invaluable help to people like
them. They viewed it as an enterprise that had moral authority
as a public good and, accordingly, they felt a responsibility to do
their best to comply with requirements imposed on them. There is
a connection here with Tom Tyler's well-known work on legitimacy
and compliance, in which he argues that a perception that one has
been treated fairly by an authority enhances an individual's willing-
ness and commitment to attempt to comply voluntarily (Tyler,
1990; Murphy et al, 2009). This posture of *commitment*, was not,
of course, a guarantee of perfect compliance but, following
Braithwaite's theory, we suggest that it is likely to be more conducive to it. It was, however, not a widely held position in our sample.
More common was a posture of *capitulation* in which it was felt to
be better to 'play by the rules' than to 'kick up a fuss'. Comments
like 'if you're alright with them, they're alright with you' were typical of this, reflecting a pragmatic recognition that if you could
manage to comply this would make life easier for you.

Resistance and *disengagement* (along with *game-playing*) are
postures of defiance that are associated with poor compliance.
Again, we found examples in our research of both these postures.
Outright *resistance* was not as common as perhaps might be
expected, although there were certainly some defendants and
offenders we interviewed and observed who were totally uncon-
vinced by the claims to moral authority of the police, the courts, and
others and who strongly doubted that those agencies would treat
them fairly or act in good faith, even if they co-operated with them.

Disengagement in its very strongest form—where the authorities are viewed as totally beyond redemption and the main goal is to keep them as distant as possible (Braithwaite, V. 2003: 18)—was not very evident in our research but a sense of disengagement certainly did characterize the motivational posture of a number of individuals. In all three sites, for example, we came across offenders who refused a DRR as they did not wish to engage with the lengthy and onerous requirements that it entailed, preferring instead the more predictable and (for them) endurable demands of a spell in prison. A magistrate in site B observed: 'Some of them'll say, "it's too hard, send me to prison". We have people ask to be sent to prison because they just don't want to do this' (Site B, magistrate (B3MG2)).

So this idea of motivational postures as the range of ways in which individuals make sense of their dealings with the police, CJIT workers, magistrates, and others, is key to understanding how these drug interventions operate as a system for the management of drug-crime risks. The regulation literature can also guide us in answering the obvious question that follows from this: what types of approach to criminal justice drug interventions might be more conducive to creating postures of deference than postures of defiance? The short answer is responsiveness. The model of responsive regulation, as set out by Ayres and Braithwaite (1992) in what is probably the most significant contribution to regulatory theory of the last 20 years, is based on the presumption that it is usually better for regulators to try persuasion first and reserve punishment for when persuasion fails. The central principle is that 'regulators should be responsive to the conduct of those they seek to regulate in deciding whether a more or less interventionist response is needed' (Braithwaite, 2008: 88). The model is summarized in the regulatory pyramid (Figure 5.1).

The idea is that we begin at the base of the pyramid with the 'most restorative dialogue-based approach we can craft for securing compliance' (Braithwaite, 2008: 88). Only when these efforts fail should we move, reluctantly, up to the next level of the pyramid. As we progress up the pyramid, interventions become more and more punitive and demanding. At each level, the knowledge that we can escalate up the pyramid is part of what helps to secure compliance. Indeed, it is the presence of the top part of the pyramid that should drive down the bulk of regulatory activity to the lower levels. When we reach a point where reform or compliance starts to

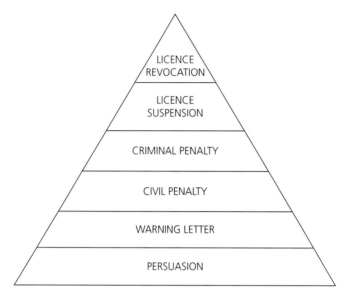

Figure 5.1 Generic business regulatory pyramid

Source: Ayres and Braithwaite (1992)

be achieved, we should de-escalate, moving back down towards the base again to reward that positive response. The pyramid is in essence a method for solving the 'puzzle of when to punish and when to persuade' (Braithwaite, 2008: 88).

What is striking about the measures we have been looking at in this chapter is how distant they are from this model of responsive regulation. There is minimal persuasion involved in the application of a RoB or DRR, nor is there any sense of escalation or de-escalation in response to conduct. Instead, as we have seen, non-compliance is dealt with in an almost chaotic variety of ways, lurching from very strict enforcement (breaches being initiated within hours of non-attendance) to extreme leniency (the practice of multiple re-RoB-ing for defendants who breach). There is an almost equally variable deployment of persuasive techniques. We saw one of the most powerful of these, informal praise and encouragement, used on occasion to great effect but opportunities to encourage were not always taken. The regulation literature suggests that praise has 'unequivocally positive effects' on compliance (Braithwaite, 2002: 24; Makkai and Braithwaite, 1993). It also engenders minimal reactance effects compared to rewards, as it tends to be viewed more as a gift, rather than as an attempt to manipulate (Braithwaite, 2002: 25). It is therefore ideally suited to co-operative dialogue-based work at the base of the pyramid. Overall, we suggest that using the model of responsive regulation to revamp strategies and practices in relation to breaching and enforcement could have a transformative effect on compliance.

We have seen then how a regulation perspective can help us to understand some of the difficulties experienced in securing compliance with efforts to direct targeted individuals into treatment and to keep them there. But to manage the risk they pose requires more than this: the treatment engagement has to lead to a reduction in their offending. In other words, the identified risk factor (heavy use of heroin or crack) needs to be reduced or eliminated. We consider this question of effectiveness and impact in chapter seven. Here, we restrict ourselves to a very brief observation about how this risk-management logic has shaped the modalities of treatment that have come to the fore within DIP. The evidence base very clearly indicates that from a narrow and exclusive crime-reduction perspective, the most effective treatment modality is methadone maintenance (eg Coid et al, 2000; Millar et al, 2008). We should not be surprised then that an efficient methadone-prescribing system was viewed in our three sites as critical to success. In site A, for example, a Rapid Prescribing Service was set up and was seen by many of the local partner agencies as one of the most important components of their local system. The prescribing modality fits neatly within the logic of the system for administering risk.

Conclusions

In this chapter, we have examined the two main interventions at the court stage, the Restriction on Bail and the Drug Rehabilitation Requirement, drawing on our empirical research in three local sites. We have attempted to break down, specify, and analyse how they operated, with the aim of understanding in some detail the 'micro-physics' of power (to borrow Foucault's phrase) as it functioned at this stage of the criminal justice process. Our central argument has been that they are best understood as elements within a system for the management of risk. In particular, we have suggested that a fruitful way of looking at them is as a risk regulation mechanism and we have drawn insights from the interdisciplinary field of regulation studies to provide a deeper perspective on their functioning.

Viewing this risk-management model through the lens of regulation brings into focus the question of the subject. What kind of subject or actor is assumed by this model for administering risk? A responsible citizen, willing and capable of compliance? A rational actor, weighing up options through cost–benefit calculations and only complying where this is the best route to maximizing utility? Or an irrational or incompetent actor who cannot voluntarily comply and requires incapacitative punishment? For Braithwaite (2002: 21), these motivational assumptions underpin the different levels of the regulatory pyramid: virtuous/responsible actors being amenable to persuasion at the base, irrational actors requiring incapacitation at the apex, and so on.

This matter of the subject is also a core concern of Foucauldian approaches to the analysis of power (Foucault, 1982) which have also influenced our approach. Our reference above to the 'microphysics of power', a phrase famously central to *Discipline and Punish* (Foucault, 1977: 26) but which Foucault was using extensively in public lectures at least as early as 1973 (see Foucault, 2006: 16), goes to the heart of the matter. What kind of subject is created and reproduced through these particular interventions? Or, to put it in the language of Foucault's later work on governmentality: how are drug-using offenders understood as governable subjects?

Both these regulatory and Foucauldian perspectives on the subject and the exercise of power point to a critical matter that we hope we have shed some light on in this chapter. Namely, that we can best understand power or authority through concrete analyses of how individuals are acted on within specific governance projects (see also Valverde, 2011). So, in this chapter, we have seen how this security governance project, that is the criminal justice turn in drug policy, is executed through micro-level interventions and mechanisms that act on the behaviour of targeted individuals. While risk management is concerned with aggregates and the distribution of risk factors across the population, it is at the level of the individual that interventions take place, even if those individuals are construed solely as members of risk categories. Our analysis, then, in this chapter (and the preceding one) has been focused on the operation and functioning of specific security techniques applied to individuals (drug testing, the bail restriction, and so on) which, taken together, constitute a system for the management of risk.

In the next chapter, while retaining our focus on a detailed examination of practice in three local sites, we shift gears a little to consider an issue that cuts across the different points of intervention
in the criminal justice system: the processing and sharing of information. We will explore the central role of local CJITs in brokering
and communicating knowledge and information about risk.

6

Drugs Work / Knowledge Work

There's now a huge [information] infrastructure around DIP. There's this management information system, DIRWeb, that's now web-based. There's still ongoing problems with it but I guess one of the other innovative things around DIP has been quite a quantum leap, going from bits of paper to much more elaborate management information systems.

[Nino Maddalena]

People spend more time filling in bloody forms than they do actually seeing punters.

[Howard Parker]

Introduction

This chapter differs a little from the previous two. While we continue our focus on the implementation of policy in our three local sites, we turn here to consideration of a significant matter that cuts across the whole system of drug interventions within criminal justice: the management and communication of risk knowledge. Drawing on Ericson and Haggerty's (1997) landmark account of policing (see also Ericson, 1994), we use our empirical findings to set out and explore our claim that criminal justice drugs work can be usefully conceptualized as a mechanism or system for brokering and communicating knowledge about risk with other agencies.

Our first trigger for developing this line of argument was the repeated lament we heard during our fieldwork from criminal justice drug workers about the time they spent filling in monitoring forms and databases, as, for example, these two experienced drug treatment workers in sites A and C, respectively, observed:

The humanistic side's gone. It's gone a bit here somewhere. You know, we're so preoccupied with producing data, cos data's the only thing that matters, that we can't concentrate on being the worker that really wants to be here just to listen to somebody offload in the way they want to offload. Because we've gotta do a TOPS [Treatment Outcomes Profile System] form and we've gotta do this. And it's really hard.

[Site A, drug treatment worker (A3TS1)]

What I have seen over the last twelve years is a mammoth increase in paperwork. Now, some of it's needed around risk assessment obviously [...] [b]ut the rest of the monitoring sometimes, you're sending something off here [...] [y]ou're sending something off there to the NTA, and it gets to the point that, 'my God, this...', you know, the paperwork becomes a massive problem.

[Site C, drug treatment worker (C3TS1)]

This reminded us very strongly of Ericson and Haggerty's (1997: 296) classic definition of the 'paper burden' experienced by police officers:

Police culture is permeated by what its members call the paper burden. 'Paper' symbolizes knowledge work in all its forms. Whether the knowledge is produced and distributed in hard copy or in electronic formats, it is seen as 'paper'. 'Burden' expresses the feeling of being overwhelmed by external demands for knowledge. Thus 'paper burden' articulates the prevailing sentiment that external knowledge demands are excessive and insatiable and detract from policework that somehow stands outside the communication process.

The second trigger was the related observation, made largely by representatives of other partner agencies and also often repeated, that criminal justice drug workers spent remarkably little time doing what would conventionally be termed 'drugs work', that is, face-to-face 'therapeutic' work with drug users. This led us to pose this question, adapted from and paraphrasing Ericson (1994: 151): if criminal justice drug workers spend relatively little time on directly helping drug users with their drug problems and associated criminality, what else are they up to? Answering this question is the focus of this chapter.

The question is important for several reasons but, above all, because it goes right to the heart of the central thesis of our book, namely that the suite of drug interventions in the criminal justice system developed in recent decades can be best understood as forming a system for the administration of risk, in pursuance of the goal of enhancing security. Grasping the operation of the structures and practices of risk communication is a vital element within our account. Risk management necessarily involves and requires the transmission and sharing of knowledge about risk.

The chapter proceeds as follows. We begin by outlining in a little more detail the central ideas of risk-communication systems, knowledge work, and the brokering of risk knowledge. We then explore how risk communication operated in our three local sites, looking in particular at the communication rules, formats, and technologies through which the transmission and brokering of risk knowledge was effected. In conclusion, we summarize the core argument presented here and in the previous two chapters, bringing together our findings about the implementation of policy on the ground.

Criminal justice drugs work and risk communication

What is meant by these notions of risk-communication systems, knowledge work, and knowledge brokering? The thesis developed by Ericson and Haggerty (1997) centres on the idea that risk has become a central organizing concept within the social world. As the title to their book suggests, they follow the grand narrative of Ulrich Beck (1992) and his claim that we have become a risk society. While we would wish to resist that totalizing account, for reasons similar to those articulated by O'Malley (1999b) but which need not detain us here, we nevertheless share their view about the 'rise of risk' (Garland, 2003) in recent decades. They also emphasize the linkage or nexus between risk and security, arguing that governance in the risk society is directed at the provision of security, with the 'yearning for security driv[ing] the insatiable quest for more and better knowledge of risk' (1997: 85). This argument would be picked up and further developed by Ericson in his 2007 book *Crime in an Insecure World*.

But how does risk-based or risk-oriented governance actually work? Here, Ericson and Haggerty introduce the idea of *risk-communication systems*. They suggest that the social meanings of risk and the operation of risk-based governance are achieved through systems for communicating risk. Different institutions create their own risk-communication systems with their own logics and processes and, together, these make up the field of risk management in a given domain (1997: 4). This plurality, that is the existence of multiple risk-communication systems within a single field, tends to make risk management a highly variegated and complex business.

A risk-communication system is not simply a mechanism for the transmission or relaying of information from one point to another; rather it is about the active construction of knowledge:

There is not just an event in the world and then communication about it. The event is called into being, made visible and responded to through the rules, formats and technologies available in the communication system. The communication system makes things real.

[Ericson and Haggerty, 1997: 4]

In this way, risk-communication systems structure, organize, constrain, and enable practice within different institutions and agencies. They are thus central to an understanding of how risk management functions. Indeed, they are the means through which it works. They provide the material for the process of the 'constitution of populations in their respective risk categories' (Ericson, 1994: 168), which is the core activity within strategies and practices for the administration of risk.

What, then, of the idea of *knowledge work*? Knowledge, in essence, consists of the forms of representation—classifications, concepts, categories—that 'stand for objects, events, processes, and states of affairs in the world' (Ericson and Haggerty, 1997: 83). Following Ericson and Haggerty, we draw no distinction between knowledge and information and treat them synonymously. Representational frameworks are based on 'forms of inscription'—writing, drawing, statistical analysis—that render people, events, and processes into information or knowledge. The conceptual forms of that information, such as, text, numbers, graphs, or pictures, then make them amenable to regulation and governance (1997: 84).

Knowledge work then is quite simply all activity that is concerned with the creation, production, processing, interpretation, distribution, sharing, reception, or utilization of knowledge or information. It can include form-filling, data entry, interviewing, data analysis, or any other kind of information-oriented work. Knowledge creation and production will usually involve the deployment of a 'technical apparatus of inscription' (1997: 84). Knowledge distribution or sharing is concerned with the conveyance of information to other institutions or institutional actors where it will be received and interpreted through the respective risk-communication systems of those institutions, while knowledge utilization is a central aspect of governance. This is a crucial point. Discourse is not simply a gloss on, or description of, practices 'in the real'. The conceptual forms of knowledge are a type of 'intellectual technology' which render reality governable through particular practices (Rose et al, 2006: 88–9; Miller and Rose, 1990; Rose and Miller, 1992). In this sense, discourse and practice are inextricably linked.

Knowledge workers thus create, distribute, and use information for governance purposes. Where that knowledge concerns risk, such workers can be described as belonging to 'risk professions':

A risk profession is an occupational group that claims some exclusive abstract knowledge concerning how to address particular risks, and some unique ability to provide expert services of risk management. Risk professions make risks visible, rationalize them through the use of processes of assessment and validation, and then offer an interpretation to constitute and enforce standards. Each risk profession exists within a system of professions defined by abstract knowledge of risk.

[Ericson and Haggerty, 1997: 447]

Knowledge brokering is a particular type of knowledge work. It involves an institution, or actor(s) within an institution, acting as a co-ordinator or distributor of knowledge within a network of institutions joined together for a particular governance purpose. In an era variously characterized as one of networked or nodal governance (Burris et al, 2005, 2008) or as an information-based network society (Castells, 1996, 1997, 1998), the brokering of knowledge is of critical importance within contemporary regulation and governance.

A knowledge broker typically acts in response to external demands for information from other institutions, for whom they are required to produce and/or communicate knowledge. For example, as Ericson and Haggerty (1997) show in great detail, many of the information demands on the police are generated in fact by the needs of insurance companies (see also O'Malley, 1991). These types of demands for information create complex inter-institutional webs of communication, in which different institutional actors at different times may take on a knowledge-brokering role. Risk professions will frequently be called upon to broker knowledge about risk because of the plurality of risk-communication systems in any given field of risk management that we referred to above.

We now turn to consideration of the risk-communication systems that operated in our three sites. We focus first of all on the ways that knowledge work creates population identities. We then examine, in turn, the communication rules, formats, and technologies through which these risk-communication systems were constituted and operated.

Population identities

The creation of categories and classifications of identity within populations is intrinsic to the risk-management enterprise. The core principle of risk management is differentiation, that is treating members of one identity category differently from those of another. And so in order to regulate behaviour and manage risk, populations need to be sorted into categories according to risk. Risk categories created by one institution may have an impact on how other institutions work.

In chapter four, we focused on the production of risk knowledge in police custody through drug testing and assessment processes and looked at how these were used as risk-filtering mechanisms. This, in effect, was a story of the creation and continual refinement of these identity categories and we refer readers back to that chapter for details on how those processes operated. Here, we wish to emphasize two points.

First, while in chapter four we looked exclusively at the category of 'drug-using offender', initially constructed through the two-step process of trigger offence and testing and then subsequently refined by the information generated in the initial assessment, some individuals were subject to further risk classifications generated by other agencies. They had, in effect, multiple identities. The most common of these was the category of 'prolific offender' (the exact label for this category varied across the sites). If an individual with a positive test had been assigned to this identity category, it would have a significant impact on the thought and action of CJIT workers in relation to that individual and the knowledge work that they would undertake. A CJIT worker in site B who was a member of a multi-agency Prolific Offender Unit captured this well:

If you're a prolific offender, being on the project means that you work with a multi-agency team and your information is shared. There's no arguing about it. Probation, NHS, CJIT, the whole lot, it's just across the board. And so I get police intelligence as well overnight from what's been happening. It's interesting when you're with somebody and you say to them, 'oh, what were you doing out in [town] last night with so and so?'. And they say, 'how do you know that?'. And you say, 'well, the police, you know, don't forget you're reporting to the Prolific Offender Unit and we all share information.' But it makes them think. And likewise, if they're doing well, the police will put on the PNC system that they're giving drug-free tests and they're engaging well et cetera. And that likewise reflects back cos if they get stopped then the PC [Police Constable] in the car could say, 'oh, I heard you were doing really well, what are you up to?'.

[Site B, DIP staff interviewee (B3DS6)]

This also illustrates our second point, which concerns the dual nature of risk identity categories as both immutable and infinitely variable. Given that the goal of sorting by risk categories is differentiation for the purpose of differential treatment, they have a binary nature: an individual either belongs to a particular identity category or they do not. In the context of our study, the drug-testing process at the police station is the clearest instance of this: an arrestee either tests positive (in which case they are included in the DIP system and must attend an assessment) or negative (in which case they are usually filtered out). But, at the same time, within each risk category, knowledge work creates ever finer gradations of 'riskiness', which can move up and down as new information is generated. An ascribed identity, or set of identities, is a dynamic and ongoing process rather than just a one-off act of labelling. In this way, and as the quote above illustrates well, it is closely connected with surveillance activity: 'Risk-communication systems require surveillance. Surveillance provides knowledge for the selection of thresholds that define acceptable risks and justify inclusion and exclusion' (Ericson and Haggerty, 1997: 448). We define 'surveillance' here in a particular and precise way as a type of knowledge work:

Surveillance is the production of knowledge about (monitoring), and the supervision of (compliance), subject populations. Knowledge production and supervision are mutually reinforcing, and together they create surveillance as a system of rule. Bureaucracy is itself a kind of surveillance system. Surveillance is THE vehicle of risk management.

[Ericson, 1994: 161, emphasis in original]

We can see then that the production of risk knowledge, and specifically in relation to identity categories, is bound up with the whole process of risk communication and risk management, to which we now turn.

Communication rules

The institutional character of risk-communication systems leads to 'professional knowledge of risk becom[ing] embedded in communication rules, formats and technologies' (Ericson and Haggerty, 1997: 447). We explore in this section the communication rules that operated in our three sites, before going on to look at communication formats and technologies in the following sections. But first we should clarify what types of risk knowledge were created and circulated within these systems. During the course of our study, we identified three basic types:

(1) *Knowledge about an individual's drug-using and offending behaviour.* This could come from drug-test results, assessments, face-to-face appointments, or police intelligence. The basic category here was the 'drug-using offender', but other classifications were also used in different contexts, including 'prolific offender', 'injector', and 'crack user'.

(2) *Knowledge concerning the presence or absence of individuals at designated times and places.* This included, for example, attendance at Required Assessments after positive drug tests at the police station and attendance at treatment appointments in the community as part of a Restriction on Bail. This type of knowledge largely took a binary form (present or absent) but 'absence' could be qualified by information considered to count as an 'acceptable reason' for non-attendance. These categories of 'acceptable reason' were largely a product of negotiation between staff and service users.

(3) *Knowledge about degrees of engagement or co-operation with treatment agencies.* Again, this was a complex and negotiated category, involving the setting of thresholds of adequate engagement, below which an individual would be considered to pose too high a risk of continuing drug-related offending.

So how are these types of risk knowledge communicated? Looking, first of all, at communication rules, these are concerned with the 'regulation of knowledge work' (Ericson and Haggerty, 1997: 321). They can be legal rules or they can take the form of guidance (which may nevertheless be described as 'mandatory'). CJIT workers often expressed to us a feeling of the complexity of the information requirements placed on them—the 'paper burden'—and that guidance and training were necessary to help them in this knowledge work. Yet, guidance could also become overwhelmingly complex. The NTA guidance document on completing the Drug Intervention Record (DIR) suite of forms, for example, ran to 85 pages and included field-by-field instructions. On the same webpage that this guidance appears, there are a further four documents about aspects of DIR completion. The field-by-field guidance offered precise and detailed specifications for filling in each field, even for the most apparently obvious and mundane parts, as the examples in Table 6.1 below demonstrate:

Table 6.1 Extracts from NTA DIR guidance

Field	Guidance	Completion guidance
Name	Full name	Name of drug worker completing the DIR rather than agency name
Phone	Full phone number (including area code)	Contact phone number of drug worker who completed the form; either landline, mobile or both
Sections completed	Tick more than one box where appropriate	Only tick to indicate a completed section if every question from that section has been completed. If the whole DIR form has been completed, tick 'all' rather than each individual section. This allows another worker or the data manager to seek clarification if required

Source: NTA (2009)

There were other national sources of guidance, too, notably from the Home Office. Indeed, the Home Office produced flowcharts, not just of the DIP process for moving individuals through the system, but also of the parallel data-collection and transmission process. The latter was at least as complex as the former, if not more so.

At a local level, in each of our sites, a series of inter-agency protocols, systems, and compacts were in place to regulate knowledge production and distribution. There were also more informal systems and conventions in place, often built up by custom over time. These types of protocols governed information communication in a range of settings and contexts. For example, in site A, a member of the CJIT team described a multi-agency meeting in which information about drug-using sex workers was shared:

I chair the Prostitutes Support Network meeting and this is a great opportunity for a multi-agency approach to target the top ten most prolific street workers […] It's a case conferencing meeting, who's engaging with treatment, who needs extra support, their [criminal justice] status. We have a very strict share of information contract that everybody has to sign. And it's become a really good meeting for people to exchange information.

[Site A, DIP staff interviewee (A3DS8)]

Although the 'strict' information-sharing contract was obviously a formal means of regulating this inter-agency knowledge work, our observations of these types of meetings suggested that informal conventions about what information could be shared in that setting were also very important. And over time, specific inter-agency groups or networks would build up their own customs of practice, setting out the boundaries of their knowledge work.

Another set of communication rules were driven by the legal requirements of criminal procedure, particularly concerning evidence (see Ericson and Haggerty, 1997: 322). We saw, for example, in chapter four, a variety of ways in which the production of drug-test results was regulated by the need to make sure that they would satisfy legal standards set by the courts for evidence. There were 'chain of custody' rules concerning the collection and storage of samples, to ensure the integrity of the testing process was robust (eg barcodes to link samples to paperwork, tamper-evident seals on sample packaging). These were based on well-established protocols developed for the collection of DNA samples and so on. Arrestees were also permitted to dispute tests, with samples sent for a confirmatory laboratory test for a definitive result. And those who did not contest the result were required to sign at the bottom of the printout slip to that effect. By these means, test results were able to be used in the courts to inform bail and sentencing decisions. Where attendance at assessments or appointments was required—either under an RA, RoB, or DRR—the evidencing of non-attendance also followed strict protocols to ensure that legal action could be taken, whether the issuing of an arrest warrant by the police or the bringing of breach proceedings to court. Only information that satisfied these communication rules 'counted' in the legal process. There was as a result a gap between 'actual' levels of non-compliance and those presented formally. And this provided a ready means, for example, for drug treatment agencies to manage breach rates, by choosing which instances of non-compliance would be processed through the formal channels and which would not, as this CJIT worker in site A observed of a specialist treatment service:

We can only deal with the paperwork we get presented with. If we don't get the paperwork, the evidence, then we can't proceed with any breaches. And obviously we don't have direct access to their appointments [log] which is confidentiality. We can't actually physically go in and say, 'well he actually had 102 breaches last month, we only got 25, what's going on?'. We don't have that access and they won't share it with us.

[Site A, DIP staff interviewee (A3DS9)]

In addition to guidance, protocols, and the requirements of criminal procedure, the other principal means for the regulation of knowledge work is based on what Ericson and Haggerty (1997: 331) call information law, in other words data protection law and policy. The distinction between law and policy is important here as agencies and institutions may place restrictions on the processing and communication of information that go beyond legal requirements. This may be partly a strategic move to develop communication rules that protect their institutional 'knowledge assets' (1997: 335). They may also claim that particular restrictions are based on data protection law when in fact this is not the case. In multi-agency working, 'confidentiality' and 'data protection' can be used as shields to fend off the knowledge demands of other agencies.

One set of these information law communication rules that we encountered in our study governed the ways in which information could be accessed by different agencies without an individual's consent. Various provisions in the Drugs Act 2005 give express or implied legal powers to share specific information for particular purposes. For example, the communication of the test result from the police to the CJIT for the purposes of the initial and follow-up assessments does not require the arrestee's consent under sections 63B(7)(ca) and 63B(7)(d) of the Police and Criminal Evidence (PACE) Act 1984 as amended by the Drugs Act 2005. Based on this legal power, particular communication rules were made. The requirement for the assessments is communicated to an arrestee using a specific form (the RA1). According to Home Office (2009: 15) guidance: 'the RA1 form must be served on the individual before they are released from custody. A copy of the RA1 form is also held on the custody record'. Similarly, section 63B(7)(a) of PACE (amended by the 2005 Act) provides for the power to share the test result for the purposes of making bail decisions, in other words deciding whether or not to apply a RoB. Again, further communication rules accompany the legal power. These systems or arrangements for conveying the result from the police to prosecutors and the courts varied locally. As we described in chapter five, this was done differently in our three sites. In site C, for example, the RoB team received a daily email from the police with the list of people with positive tests due in court that day. Results were also part of the Crown Prosecution Service (CPS) file. In sites A and B, the arrangements were different. The experience of the RoB pilots was that despite the legal power to share information, it proved difficult to establish effective mechanisms for ensuring test results arrived in court in a consistent way, not least because at the start of the pilots it was unclear to local partners how information actually entered into court systems (see Hucklesby et al, 2005, 2007).

Another set of communication rules concerned the gaining of consent from individuals to share information about them with other agencies. Obtaining consent to share obviously circumvents any restrictions raised by information law. We note in passing that workers stated that it was very rare indeed for individuals when asked for consent to question this or indeed to express any concern at all about data-sharing, and even rarer for that consent to be withheld. A court-based drugs worker quoted in Seddon (2007a: 281), in fact interviewed as part of the evaluation of the RoB pilots, captures the prosaic reality of consent-seeking in this context: 'You're assessing somebody who's literally holding the wastepaper basket in front of them, heaving into it. And then you say, "I'd just like you to sign these forms", and they will sign anything.' Gaining consent to share information is clearly in large part an aspect of rules concerning inter-agency knowledge work rather than about safeguarding the rights of individual drug users. This CJIT worker in site A described, in more benign and less graphic terms, a typical arrangement for obtaining consent:

We've got a tool. We get them to sign the confidentiality tool and we go through with them who they want us to share information with. Nine times out of ten it's the GP because that is important for the treatment anyway. And then we'll check where else they go and then we can write that in for them or they can write it in and then they sign it at the bottom. And that's done with them, I do that, you know workers do that with them. Some may want family, some may not. They sign that, then we sign it and then that shows that these are the people we can share information with.

[Site A, DIP staff interviewee (A3DS10)]

Taken as a whole, communication rules structured and organized the ways in which risk knowledge was communicated between agencies. Given the strong knowledge-brokering role played by criminal justice drug workers, these rules were central both to the strategic context in which they operated and also to their day-to-day working.

Communication formats

Alongside communication rules, another crucial aspect of risk-communication systems is communication formats. These are incorporated into the mundane media of paper forms, electronic databases, and report templates. Despite their apparent routine nature, these formats are in fact of great significance. The knowledge recorded in a report, for instance, depends on the template or format used. In this sense, communication formats 'govern how knowledge is conceived, recognized, and communicated as a capacity for action' (Ericson and Haggerty, 1997: 357).

It was evident from our fieldwork in the three local sites that communication formats were indeed central to risk-communication systems. As we have already noted, the suite of DIR forms, which formed the backbone of information recorded about the target group of drug-using offenders, was very tightly formatted and regulated. The DIRs had a highly restrictive 'narrative capacity' with very limited and circumscribed spaces for free text entry (Ericson and Haggerty, 1997: 370). For example, on the DIR activity form for completion by CJIT workers in the community, only six fields out of 47 allowed for any free text to be entered. And all six of these fields restricted the text to just 50 characters (equivalent to one short sentence). The other 41 fields involved either ticking a box, entering a date or a name.

These restrictions on what data can be entered provide a type of 'regulation of formats' (1997: 364). Within electronic databases these were often automatically triggered within the architecture of the software, making it, for example, impossible to enter more than 50 characters within a space for free text. Paper forms also restricted deviations from the format by their layout (eg the size of box available for free text, or by having other limitations on the type of response possible). A good example of this is the DT2 form reproduced in Figure 6.1 below, which is completed after a drug test has been carried out in the police station. As can be seen, this very tightly circumscribes what information can be included and the ways in which it can be recorded.

The DT1 form, which is completed when the drug-testing process is initiated, provides a combination of information-recording form and legal/procedural guide, even including specific forms of words that must be read out at different times. It presents a basis and guide for action and also accounts for the action taken (with multiple opportunities for different parties to add signatures to the form). An extract is included in Figure 6.2 below.

Court Information Pro-forma   DT2
To be submitted with Prosecution File for First Hearing

TESTING FOR SPECIFIED 'CLASS A' DRUGS AT POLICE STATIONS
Result of Drug Test

Name of person tested _____

Custody Record No. _____

Case Unique Ref. No. _____

Tested:	*On arrest / On charge
Tested after 'trigger' offence:	*Yes / No
Authority granted by Inspector or above:	*Yes / No
Test refused?	*Yes / No
Drug Test Result: Cocaine:	*Yes / No
Opiates:	*Yes / No
Sample sent to Confirmatory service?	*Yes / No
If yes, reason:	*Disputed / Medication / Quality Assurance

Charged in same period of detention with arrest offence or other relevant offence (sample to be treated as relating to charge offence)   *Yes / No

Date of 1st Court Hearing:_____

Drug Test Result from Cocaine:	*Yes / No
Confirmatory Laboratory: Opiates:	*Yes / No

Court informed of result on 1st Hearing_____Signed CPS Prosecutor

Detainee required to attend initial assessment: *Yes / No

If yes, date and location of appointment: _ _/_ _/_ _ _ _   _____

If no, state reason: _____

Paste 3rd copy of

Cozart RapiScan test result

here for Court

This Document to be submitted with the file for the First Court Hearing
* Please tick/circle where relevant.

Figure 6.1 DT2 form

REQUESTING A SAMPLE FOR TESTING

Either section 2A (before charge) or 2B (after charge) should be read to the detainee by a custody officer *(whichever is appropriate)*:

2A Before charge:

"You are 18 years old or older and have been arrested for:

    a) a trigger offence*

        OR

    b) an offence for which the inspector has authorised a drug test on the grounds that*
        [explain grounds from section 1 above]

I (name, rank, number) am now going to ask you to provide a sample of saliva for testing in accordance with the Police and Criminal Evidence Act 1984.

    a) The purpose of the test is to find out whether you have evidence of the presence of crack/cocaine or heroin in your body.

    b) If the result of the test is positive, you may be required to attend an initial and follow up assessment with a drugs worker and to remain for its duration. Failure, without good cause, to attend and remain for the duration of either of these assessments, when required to do so, may result in prosecution.

    c) If you are later charged the result will be passed to the Court for use in making decisions on bail.

    d) If you are found guilty of the offence charged the Court may use the result to help inform your sentence.

I remind you that whilst you are in custody you are entitled to:

    I)   the right to have someone informed of your arrest;
    II)   free and independent legal advice and have the right to consult privately with a solicitor;
    III) the right to consult a copy of the Codes of Practice

You may also speak to a drugs worker.
These rights and entitlements may be exercised at anytime whilst you are in custody.

Do you wish to exercise any of these entitlements?"

Note any reply..

Signed by detainee............................ Signed by App. Adult *(if applicable)*...............

Time .... Date.......................................

Signature of officer, name, rank, No...

"Do you agree to provide a sample of saliva?"

"You do not have to, but I must warn you that, if you fail to provide a sample of saliva without good cause, you will commit an offence for which you may be imprisoned, fined or both."

YES* *(note any reply, go to 4)*..
NO* *(note any reply and go to 3)*...

Signed by detainee............................ Signed by App. Adult *(if applicable)*...............

Time................................ Date....................................

Signature of officer, name, rank, NO..

April 2009

Figure 6.2 Extract from DT1 form

Another mechanism for the regulation of formats is what Ericson and Haggerty (1997: 364–7) describe as 'forms about forms'. These are forms used to trace, monitor, or otherwise regulate the use of other forms. So, for example, we came across forms attached to the front of files that included spaces to tick a box indicating a particular form had been completed and included in the file and databases that recorded the completion of various forms rather than the information collected by them.

Some of these 'forms about forms' were ones created locally rather than centrally at national level. Other locally created forms were used to solve local problems in communication. A good example of this was in site A, where a new paper form was created as a means of ensuring the RoB team got to know the court outcomes where they were not able to attend in person:

One of the things with Restrictions on Bail is that to get all the results that we need we ask the [court] ushers to get them for us. We give them a slip of paper. So the names are on it and there's a space there for them to write the outcomes.

[Site A, DIP staff interviewee (A3DS8)]

Forms created in the microcontexts of everyday practice are what Ericson and Haggerty (1997: 367–70) term 'bootleg forms'. They describe the reasons for the proliferation of these forms as including: 'The need to further rationalize complex procedures, the problems posed by unique local circumstances, administrative peculiarities concerning what should be reported, and the ease with which forms can be created using personal computers' (1997: 367). The spread of 'bootleg forms' in our three sites appeared to be fuelled in part by cultures of practice in which the creation of new forms, or additions to existing forms, were seen as key ways of solving problems. A legal adviser in site B, for example, described his experience of the use of a form in court in another area that he had worked in on a temporary basis as a solution to the problem of the court on occasion being unaware of a defendant's test result:

When I did court in [town], for every case whether it's positive or negative a sheet is handed up to the bench. Which I thought is very good practice because even if there isn't a DIP worker present in court, the bench know and the other advantage is if a prosecutor's busy the bench can instigate it. But here we don't have that system.

[Site B, court staff interviewee (B3CS1)]

Through these various communication formats, there is a direct effect on the structure and organization of risk communication. The formats provide, in a sense, an architecture or infrastructure for knowledge work. The format of the DT1 form, for example, literally and figuratively provides a script for action. Individual agency is tightly circumscribed and a limited set of possibilities is created. This leads to an increase in enactments and interactions in practice that are largely routine (see Ericson and Haggerty, 1997: 100–1). In other words, individual extemporization and improvisation are almost entirely eliminated. These institutionalized communication formats also provide for systemic relations across agencies and institutions (1997: 101). The various forms produced by the police, for instance, become standard parts of prosecution files, shaping how CPS lawyers act in court, including the ways in which they communicate risk knowledge to magistrates. The brokering of risk knowledge is facilitated by communication formats.

To summarize, within the risk-communication systems through which the administration of risk is actualized, formats for communication are a critical element. They structure and organize knowledge work. At the level of individual actors within the system, the initiation and conduct of standard tasks are shaped by the formats within which information will have to be recorded. There is, in other words, a 'format effect' in which knowledge workers like those within CJITs 'inevitably must think and act according to the concrete and discrete terms of the formats within which they communicate' (Ericson and Haggerty, 1997: 383). So the apparently mundane matter of forms and form-filling, databases and data-entry, turn out to be highly significant when criminal justice drugs work is understood as risk knowledge work.

Communication technologies

Communication technologies are the mechanisms through which communication occurs. In our research these included: phone calls, emails, faxes, face-to-face conversation, meetings, databases, and the distribution of lists (eg daily court lists). As with communication formats and rules, these technologies also shape the ways in which risk communication is achieved. They are not simply neutral vessels carrying information from one point to the next.

The drug-testing equipment was a vital piece of technology for risk knowledge production. This was viewed by many as a technological solution to the problem of not being able to identify in a comprehensive or effective way the population of drug-using offenders coming through the criminal justice system (Seddon, 2005). Prior to the introduction of drug testing, arrest referral schemes, for example, were largely dependent on arrestee admissions of drug use. The testing equipment that has been used in police stations since the drug-testing pilots in 2001, the Cozart Drug Detection System (DDS) (previously Cozart RapiScan), was selected as an easy-to-use technology that provided screening results within minutes. Other features were also important for its suitability in the police custody environment: multiple printouts of test results (required for inclusion in various files and records); 'sample adequacy indicator' (blue light indicating successful test completion to the detention officer); and no interpretation of results required (results simply indicate the presence of opiates or cocaine).

But, as we saw in chapter four, the Cozart DDS did not provide an entirely effective technological solution. Despite its ease of use, there were, from time to time, problems with its administration (taking as long as 10 minutes to collect an adequate saliva sample, paddles breaking off, collection swabs being dropped etc). More critically, as a quick screening rather than a confirmatory test, the cut-off level created a band of uncertainty that caused difficulties for the risk-communication system (see chapter four for further discussion of this).

A further implication for practice derived from the fact that the DDS did not distinguish between powder cocaine and crack cocaine. This led to 'recreational' powder cocaine users being caught in the DIP net and, as we noted in chapter four, in site C this involved a sufficient number of people that a new cocaine-focused treatment initiative was established to provide a pathway for this group of positive testers. In our view, the establishment of this new service was almost entirely an effect of this aspect of the functioning of the technology for the production of risk knowledge. In many respects, this encapsulates the centrality of risk communication to the operation of criminal justice drugs work: a new drug service triggered by a communication technology effect, rather than by an emerging new area of client need. This is not to say that there was no concern at all about increased cocaine use and how to deal with it but rather that the translation of this concern into a practical intervention was strongly driven by this functioning of the technology.

Other communication technologies we found in operation in the three sites were a mixed bag of old and new technology. An example of the former that was arguably one of the most important was the phone call, as this specialist drug treatment worker in site A described:

We obviously liaise with the Restrictions on Bail team and they phone up to make sure people have come for appointments, and when their next appointment is. And if they don't attend an appointment here they can be breached but we don't do that. We just pass on the information whether they've attended the appointment or not [...] It's their [the client's] responsibility to make it to an appointment and if they phone to cancel I make sure that the RoB officer knows they've rang to cancel and to re-appoint.

[Site A, drug treatment worker (A3TS2)]

Another vital 'old' communication technology was the face-to-face meeting. In all three sites, workers described 'two-way' and 'three-way' meetings as important means of communicating risk knowledge about individuals. There were also larger multi-agency group meetings. Some of these focused on discussing individuals (eg the 'top testers' meeting in site A and its equivalent in site B), while others sought to share information about more systemic issues concerning the operation of processes and procedures on the ground. In site A, there was also a move to co-locate different parts of the criminal justice and treatment services within a single building, precisely to improve these face-to-face contacts between professionals:

There is a suggestion from the powers that be that it would be better if it was all in one building, all the criminal justice stuff, in that they think there'll be even better liaison between the aspects of the service.

[Site A, drug treatment worker (A3TS3)]

Newer technologies, primarily electronic databases, provided different communication opportunities and possibilities. One of these was the capacity to allow for a much wider potential to access information, as Ericson and Haggerty (1997: 448) note: 'Communication technologies [...] facilitate immediate production of and access to precise risk communications from dispersed locations' (Ericson and Haggerty, 1997: 448). This was an aspiration in all three of the sites and viewed as an important way of achieving inter-agency communication of risk (and other) knowledge:

I've been to [site A] prison, I've spoken to the teams there. They've got access to our database as well. We're trying to make it as seamless as possible that once someone comes in our doors here, we've got an up-to-date picture that we'll pass on to the prisons, so the prison is then aware of it, so they're not doing the same work twice.

[Site A, DIP staff interviewee (A3DS9)]

In practice, this was often difficult to achieve because of the problem of different agency databases not 'talking' to each other, that is not easily being linked or harmonized, as this specialist drug worker in site A complained:

At the moment, NHS [services] don't have a computer case recording system, they use notes. CJIT use [name of database]. And read-only CRAMS, which is the probation recording system. So we've got three separate recording systems. And I think that's the most frustrating thing because it's all reliant on phone calls to find out who's in treatment with who […] Fortunately we have access to CRAMS, which is the probation one, because we have to input our prolific offenders onto that. But we don't have access to [name of database] which is the one CJIT use.

[Site A, drug treatment worker (A3TS4)]

A similar state of affairs existed in site B, with multiple databases in existence. Here, even when access to all the systems was possible, a new problem arose of ensuring that information was consistent across those systems:

[Drug agency] has a database, and also DIP [CJIT team] does, you know the [name of database]. And equally then there's CRAMS which is probation. I'm now party to all of those databases. And it's trying to collate the information so it tallies. So we've been doing a bit of work with admin recently to try and get the stats to tally across databases.

[Site B, DIP staff interviewee (B3DS7)]

In site C, the structure of the CJIT system was different from the other two, with the entire criminal justice service delivered by a single drug agency, which used one database to store information about all its clients. As a result, CJIT workers at any point in the criminal justice system were able to access information, not only about CJIT activity in other parts of the system but also about any previous treatment contacts there might have been with an individual outside the criminal justice process. Yet even here, the complexity of the information requirements proved highly challenging, as this senior DIP worker recounted:

What we had to do was we got in a business manager […] to kind of ground zero it all, because it had reached the stage where it had got so confused that people weren't sure what they were doing anymore. They knew what they were doing with clients but in terms of form completion and [name of database] involvement and that side of things, it was a mess. And what we did was to get somebody in for a set period of time, to analyse where we were at, to try and go, 'right, OK, forget all that now, this is what we have to do'.

[Site C, DIP worker, (C3DS1)]

Despite these difficulties with electronic data storage and retrieval, the use of communication technologies that did not require physical face-to-face meetings was viewed by some as increasing the efficiency of information exchange:

[Multi-agency meetings are] very hard to co-ordinate. They look nice on paper, joint working, it's a lovely idea. But in reality joint working is much better done in a virtual space, by phones, by calls, by messages, by linking up. It's a sort of constant stream of virtual co-working.

[Site A, drug treatment worker (A3TS3)]

The idea of 'virtual co-working' nicely conveys the way in which risk communication operates in a 'regulatory space' (Hancher and Moran, 1989) that cuts across sectors, agencies, levels, and even geographies (where liaison is required between CJITs in different areas). The 'constant stream' this drug worker refers to is, of course, a stream of information or knowledge, and the 'co-working' consists of risk communication or knowledge work. In this respect, we should perhaps not be so surprised if some critical commentators see nothing but 'paper work' here:

The field's supported this enormous bureaucracy that doesn't deliver anything, that really just pushes paper around.

[Peter McDermott, drug policy consultant]

There's just thousands of people measuring and filling in forms and it's just become a whole industry of bureaucrats.

[Senior manager, voluntary sector drug agency]

Communication technologies also provide a surveillance mechanism for the activities of knowledge workers themselves. They become objects or participants in the surveillance system, as their work is immediately available for scrutiny within information systems (Ericson and Haggerty, 1997: 410). In local multi-agency partnership meetings in our sites, data reports would be interrogated and 'poor' performance identified. Indeed, activity not captured by an information system would often escape partnership attention in these meetings. Further, as we saw in chapter three, at national level, local data reports were also the means for Home Office officials, and even the Prime Minister, to scrutinize local CJIT activity. The three-monthly prime ministerial stock-take meetings were based around such reports, as Justin Russell, special adviser to Tony Blair from 2001 to 2005, described:

> Very regular DIP delivery stock-takes to just hold people's feet to the fire in terms of actually delivering. They became every three months, I think. The Home Secretary would have to come in and the relevant Permanent Secretary [civil servant]. What was really great was you had all of them. You had the health people, you had all the relevant Health Ministers. What I thought was really good, we had front line people as well, who could keep everyone honest and say, 'Well, you know, you may be saying all this, but it's not how it really looks in Camden', and that was a really powerful coalition to start driving delivery. And the PM himself continually saying, 'Well, why aren't you taking this more seriously? Why are you only testing people that are charged if you're arresting far more people than that? Why were you allowing people to breach their bail conditions or carry on using while they were on bail?' You know, it was that relentless.

So the prime ministerial singeing of senior ministerial feet was based on reports drawn from local information systems! Badly singed feet would inevitably lead to the Home Office or NTA DIP team contacting or visiting areas that had been highlighted as performing poorly. In an important sense, then, the visibility of knowledge work created a degree of accountability that could extend from local partnership meetings up to the Prime Minister.

It is unsurprising that, as a result, local teams found their practice to be increasingly directed and shaped by this type of information-system accountability, as this DIP worker in site C remarked:

> When we reviewed what we were doing, the fundamental aim wasn't 'let's get using [name of database] as a case management tool,' it was, 'Christ, what do I have to put on [name of database] to make the KPIs [Key Performance Indicators] look better.' Do you know what I mean? And that's an entirely different consideration. And unfortunately, again, the case management, the client-centred aspect was of secondary importance in comparison to us fulfilling our KPIs.
>
> [Site C, DIP worker, (C3DS1)]

Systems of risk communication

We have seen in the main sections of this chapter that criminal justice drugs work can be understood as a form of knowledge work based on risk-communication systems. These systems are structured around particular rules, formats, and technologies for communicating knowledge about risk:

> [Knowledge work] fabricates people around institutionally established norms [...] These norms [...] emerge from the interinstitutional politics of risk in which rules for classifying populations are negotiated, the formats for communicating these classifications are devised, and the ways of acting on the knowledge so formatted are considered.
>
> [Ericson and Haggerty, 1997: 450]

Drug workers acted as brokers of knowledge that fed into key risk-based decisions by criminal justice actors, specifically decisions about bail and sentencing. The risk knowledge they communicated included drug-test results, information from assessments, details of attendance at appointments, and information about engagement with treatment. It was through these complex systems for communicating risk knowledge that the operation of the suite of drug interventions was made possible. Indeed, in the early stages of our fieldwork in the three sites, we found that such was the centrality of this information to the whole system that one effective way of mapping out the operational processes in each site was to trace the lines along which this knowledge was communicated.

Conclusions

In this chapter and the previous two, we have presented an argument for understanding the drug interventions in the criminal justice process as a security project based on a system for the management of risk across a population. In chapter four, we looked at the police station as a site for risk filtering, that is for identifying and selecting the target population defined in terms of the presence of a specific 'combinatory of factors' of risk (Castel, 1991: 281) (involvement in acquisitive offending and use of heroin/cocaine). In chapter five, we examined two court-based drug interventions—the RoB and the DRR—as mechanisms for managing risk across this population. And in the present chapter, we have set out the argument that criminal justice drugs work can be best understood as knowledge work, in which the communication and brokering of knowledge about risk forms the core of activity.

In this trilogy of chapters, we have attempted to generate a new perspective on this area, using the lens of the risk-security nexus to bring new aspects and dimensions into focus. We have also tried to connect our analyses of practice on the ground with our earlier discussions in chapters two and three of the 'big picture' of social change. It is a central element of our approach that the micro-interactions that take place in police stations, criminal courts, and drug treatment services can tell us as much about the nature of contemporary governance as the blueprints of rule contained in national policy and strategy documents.

In the next chapter, we turn to consideration of the difficult but important question of impact. What has been the impact of the criminal justice turn in recent British drug policy? Has it been effective in directing more drug-using offenders into treatment? And has this had an impact on drug-related criminality? As we will see, these are complex questions to answer and our approach to thinking about 'impact' will, by necessity, be broader than is conventional.

7

The Impact of the Criminal Justice Turn

I would actually say it's a huge success.

[NTA representative]

Bottom line, if you had to sum it up, you know, it just looks like a huge waste of money.

[Drug policy consultant]

I think everybody said that *Tough Choices* was a success.

[Home Office representative]

I just regard it as an ill-conceived adventure and I think it's been a waste of money, basically.

[Howard Parker]

Introduction

The focus of the research on which this book draws was not on evaluating the impact of the policy. We did not conduct an outcome-focused study and, in that sense, we have no primary data or findings to report here on whether this ambitious criminal justice project that we have been describing actually achieved its self-stated purpose of reducing drug-driven crime. To a large extent, this reflects our interest in understanding this policy development in the wider context of transitions in governance—in other words, we are mainly concerned with questions about the 'what', 'why', and 'how' of the criminal justice turn in British drug policy, rather than evaluating whether it 'worked' in a narrow sense. Indeed, as we suggested in chapter one, the very possibility of conducting an outcome evaluation defined in that way depends on accepting the idea of 'drug-driven crime' as a *description* of a pattern of behaviour rather than as a *construct* for the regulation of behaviour. This is not a tenable position, in our view. But this does not mean that we have nothing at all to say about impact. In the course of our research, we have developed insights into the matter, which we believe to be significant. Accordingly, in this chapter we set out some of our reflections on what we have learnt about this thorny question of impact. One of our intentions in doing so is to encourage more nuanced discussions in the future about the idea of policy impact, both in general and in the specific arena of drug policy. Our other main purpose is to develop the argument that the politics of drug policy needs to be understood more fully as extending beyond the phase of the making of policy (which we have considered in some detail in chapter three) to the ongoing discursive battle over competing claims for policy success or failure. In other words, the evaluation of policy impact, far from being solely a technical issue to be resolved by scientific expertise, is also a deeply political one.

But we are perhaps already getting ahead of ourselves, for there is a prior question here that we need to address: what exactly *is* 'impact'? This may seem too obvious or self-evident to require spelling out and, indeed, it is rarely considered a matter worth dwelling on. In the evaluation literature, it tends to be defined in relation to the idea of the 'counterfactual': impact is evaluated by comparison to the alternative scenario in which the policy or intervention was not implemented. For example, the UK government's guide to policy evaluation, known as *The Magenta Book*, describes impact evaluation as an attempt 'to estimate the counterfactual—that is, what would have happened to the outcome of interest had the policy not taken place—by controlling for other factors which might have caused the observed outcome to occur' (Cabinet Office, 2011: 97).

The *Collins English Dictionary* defines the noun 'impact' as follows:

1. the effect or impression made by something
2. the act of one object striking another; collision
3. the force of a collision.

It notes the origin of the word in the Latin *impactus*, past participle of *impingere*, meaning 'to push against'. We can draw from this two broad types of policy impact that we might be interested in considering; first, the idea of an 'effect' made or caused by a policy—this most closely resembles standard definitions of impact, such as that in *The Magenta Book*; second, the idea of a 'collision', caused by a policy striking or pushing against an existing process, system, or set of practices—this is rather different but opens up consideration of a wider range of consequences of policy. It also conveys something of the sense of forceful disruption that can be associated with major policy change. In the first two parts of this chapter, we look at these two types of impact in relation to the criminal justice turn, starting with 'impact as collision' then 'impact as effect'. In the third part, we situate the question of impact in the context of the overall theoretical argument of the book.

Impact as collision

One of the most distinctive aspects of the development of drug interventions within the criminal justice system has been the impact of these two rather different sectors coming together. In this sense, the notion of impact as collision provides quite a useful lens for exploring this. One aspect of this is a fairly familiar issue concerning inter-agency working, namely the difficulties experienced at the level of practice when bringing together staff from agencies with very different aims, values, and cultures. This finding appears in research on partnership work in diverse fields. Criminologists will be most familiar with classic works by Crawford (1994, 1997; Crawford and Jones, 1995), Sampson et al (1988; Pearson et al, 1992) and Liddle and Gelsthorpe (1994a, 1994b, 1994c), although it is a commonplace of many criminal justice evaluations in the last 20 years.

In the context of the criminal justice turn in drug policy, the problem was most pithily expressed in interview by David Best, a drug treatment researcher:

> We still have the problem, what, seven years after DRRs were piloted [of] a fundamental culture clash between the treatment provider and the probation service. So you will frequently get [treatment staff] not reporting non-attendance, not reporting dirty urines or oral swabs.
>
> [David Best]

In a review article, Mike Hough (2002: 993) identifies this gap between the criminal justice system and treatment services as one of the most significant problems encountered in the implementation of this area of drug policy:

> Agencies with different objectives and values find it difficult to establish effective partnerships, especially when they are *required* to do so [...Inter-agency] partnership work often fails. The reason, in short, is that agencies are required to do things which in the short term advance their partners' organizational goals rather than their own. The mutual trust and commitment needed to pursue shared long-term benefits often proves fragile. It is easily shattered by fundamental conflicts of approach.

Our own favourite encapsulation of these types of difficulties was the story we recounted in chapter three of the Southwark police officer claiming to have 'distributed' drug referral cards by emptying boxes of them out of the window of the police station! Other more prosaic versions of this type of problem were certainly evident in the research we described in the previous three chapters.

But in thinking about this aspect of policy impact, we need to go beyond this well-established idea of inter-agency 'culture clash'. In some settings and contexts, working together in partnership appears to have the potential to *change* the participating agencies, sometimes in important ways. Through engaging in a joint enterprise, agencies can experience a mutation of their purpose, values, or practices. We might think of this as two colliding objects changing each other's shape or leaving an imprint. This idea was certainly expressed by many of our interviewees. A national representative of the NTA, for example, discussing the significance of the criminal justice turn, asserted that 'what I think it's done is change the whole view of treatment and the criminal justice system and like I said the way we do business now'. Often, this idea that the very nature of an agency or sector was being transformed through this policy was cast in a negative light. Charlie Lloyd, formerly of the Home Office, suggested that the focus on crime reduction as an overarching objective had had a detrimental impact on the treatment system:

A worry that I have with how the system works at present is around the nature of the treatment that's delivered [...] There's a worry of everyone just getting put on a [methadone] script with rather minimal other interventions alongside it [...] There would be some that would say that it was a fairly cynical ploy by the Government just to reduce offending and scripts are quite cheap to dole out and so a rather sort of pared down form of treatment came out of this investment.

Similarly, Professor Gerry Stimson, a public health drugs researcher, contrasted the model of harm reduction from a decade earlier with the contemporary involvement of treatment services in the criminal justice system:

The whole ethos of needle exchange and outreach and making access to treatment easier was presaged on an implicit model of the relationship between staff and clients that we're in this battle together and we can only do it together. Whereas I think adding coercion to treatment changes fundamentally that relationship because the treater or the service staff become watchdogs for the courts, they become potentially more coercive in their relationships.

Others saw the impact on the treatment sector in an altogether different and more positive light. Peter Wheelhouse, head of the Drug Interventions Programme in the Home Office from 2003 to 2008, observed:

The ripple effects of DIP on the wider drug treatment system were significantly beneficial because there's no doubt in some places DATs [Drug Action Teams] were pretty ineffective, commissioning was, I think, pretty hopeless and the mainstream services, if you want to call them that, or the services that were there at the start, weren't very good either and some of those people got a massive shake-up as a consequence of the high profile of this. So I think there was the opposite of what some people feared actually, the ripple effect was backwards then to dragging up some of the existing treatment services.

Inevitably, judgements about the desirability of these impacts varied considerably. This variation was no doubt driven partly by the particular vantage point of those making such evaluations. We suggest, however, that rather than dwelling on whether impacts of this kind should be judged as 'good' or 'bad', it may be more fruitful to try to specify with more precision exactly what these impacts have been. Drawing loosely on Feeley and Simon's (1992, 1994) classic account of transformation in the criminal justice context, we suggest that mutations in the two sectors can be seen in three areas: *language*, *purposes*, and *techniques*.

If we look at the *language* and discourse of the two sectors, it is clear that much is unchanged. The dominant discourse within the treatment service sector remains centred on ideas of health and welfare, whether articulated in terms of 'management' of a condition, improving health outcomes, or preventing specific health problems. Similarly, the criminal justice system continues to use the language of law enforcement, due process, punishment, and so on. Over the last couple of decades, both sectors have also seen a more future-oriented risk-based discourse take its place alongside these older elements, in the respective emergence of harm reduction (see Mugford, 1993) and crime prevention (see Crawford, 1998). But can we see any impacts on language that have resulted specifically from the coming together of treatment and criminal justice?

We suggest that there are (at least) two discernible imprints that the two sectors have left on each other. First, the language of 'interventions' has become embedded in certain parts of criminal justice practice. While the term has always had a generic sense (an action designed to achieve a certain desired outcome) and so has been used across a range of social policy fields including criminal justice, it has been particularly prominent in the health care sector and especially nursing (eg Burns and Grove, 2010). So, the local Criminal Justice Interventions Teams (CJITs) and the national Drug Interventions Programme mark an important change of language. Its significance is that it expresses the idea that the core criminal justice agencies, like the police and the courts, are concerned with behavioural change and not simply with the enforcement of the criminal law and the conviction and punishment of offenders. Clearly, to some extent this chimes with the broader preventive turn in criminal justice that we have already mentioned; but, in our view, it goes considerably beyond that. As commentators like Adam Crawford (1998, 2007, 2009) have observed, crime prevention has emerged partly as an adjunct or even an alternative to criminal justice, an adaptation to the perceived failures of the formal apparatus of law and punishment. In that sense, it has developed along its own separate track. In contrast, the embedding of the notion of delivering 'interventions' within the core business of the police and the courts, as in DIP, has put behaviour change into the heart of the system. Time will tell, of course, as to whether this mutation of language has a long-lasting impact on criminal justice.

The second imprint or mutation concerns the term 'harm'. Emerging initially in the mid-1980s in the drug treatment sector, 'harm' signified health-related risks and specifically the threat of transmission of HIV. But as the criminal justice turn within drug policy has unfolded, 'harm' has come to cover a wider range of undesired effects, including those related to criminality. As its scope has expanded in this way, it has become a concept used in both sectors. To give a striking example, the Home Office evaluation report on 'Tough Choices' uses the term 'harm' several times, referring to frequent offenders as those 'causing a high level of harm' (Skodbo et al, 2007: 7). So the language has changed its meaning in the drug treatment sector and also transferred across to criminal justice. Again, we do not know whether, or to what extent, these mutations will persist over time, but certainly in the short run this collision between the two sectors has significantly altered the ways and places in which the language of 'harm' is used.

In terms of the *purposes* of each sector, it is perhaps here that we can see the force of the collision between the two most vividly, with one of the two colliding objects much more affected than the other. Paul Hayes, head of the NTA, spelt this out in interview:

The overarching mission [of the NTA] was to improve the availability and quality of drug treatment to reduce crime. Now our view was always, and still is, every time you get someone in to treatment, you will impact on their criminality, you will improve their health and you'll lower the risk to the health of other people. You don't have to choose which you're doing [...] Every time you get an individual in to treatment you'll deliver in all those three dimensions. We will always deliver health gain and crime gain and improve their social functioning every time we get someone in to good-enough treatment [...] So our argument's always been that although the main driver for it, the reason the public are happy for their money to be spent on it, is because of their fear about the link between drug use and acquisitive crime, [that...] isn't the only benefit that accrues from that money being available. So although it's health money, the reason the Treasury [made the money available...] wasn't to help drug users, it was to impact on criminality. So that's always been central to everything we've done.

In other words, the goal of crime reduction has now become not just one of the central purposes of drug treatment but also the principal justification for its funding at the present level. Again, Paul Hayes nicely captured this point in interview:

Left to their own devices, the Department of Health would invest very little in drug treatment. Drug dependency kills very few people, compared to alcohol, tobacco, suicide, road deaths. It's not a great killer. It doesn't cause that much illness either, again compared to lots of other things. So in strict health economics terms, it's not that good an investment [...] It shoots up the health pecking order because of the crime link.

This is an important point. As we observed in chapter three, many of the policy actors we interviewed agreed that the enormous expansion of treatment in the period after the establishment of the NTA in 2001 was largely dependent on this connection with crime. In this sense, the shared goal of crime reduction is not just an impact from the collision of the two sectors but the very reason for them being brought together in the first place.

Lastly, we can also see an impact from the two sectors colliding together at the level of the *techniques* deployed in each field. Here, perhaps the impact has been less marked or dramatic but nevertheless is still important. An obvious example concerns drug testing. While this has been a tool used within drug treatment services for decades, notably in residential rehab and detox centres, the criminal justice turn has seen it inserted right across the criminal justice system, from police custody suites through to prisons. It has rapidly become embedded in the everyday practices of criminal justice personnel. In the police station, for example, as we saw in chapter four, it has taken its place within custody procedures alongside fingerprinting and other standard processes. The information from drug tests has, in turn, become 'folded into the decision-making algorithms of the system', as Feeley and Simon (1994: 179) put it, particularly in remand and sentencing decisions made by the criminal courts. The drug test has rapidly become a central technique within criminal justice for the management of the risks understood to be posed by the sub-population of drug-driven offenders. For the police, this development has no doubt been aided in part by the 'family resemblance' with the alcohol breathalyser test, which has been a staple of British police practice since the late 1960s.

A slightly less obvious example concerns an impact in the other direction, to which we have already alluded. This relates to the effect of the new criminal justice agenda on treatment modalities and the view that the prescribing of methadone (and other opiates) has become the dominant treatment offering as a consequence of the criminal justice turn (as prescribing has a well-established evidence base for its crime-reduction effect—eg Coid et al, 2000; Millar et al, 2008). This claim is difficult to assess or evaluate because the entire treatment sector has been through an enormous expansion during this period, making meaningful 'before and after' comparisons problematic. We can certainly say that this was a view expressed by several of the policy actors we interviewed, and also by some practitioners in the local sites we studied. Again, it is unclear how lasting an impact this will prove to be. At the time of writing in mid-2011, there have been calls for a rowing back from methadone prescribing, in the context of the debate about the need for provision to become more 'recovery-oriented' (Home Office, 2010), although whether these calls will be translated into change at the level of service provision is not yet known.

Impact as effect

What about the impact of the criminal justice turn, in the sense of its effects or outcomes? We can separate this into two questions. Did the initiative get the intended population into treatment services? Did it reduce crime? These seemingly straightforward questions are inevitably more difficult to answer than might be imagined. In this section, we attempt to provide a critical summary of some of the published evidence on these outcomes. We then go on in the section that follows to contextualize and explain these findings, drawing on insights we have gained from our own research.

We will consider here two key studies:

(1) a piece of large-scale secondary analysis focusing on the 'Tough Choices' measures in particular, carried out by the Home Office with some external input and published as Skodbo et al (2007); and

(2) an independent evaluation commissioned by the Home Office and conducted by a team led by Mike Hough's research unit, published as ICPR et al (2007).

Looking at the first of these two studies, this draws on secondary data-sets in order to examine how effective DIP has been in retaining individuals in treatment and in reducing their offending. Two different cohorts were constructed:

- the Testing on Charge (ToC) cohort, consisting of 7,727 individuals who tested positive during a four-month period in 2005 and were matched with offending data held on the Police National Computer (PNC);
- the Testing on Arrest (ToA) cohort, consisting of 11,015 individuals who tested positive during a three-month period in 2006 and were matched with PNC data.

The purpose of having these two cohorts was to enable a comparison before and after the implementation of 'Tough Choices', in terms of the profiles of positive testers, patterns of attrition, and impact on offending. The published report of this study, Skodbo et al (2007), is worth reading closely and in detail. Here, we summarize some of the key points.

There are two headline findings in terms of the profiles of positive testers:

- the net has widened considerably following implementation of 'Tough Choices', and the shift from ToC to ToA, with throughput moving from a monthly average of just under 2,000 to an average of just over 3,500;
- the demographic profile has not discernibly changed with this increase in throughput but the ToA cohort contains lower proportions of frequent and serious offenders.

Findings on drop-out through the process are mixed. The study clearly found that the 'Tough Choices' measures reduced attrition at the front end, in terms of the proportion of positive testers having initial contact with a drug worker (77 per cent compared to 53 per cent) and then receiving an assessment (93 per cent of those contacted compared to 77 per cent) (Skodbo et al, 2007: 9–10). However, the picture is less clear after this. For example, it was found that the proportion of those assessed as requiring further intervention who consented to that intervention actually fell from 96 to 83 per cent, indicating worse attrition at this point for the ToA cohort.

Perhaps the most critical part of attrition concerns the proportion of positive testers who actually get to specialist treatment. Here, in both cohorts the level of attrition was high. In the ToC cohort, only 652 individuals out of 7,727 positive testers entered treatment (8 per cent), while for the ToA cohort it was slightly higher at 1,197 out of 11,015 (11 per cent). Part of the attrition at this point is actually indicative of population recycling—in other words, individuals already on the DIP caseload and in treatment who are arrested and test positive at the police station are obviously not counted as 'new' treatment entrants. Another sizeable chunk of the drop-outs consists of those who end up in custody. And some, of course, are assessed as not requiring any further intervention. But there remains a big group who are either unable or unwilling to engage with treatment.

Even among that small group who arrive at the doors of a community treatment service, not all will stay the course. The final measure of attrition is therefore equally critical: of those who arrive in specialist treatment, how many are retained there long enough for that treatment to make a difference? The standard proxy measure for this is the percentage of treatment entrants who stay engaged for 12 weeks or more. Skodbo et al (2007: 12) note that the general retention rate for drug treatment as a whole is 76 per cent, while the comparative figures for the ToC and ToA cohorts were 79 per cent and 74 per cent respectively. This suggests that while criminal justice leverage may help to deliver people to the door of treatment (although drop-out through the process is high), it has little additional impact after that in keeping them there, a point made in interview by drugs-crime researcher Tim McSweeney:

People do feel a coercive pressure, or influence, to get them into treatment. But that generally wanes over time, particularly as people do get into services and accept, or realise, that what's on offer can actually be of benefit to them. And those that don't, leave very quickly.

In relation to the impact on offending, the study examined PNC data for the ToC cohort only, looking at convictions in the six months before and six months after the positive test that brought them into the cohort. The headline finding that the study reports is a 26 per cent reduction in convictions post-DIP. Setting aside the obvious methodological qualms we might have here (reliance on convictions as a proxy for offending, lack of a control group etc), this may appear to show a positive impact on criminality. It masks, however, some significant variations within the cohort. In fact, only a minority (47 per cent) had a decline in convictions, while the majority either saw no change (25 per cent) or a rise (28 per cent). This indicates a decidedly mixed picture of impact on offending.

The second of the two studies we are focusing on here was not formally published by the Home Office. Here, we draw on findings in a self-published report by the research team (ICPR et al, 2007). Specifically, we consider analysis of data from interviews conducted with 209 individuals at three time points:

- time one (one to three months after initial assessment by the local CJIT);
- time two (three to six months after time one); and
- time three (six to nine months after time one).

Time one represents the baseline measure, with times two and three as follow-ups. Basic data on changes over time in drug use and offending are summarized in Table 7.1 below.

In broad terms, comparing measures at the two follow-ups with those at the baseline, we see reductions in drug use, spending on drugs, and offending. On the face of it, these are arguably positive findings but we can make several critical observations. First, and as

Table 7.1 Headline findings from ICPR evaluation

Outcome area	Time 1	Time 2	Time 3
Proportion reporting any crime in last month	34%	24%	20%
Mean number of crimes in last month	8.4	2.7	2.7
Regular/daily heroin use in last month	68%	15%	12%
Regular/daily crack use in last month	24%	5%	6%
Drug spend > £1000 per month in last month	65%	18%	16%

Source: ICPR et al (2007: 25)

the research team themselves notes (ICPR et al, 2007: 29), the levels of offending at baseline are strikingly low. Indeed, two-thirds reported no involvement in crime in the previous month. This rather undercuts claims to be 'gripping' serious drug-driven offenders. Second, and again as acknowledged by the research team, the 'before and after' research design is unable to determine what proportion (if any) of these apparent reductions in drug use and offending were the result of CJIT interventions. In other words, we do not know whether some or all of these reductions would have occurred anyway. An (unknown) part may also be a statistical artefact known as 'regression to the mean' rather than a 'real' reduction (see Bland and Altman, 1994). It would be unwise, therefore, to conclude that these findings are anything more than 'indicative' or suggestive of some impact. Third, it is evident that the apparent falls in drug use are much greater than those in offending. This implies the connection between the two is rather looser than the behavioural model that underpins the policy would suggest.

To summarize, these two studies present us with a mixed and, to some extent, puzzling picture of the outcomes of DIP and related interventions. Certainly, we can say that the drug testing net captures significant numbers of drug users who have been arrested, and that it manages to channel some of these into treatment. Attrition through the process remains very high but appears to compare favourably with earlier initiatives like arrest referral (eg Millar et al, 2002; Oerton et al, 2003). This prompts an obvious public policy question concerning costs: does the expenditure on the testing and DIP infrastructure deliver an adequate return in terms of 'new' treatment entrants? Part of the answer to this question turns, of course, on the thorny question of the extent to which those who engage in treatment stop or reduce their offending. And on this, we are faced with an equivocal and limited evidence base, as the brief account above indicates. How, then, should we make sense of all this evidence on impact? We consider this in the next section in which we return to our central argument about how we should understand the criminal justice turn.

Drug policy as problem-solving action

In chapter two, we outlined our theoretical framework in which, drawing on but extending Garland (2001), we conceptualized recent British drug policy as a (socially structured and culturally shaped)

process of problem-solving action in the face of new (socially structured and politically constructed) policy predicaments. Can this
help us better understand these difficult questions of impact?

One way to use this framework is to pose a blunt question: did
the new policy solve the problem it was meant to? This suggests (at
least) two elements that we might examine to contextualize and
understand impact findings: first, the framing and construction of
the problem; second, the form and functioning of the solution.

If we look, then, first of all, at the framing of the problem, we
have already noted in chapter one that the evidence for the idea
of 'drug-driven crime', on which the criminal justice turn fundamentally rests, is at best equivocal. In the plainest terms, the
'economic necessity' model of the drug–crime link is crude and
simplistic, failing to capture the causal complexity and variation
involved (see Seddon, 2006, 2010c). It follows then that any crime-
reduction impact of drug interventions is likely to be highly
variable between sub-groups and limited in scale at the aggregate
level. From this perspective, the otherwise puzzling finding from
the Skodbo et al (2007) study that over a quarter of their cohort
saw a *rise* in their convictions post-intervention starts to become
more explicable.

A more sophisticated version of this type of critique was outlined in interview by Howard Parker. Drawing on his own research
in Merseyside in the 1980s (Parker et al, 1988; Parker, 2005), as
well as earlier North American work on the post-war heroin epidemics (Hunt and Chambers, 1976; Hughes, 1977; Hughes and
Rieche, 1995; see also Ditton and Frischer, 2001), he argued that a
failure to understand the epidemiological life-cycle of local heroin
outbreaks significantly undermined the potential impact on crime
of these criminal justice drug interventions:

They [the Home Office] were still relying on the 80s research, but we had
a second wave of heroin outbreaks in the 90s, which went into the East
Midlands, Yorkshire, Welsh valleys, along the east coast and so on. So we
got to the situation in the [early 2000s] where they said, 'Right. We want
to put the DIP intensive programme into the high heroin/crack areas.'
And of course they picked up the Salfords, the Manchesters, the Liverpools,
the Knowsleys, the inner London boroughs, nearly all first-wave heroin
epidemics, so they were actually coming to the end of the incidence period
of their heroin use. So you get to the situation in Salford now where
there's no young heroin users, and all the heroin users are getting older […]
And yet, I've been working in Derbyshire, which is a second-wave area,

I've been down there recently, they've got 3000 problem drug users. They've got a complete correlation between the PPO [Prolific & Priority Offender] targets and known problem drug users at 93 percent. It's about 15 percent in Salford [...] The problem for DIP was that, come the millennium, as it started to be a hot political idea, it got caught in not understanding the [epidemiology], it got caught in using an old evidence base.

In other words, the coupling together of problem drug use and crime varies quite significantly between different localities, depending on what stage of the life-cycle of the outbreak is being experienced. This type of epidemiological insight seems to have been entirely absent from policy discourse, both in public and in private.

Developing this idea, Parker (2007) has argued elsewhere that patterns of drug-related crime do not just vary between localities but have also undergone a significant shift nationally over the last couple of decades. It is a common argument in the literature on regulation that regulators tend to act to fix yesterday's problems rather than tomorrow's, leading to regulatory regimes that seem to be perennially unfit for purpose (Braithwaite, 2008). This provides a good analogy for what appears to have happened in this area of drug policy. The typical heroin user of the 1980s was involved in burglary or theft of/from vehicles to fund their drug purchases (see Parker and Newcombe, 1987). Twenty or so years later, in our study, most of the people we interviewed had committed relatively minor offences, sometimes almost trivial, with shoplifting by far the most common and burglary relatively rare. The proportion of people using only heroin has dwindled, as it is increasingly used alongside crack. At the same time, the use of powder cocaine has also risen significantly. This has presented a challenge for drug treatment services, in terms of developing appropriate interventions. It has also cast serious doubt on the capacity of the system to reduce the types of crime viewed as most harmful to communities. While a major reduction in shoplifting might be welcomed by Mr Marks and Mr Spencer, it would no doubt cut much less ice with residents in high crime neighbourhoods.

We might say then that the materiality of the problem was arguably not fully or properly captured in its framing by policy-makers and that this affected the resulting outcomes and impact. But this is only a narrow part of the story. As we have argued, problem-framing is a *socially structured* and *politically constructed* process rather than an unmediated descriptive one. It has been a core argument of this book that the particular framing of the drug–crime link has had a distinctive focus as a result of being viewed through the lens of late modern anxieties about risk and security.

This helps us explain some otherwise perplexing aspects of the way that the debate about impact has been conducted. One of the points of criticism that many policy commentators have made (eg Stevens, 2011b) concerns the repeated claim that between one-third and one-half of all acquisitive crime is drug-related. There is no basis or source for this claim, and there are strong grounds for believing it to be a significant overstatement (eg Baker et al, 1994; Dorn et al, 1994; Stevens, 2008). So why, one might ask, has it been repeated so often in policy discourse? We suggest that this is best understood as connected with the securitization of the issue. To frame the drug–crime link as a matter of public safety requires it to be constructed as a significant driver of local crime rates. We see a good example of this in the *Updated Drug Strategy* published by the Home Office in 2002, which claimed that: 'Nothing affects the well-being of local communities as much as drug misuse, drug-related crime and the fear of such crime' (Home Office, 2002: 10). For the same reason, the debate about the impact of the criminal justice turn has tended to become most heated when claims are made about the overall effect on crime in communities. In interview, Paul Turnbull described the extraordinary level of concern and anxiety that Home Office officials demonstrated during the evaluation of CJITs that we referred to above:

We delivered this [interim] report [...] you know, we did our usual warts and all thing, and it didn't go down well at all. It didn't go down well at all. So following that, [Home Office] policy [staff] became very involved in the research, attended all the meetings about the research, looked at every bit of paperwork we did, every instrument, every letter. Very hands on after that. I think they were fearful that we were going to rubbish the whole thing really. So they became very active.

As we noted above, such was the 'disappointment' with the findings that the Home Office eventually did not formally publish a final evaluation report. This is a nice example of that enduring insight that Foucault (1972) wrote about some 40 years ago in *The Archaeology of Knowledge* that science and knowledge must be understood as the *product* of power relations and conflict, rather than as something that precedes or stands outside them. The debate about the impact of these drug interventions is profoundly 'political' in this sense. Stevens (2011a) describes this struggle over claims about the impact and effectiveness of the policy as the select-ive use of evidence to 'tell policy stories'. He argues that this can be most fruitfully analysed as an ideological process designed to fur-ther the interests of the powerful. We do not see it quite like that. Rather than being a matter of serving the interests of the powerful, the politics of evidence within drug policy is better understood as embedded within a more multifaceted and multivocal discourse about the capacity of policy-makers to respond adequately to the cultural anxieties and preoccupations of the time (which in early twenty-first-century Britain revolve around risk and security). In other words, and inspired by Loader and Sparks (2004), we see the concept of *political culture* as helpful here, in contrast to a con-struction of politics as a pure tool of power.

So the struggle to 'name' the problem, as Loader and Sparks (2004: 19) put it, provides a useful way in to some of these ques-tions of impact. What then about the conflicts over preferred solutions? As we saw in chapters four and five in particular, the responses to this public safety or securitized construction of the problem are based on the idea that the required task is the admin-istration of risk across a population. This helps us make further sense of the question of impact. The logic of this risk-management model is that the starting point of the process needs to be sure of capturing the highest-risk group within the population (defined as the most serious and/or frequent property offenders). At this stage, it matters much less that many minnows are also caught in the net, provided that most or all of the big fish are there. This partly explains the strong desire to widen the scope of testing from on charge to on arrest, which, as we noted earlier, greatly expanded the haul of positive tests. For some, this was a major mistake. Howard Parker, for example, sharing our fishing metaphor, observed in interview:

By over netting, DIP is now getting loads and loads of petty, petty offenders who take [powder cocaine]. Are they crime-causing? No. Are they problem drug users? No. Are they amenable to treatment? No. So the whole system is clogging up.

But within a risk-management model, an over-inclusive initial net is not such a problem at this point in the system, as the low-risk can be filtered out at later stages. We described this filtering process in some detail in chapter four. Termed as attrition, this can be seen as a significant failing of the system. Again, Howard Parker gave a superbly incisive version of this type of criticism:

The attrition all the way through from mandatory drug testing, right through to staying in treatment is absolutely enormous […] If you look at Salford, it used to be half tested positive/half tested negative, and that's gradually moved up now over the last three years to 60 percent testing negative. So immediately 60 percent go. Then of the ones that come through, the biggest single group now are recreational cocaine powder users, who are low crime-causing offenders, who refused treatment straight after the Required Assessment because they don't think they need it, so no further intervention required. So another great big group go out. And then you've got the ones that are already in treatment who are part of the revolving door, so you get an activity sheet for them and you get a tick, but they're not new […] And then you've got another group who say, 'Yeah, yeah I'll go into treatment,' so they open a care plan, and then half of them don't turn up to the service. And then the other side of comprehensive assessment, a few more don't turn up, and then a few more go back into prison. And by the time you've finished, the attrition is absolutely enormous.

Evaluated as a 'service' or 'intervention', this level of attrition is poor. Viewed, however, as a system for the administration of risk, much (although not all) of this 'attrition' can be conceived as effective risk-based filtering. So, from this perspective, those who test negative or who are cocaine powder users with minimal criminal involvement are quite correctly and appropriately identified and diverted out of the process.

Another area of concern relating to the question of impact has centred on the nature of the interventions delivered to individuals. The experienced drug treatment researcher David Best described in interview a study of a local partnership in the West Midlands:

We looked at what interventions people get in DIP and most of our clients get seen once a fortnight for about 40 minutes, and you think, 'this isn't treatment,' you know, 'this is not anything therapeutic,' and only a tiny minority were getting an actual structured intervention. So it basically was medication plus chatting, and this is not drug treatment […] It's not a palatable thing to say, but it's a population management medication model. That's fine if that's what you want DIP to be, but to pretend it's a treatment package is meaningless.

For Best, this type of intervention is clearly undesirable and inadequate and he sees it as one reason for the mixed findings on impact. But he also pinpoints precisely the intended purpose of the model, namely population management. In other words, as we have argued throughout this book, the overarching goal is not to make drug users 'better' but to make communities safer. The latter is to be achieved by intervening not at the level of individuals as such but at the level of the factors, or combinations of factors, that render individuals high-risk. Within the framing of the problem that we have described, the single most important of these factors was constructed as regular use of heroin and/or crack. And so the core of the response has centred almost entirely on drug treatment in general and methadone prescribing in particular, with many local partnerships placing great importance on developing rapid prescribing services to provide quick and easy access to methadone. This also partly explains the narrow way in which policy-makers have tended to conceive of the interventions. Paul Turnbull commented on this in interview:

It's this idea that drug treatment is this uniform thing that can be delivered to anybody and in a uniform way. And that it will have this result. And that's how the [Home Office] policy people I think responded to the [research evidence]. All I had was, you know, treatment works and it costs this much and you save this much. And they took those messages and thought, 'Right, great, somebody's telling us this, we must apply this to this population and we'll have the outcome that we want.'

In this way, many of the limitations of the policy that have been identified as constraining its crime-reduction impact—the narrow understanding of treatment, the high attrition through the process, the 'over-netting' of police drug testing—can be understood as linked to the logic of the risk-management model. In other words, they are products of this distinctive form of problem-solving action, which has been shaped by wider social, political, and cultural forces.

Conclusions

In this chapter, we have sought to provide a contextualized account and consideration of the impact that this drug policy development has produced. Rather than simply review or evaluate the evidence, a task to which others may be better suited than us in any case, we have tried to examine the question of impact in a more rounded and nuanced way, in part by using our theoretical framework. An important idea that we have attempted to get across here has been that debates about impact are profoundly political and need to be interpreted in that light. The thorny question of whether a particular policy has 'worked' or not cannot be definitively settled simply by appeal to the 'science' or 'evidence'. We note, in passing, that the repeated calls for drug policy to be based on science and not politics or ideology are misguided on this point. Drug policy *is* politics.

One obvious question about impact that we have not addressed follows quite closely from our argument about the significance of anxieties about insecurity to an understanding of the criminal justice turn. Has it alleviated at all, or dampened down, these anxieties? In other words, has this development in British drug policy made us feel safer and more secure? A proper answer to this question would require an entire new research study and it is beyond our scope and capability even to begin to respond to the question in an empirical way. Nevertheless, some of the criminological literature on fear of crime provides a clue to some important matters relevant to our central argument in this book and to which we return in the final chapter. Building on an important early essay by Richard Sparks (1992), the most sophisticated recent work on fear of crime has demonstrated that worries about crime are deeply entangled with wider anxieties about politics, social order, and justice (eg Farrall et al, 2009). It is for this reason that our 'case study' of this drug policy episode can tell us something about these broader issues concerning society in the early twenty-first century. Part of our task in the concluding chapter is to make sense of what we have learnt about the 'big picture' from this examination of a small corner of public policy action.

8

Conclusions: Reimagining Risk and Security

The liberal social imaginary promises security as freedom from harm to life and its potential. Security is safety, something that guarantees and guards a secure condition and thus provides freedom from danger. Security contributes to certainty: freedom from doubt, fear, and anxiety about danger.

[Ericson, 2007: 216]

It has been mostly in Europe and its former dominions, overseas offshoots, branches and sedimentations […] that the ambient fears and securitarian obsessions have made the most spectacular career in recent years.

[Bauman, 2007: 55]

Introduction

At the heart of the debate explored in this book are a series of questions about the place of risk and security within the contemporary landscape of social control. This is terrain that has been charted over the last 25 years by some of our leading criminological and socio-legal scholars, with notable contributions from, among others, Pat O'Malley (1992, 1999a, 2004), Jonathan Simon (1987, 1988, 2007; Feeley and Simon, 1992, 1994), Lucia Zedner (2003, 2007), Richard Ericson (2007; Ericson and Haggerty, 1997), David Garland (1995, 2001, 2003), and Richard Sparks (2000, 2001). Looking further afield, entire sub-disciplines of security studies and risk scholarship have been established with their own journals, book series, and academic conferences. One of the reasons that these ideas have provided such fertile ground for enquiry is that they are connected with much wider concerns about the nature of politics and government at the beginning of the twenty-first century. For many criminologists, this link with the 'big picture' has made risk and security immensely seductive and exciting topics for investigation.

It is perhaps this sense of engaging with such big questions that has encouraged a tendency towards grand narratives and epochal accounts (eg Ericson, 2007; Simon, 2007). These have no doubt had an exceptionally bracing and productive impact on criminology but, as we suggested at the beginning of this book, a space has also emerged for more 'focused case studies' (Garland, 2001: vii), which can add specificity and detail, refining and revising those broader accounts. With this in mind, our objective in this book has been to examine in depth a particular corner of the public policy world, namely the criminal justice turn taken by recent British drug policy. We believe this is of substantive interest and significance in its own right, not only to drug policy researchers but also to criminologists and criminal justice scholars. But we also believe that our study can make a contribution to these larger debates. We do not mean by this that we are claiming to be able to generalize from our case study to make grand assertions about the state of contemporary society and governance. Rather, our contribution comes from seeing how those higher-level arguments look when brought to bear on a specific policy area in a specific time and place. And when viewed from that end of the telescope do those arguments require any revision or adjustment?

We begin this chapter by providing a very brief summary of the core arguments of the book. We then go on to consider how our study provides some new perspectives on these wider questions of risk and security and the nature of contemporary governance. We focus here on three key theses in the literature, which our study has indicated require some revision: the ways in which the crime problem has become central to the exercise of power and authority (Simon's governing-through-crime thesis); the emergence of a new crime-control complex (Garland's account of the late modern 'culture of control'); and the trumping of due process standards by the security imperative (Ericson's concept of counter-law).

Understanding the criminal justice turn

Our central task in this book has been to attempt to understand the emergence of the criminal justice turn within British drug policy. Why has the drug–crime link become in recent decades so central to how we view the drug question? And why has policy taken on the particular forms that it has, with the emphasis on using the criminal justice system to identify and target drug-using offenders in order to channel them into treatment? We briefly summarize here our main arguments.

In chapters two and three, we sought to answer these questions by setting the development of drug policy within the context of the 'big picture' of social change. We argued that the transition over the last 40 or so years from the welfare-liberalism of the middle twentieth century to an era of neo-liberalism at the turn of the twenty-first has changed the nature of the drug situation in Britain, greatly extending the reach and prevalence of 'recreational' drug use among young people and creating new pockets of severe neighbourhood drug problems (in which drugs, poverty, crime, and worklessness coalesce). This transformation has generated new risks and insecurities that have, in turn, been understood and problematized in a distinctively neo-liberal way. These problematizations have posed new policy predicaments: drugs are everywhere (in the media, popular culture, and society) and at the same time deeply problematic (linked to intractable problems of social exclusion and crime). The responses to these predicaments, of which the criminal justice turn is one part, have also, in turn, been shaped by the transition to neo-liberalism, becoming entwined with questions of risk and the governance of security. In chapter three, drawing on interviews with national policy actors, we sought to piece together in more fine-grained detail exactly how the policy was put together and developed at national level, focusing on the motives and intentions of these actors. Together, these two chapters set out an original account of how the evolution of the criminal justice turn in recent British drug policy can be understood as a (socially structured and culturally shaped) process of problem-solving action in the face of a new (socially structured and politically constructed) drug policy predicament.

We then explored the implementation of the criminal justice turn by local partnerships in chapters four to six, drawing on data from three multi-method local case studies we conducted. We framed our analysis here by viewing the drug interventions delivered through the criminal justice process as a risk-management system aligned to a security project. In chapter four, we focused on drug testing and assessment processes in the police station, understood as elements of a risk-filtering machine. In chapter five, we examined interventions at the court stage, conceptualized as parts of a system for the administration and management of risk. In chapter six, we explored the ways in which the role of criminal justice drug workers could be understood as brokers of risk knowledge within the system, rather than as therapeutic professionals conventionally defined.

In chapter seven, we addressed the thorny question of the impact of the criminal justice turn: has it worked? We argued that there is insufficient evidence currently to claim that it has been effective in reducing crime. We also suggested that there were some good reasons to believe that such an impact would in fact be unlikely anyway. We argued, too, that it is helpful to widen what is meant by the idea of impact, to provide a more rounded and nuanced assessment. We turn now to consideration of the wider significance of our study.

Governing drugs through crime

One of the most interesting contributions to the debate about the place of risk and security in contemporary governance has been provided by Jonathan Simon (2007) in his book *Governing Through Crime*. His thesis is encapsulated in the title and can be simply put: increasingly, at the turn of the twenty-first century, crime and metaphors of crime have become central to the exercise of authority. He outlines three dimensions along which this can be observed. First, 'crime has now become a significant strategic issue' (2007: 4). In other words, taking action to prevent or deal with criminality has become an important focus and purpose of legitimate activity across diverse settings and institutions. Second, the category of crime is deployed to 'legitimate interventions that have other motivations' (2007: 4). Third, 'technologies, discourses, and metaphors of crime and criminal justice have become more visible features of all kinds of institutions, where they can easily gravitate into new opportunities for governance' (2007: 4–5).

Simon gives numerous examples to illustrate this thesis. He looks not only at the apparatus of the state but also at key institutions of social life, from the family, to schools, to the workplace. It is a wide-ranging and ambitious account, which seeks to describe and explain the ways in which fear and anxieties about crime have fundamentally transformed the nature of how we are governed. Adopting a powerful normative voice, Simon argues that governing through crime has distorted American democracy, fuelling a 'culture of fear and control' (2007: 6), while at the same time ironically failing to make citizens more secure.

On the face of it, the area of policy we have examined in this book looks like an exemplar of Simon's thesis. A social problem previously treated as a question of welfare or public health becomes governed through its purported links with crime, legitimating new strategies and interventions (eg coerced treatment) that would otherwise be difficult to justify. Up to a point, this is of course exactly what the notions of criminalization and the criminal justice turn are meant to convey in relation to drug policy. We argue, however, that our study points to a more mixed picture in the domain of drug policy, indicating a need to develop or refine Simon's argument.

Our first observation is that we should perhaps not be surprised that a leading criminologist should interpret the world as revolving around the category of crime! The question is whether this perspective involves its own form of myopia or blinkered vision. To be fair to Simon, he warns in the introduction to his book that the title claim is 'polemical, and perhaps overstated' but nevertheless goes on to add that 'it has as its core a key insight into a central feature of contemporary American law and society' (2007: 4). In the domain of drug policy, our analysis in this book suggests that while it captures one dimension of what has been happening, the idea of governing through crime offers a relatively limited and narrow vista onto the policy landscape. Indeed, from an historical perspective, as we noted in chapter one, a crime-focused orientation to the drug question is embedded in the origins of contemporary drug control in the early twentieth century. In the British context, the Dangerous Drugs Act 1920 first introduced a criminal law regulatory regime for the manufacture, distribution, and sale of certain substances, including heroin and cocaine, providing police powers of search and arrest in pursuance of breaches of the Act and punishments of fines, imprisonment, and forfeiture. The very concept of 'drugs' in its modern sense is a regulatory construct based on the criminal law (Seddon, 2010a, 2010b). The governance of drugs has, in this respect, always been through crime.

What we need to consider then is whether, and in what ways, the criminal justice turn represents anything different. Is it a new or distinctive form of governing drugs through crime of the kind that Simon describes? Our analysis in chapters two and three points to a mixed answer. It is certainly evident that crime, as a lens for viewing the drug problem, became significantly more prominent from the 1980s onwards. To this extent, we accept that Simon's thesis offers a powerful way of encapsulating the character of recent

British drug policy. But, we suggest, its power as a slogan comes at the expense of some analytical precision and nuance. In those earlier chapters of the book, we set out the view that in fact there has been no switch or transformation from a public health approach to a criminal justice one, contrary to the claims of commentators like Stimson (2000) and Hunt and Stevens (2004). The two strategies have in fact co-existed and developed together over the last three decades. They are, in this sense, two intertwined aspects of the same phenomenon, namely, the rise of risk-based forms of governance in the context of the transition to neo-liberalism in the last part of the twentieth century. We argued in those chapters that the most useful way of understanding drug policy developments during this period is therefore not in relation to crime but rather to the broader category of risk.

It might be countered here that this misses the distinctive 'flavour' of the criminal justice turn, which was quite unlike the period of pre-eminence for harm reduction from the late 1980s to the early 1990s when the goal of preventing the spread of HIV led to real service innovation. But this confuses what Melossi (1985) has helpfully described as the long wave of structural or strategic patterns with shorter-term fluctuations shaped by political culture. As we saw in chapter three, social and cultural preoccupations about security did indeed infuse the perspectives of many of the key policy actors during this period and led to a distinctive crime-focused direction for drug policy. However, this unfolded within the wider framework of risk, as a way of organizing and acting upon the social world.

In our view, then, from the perspective of British drug policy, Simon's thesis highlights a political–cultural phenomenon but interprets it as a structural one. Recalling the theoretical framework we set out in chapter two, in effect he elides the first two elements of our explanatory account. We can see this with some clarity if we look at very recent developments in British drug policy. In the last year or so, the focus on crime has ebbed somewhat, with the new national drug policy from 2010 emphasizing the importance of 'recovery' and the need to move problem drug users off social security benefits and into work (Home Office, 2010). One way to read this shift could be in 'epochal' terms: indicating a likely transition in the near future from a governing-through-crime strategy to a recovery-oriented one. And for those engaged today in the drugs field on the ground as planners, commissioners, and practitioners, it certainly feels to many as if big change is in the air. A noisy grassroots recovery movement even talks of a paradigm shift. But this misses the picture at the strategic level where continuity is much more apparent. The new direction in drug policy retains the same problematization (heroin/crack users as sources of risk to the community), the same conception of drug-using subjects (rational calculating choice-makers), and the same strategic response (encouraging/cajoling responsible choice-making to reduce risk). What has changed is that the most significant type of risk posed by drug users is now seen as being a burden on the public purse by drawing social security benefits and failing to contribute to the economy through employment and tax-paying. During a period of economic recession and public sector cuts, we can best understand this development in terms of a new politics of drug policy. There are new social and cultural preoccupations and anxieties (coded in the language of 'cuts', 'austerity', and so on) that are influencing policy change; but the underlying strategic framework or pattern remains the same.

This suggests that Simon's thesis would be better recast as an account of the politics of crime control rather than one about social change or social control more broadly. In fact, Simon is a little unclear about which of these related but different tasks he is engaged in. He frames his narrative variously as concerned with a 'central feature of contemporary American law and society' (2007: 4), the 'reshaping [of] political authority around crime' (2007: 8), 'crime as a model problem' (2007: 10), 'crime as a governmental rationality' (2007: 16), and 'crime as a locus of governance' (2007: 27). To be fair to Simon, this is partly because his book appears to be intended as a normative as well as a scholarly contribution. It is therefore written in a quite different style and register from some of his earlier work, which offered a rare and often scintillating mix of theoretical rigour, analytical detail, immense readability, and genuinely original insight (eg Simon, 1987, 1988, 1998; Feeley and Simon, 1992, 1994). In *Governing Through Crime*, he is attempting something rather different and in certain respects even more challenging: to make a persuasive case for a major shift in American social and crime policy. In our view, this means that the best way to read his book is as a contribution to understanding the political culture of crime control and not as a general thesis about contemporary strategies of governance. And from this perspective it is certainly an outstanding addition to the literature.

A final observation we wish to make concerns the place of explanation within Simon's account. In his introduction (2007: 5), he notes: 'Much of this book is descriptive, seeking to provide a thick account of the ways that crime as a problem influences the way we know and act on our selves, our families, and our communities.' He takes this a step further later on and entirely eschews the explanatory project, on the grounds that is unnecessary for the purposes of his policy critique:

Most studies adopt the view that the causes of our 'war on crime' are crucial to any effort to reverse or even modify this development. The question of causation is fascinating but ultimately less important than the question of what the 'war on crime' actually does to American democracy, our government and legal system, and the open society we have historically enjoyed.

[2007: 25]

He argues, in other words, that answering 'the "why" question', as he puts it (2007: 25), is intellectually interesting but essentially a sideshow to his own project, which, as we have already noted, is focused on making the case for policy change. This is, of course, an entirely defensible and even honourable position. It also has something in common with a Foucauldian governmentality perspective, on which Simon's analysis is (very loosely) based. As Rose et al (2006: 93) state in a review paper on the approach, governmentality involves a 'common agnosticism about "why" and "in whose interests" questions, accompanied by a commitment to studying how things get done'. In our study, we followed a different path and in chapters two and three attempted to set out an explanatory account for the criminal justice turn in British drug policy, drawing in part on a framework elaborated by Garland (2001). This was an explicit and direct attempt to answer the 'why' question. But, as will be evident to readers who have got this far in the book, the architecture of our explanation was also relevant to how we built our analysis of policy implementation and practice on the ground (in chapters four to six) and of policy impact (in chapter seven). In fact, it pervades the entire book. In this sense, we argue that Simon's refusal of the explanatory question potentially weakens his capacity to analyse what the governing-through-crime strategy 'actually does' to American law and society.

A new crime control complex

Perhaps the single most influential and certainly most widely cited contribution to this debate about the contemporary governance of security has been David Garland's (2001) book *The Culture of Control*. A check on Google Scholar as we write this chapter indicates that its citations can be counted in thousands rather than hundreds. It has led to several symposia (eg a special issue in 2004 of the *Critical Review of International Social and Political Philosophy*), as well as some exceptional review essays that constitute significant contributions to the field in their own right (eg Zedner, 2002; Braithwaite, 2003; Young, 2003a). We, too, have found *The Culture of Control* to be an extremely stimulating and important work for our own research. Indeed, the theoretical framework we set out in chapter two draws closely on Garland's notion of policy as situated problem-solving action.

Garland's argument is sophisticated and multifaceted and does not lend itself readily to condensed summary. We see the heart of his account as concerning the idea of the emergence of a new 'crime control complex'. He argues that this complex consists of a new cultural formation (a reworked pattern of assumptions, values, and sensibilities) that has developed as a response to a distinctive late modern policy predicament based around high crime rates and increased feelings of insecurity. The resulting crime-control strategies 'represent a particular kind of response, a particular adaptation, to the specific problems of social order produced by late modern social organisation' (Garland, 2001: 201). They are made up of two principal strands: an expressive punitive strategy (mass imprisonment, authoritarianism, etc) and a preventative responsibilization strategy (inter-agency partnerships, community self-help, etc).

The title of our book, *Tough Choices*, although it obviously alludes to the specific drug-crime policy initiative of that name, also refers more obliquely to these two strands that Garland argues make up the new crime control complex. As should be clear from our analysis in earlier chapters, notably chapter three, the expressive dimension is absolutely central to an understanding of how the criminal justice turn has unfolded over recent decades. Indeed, it is impossible to grasp fully without an appreciation of the wider politics of crime and social order through this period. The second strand is equally important for our account. As we saw, for example, in chapter five, the idea of encouraging drug-using offenders to make responsible risk-reducing choices is fundamental to the way interventions like the Required Assessment and Restriction on Bail (RoB) are conceived and structured. We will return to this notion of responsibilization below.

One of the main criticisms of Garland's thesis is that it operates at such a high level of generality and abstraction that it involves an unwarranted degree of simplification, riding roughshod over local variation. Well-known essays by Zedner (2002) and Young (2003a) make this point particularly effectively. We agree, up to a point, with this critique and so do not repeat or add to it here as this is well-trodden ground, although we would add that Garland deliberately paints on a large canvas and is entirely aware that this involves some skating over localized specificities (Garland, 2001: vii). Instead, we wish to focus on some implications for his central arguments that can be drawn from our study. We consider, in particular, this idea of responsibilization. Garland explains how he uses the term:

A *responsibilization strategy* [...] involves a way of thinking and a variety of techniques designed to change the manner in which governments act upon crime. Instead of addressing crime in a direct fashion [...] this approach promotes a new kind of indirect action, in which state agencies activate action by non-state organizations and actors. The intended result is an enhanced network of more or less directed, more or less informal crime control, complementing and extending the formal controls of the criminal justice state [...It] involves the enlistment of others, the shaping of incentives, and the creation of new forms of co-operative action.

[2001: 124–5, emphasis in original]

The idea of responsibilization has multiple roots and was developed simultaneously in several areas of scholarship in the 1990s. As Garland (2001: 124, n 51) acknowledges in a footnote, the concept was developed initially by O'Malley (1992) in his pioneering article 'Risk, Power and Crime Prevention'. Other Foucauldian governmentality scholars were coining similar ideas, too, at around the same time, most strikingly the notion of 'governing at a distance' (see Rose and Miller, 1992). There is also a strong affinity with the concept of meta-regulation developed by regulation scholars during that decade (see: Grabosky, 1995; Gunningham and Grabosky, 1998; Parker, 2002) and the notion of third-party policing (Mazerolle and Ransley, 2005). This strategy, then, of power operating beyond the state, with multiple and diverse actors enlisted for governmental purposes, was clearly a significant trend in diverse policy domains.

In our study, we found that several of the criminal justice interventions that we were focusing on could be usefully framed in this way. And, in fact, policy-makers also did so, the most striking version of this appearing in a Home Office factsheet about the 'Tough Choices' project: 'Tough Choices was chosen as a name because it was felt to succinctly describe the change in the consequences drug misusers face if they do not take advantage of the opportunities for treatment and support that exist' (Home Office, 2006b). But when examining how these interventions actually operated on the ground, things seemed less clear-cut. When we sat in magistrates' courts and observed the application of the RoB, for instance, we tended not to find it offered as a choice or 'opportunity'. Rather, eligible defendants (that is candidates for bail with a positive test) would simply have it applied, more often than not. As we reported in chapter five, many criminal justice personnel and drug treatment practitioners that we interviewed were critical of this apparent erosion of the intended functioning of these interventions.

We suggest that this implies an important shortcoming of Garland's work. This concerns the distinction between the blueprints of rule—the strategies, action plans, and policy documents—and the translation of those blueprints into practice. We are not at all dismissive of the importance of examining governmental blueprints in their own right. We share the view with governmentality scholars that the language of programmes is not to be 'regarded as an epiphenomenon, a gloss on the practices of rule' but is what can be termed an 'intellectual technology' that renders reality amenable to particular practices of government (Rose et al, 2006: 88–9; Miller and Rose, 1990; Rose and Miller, 1992). In other words, it is an absolutely essential point of analysis. However, it is equally important to look at practice, as well. As Zedner (2002: 355) observes, by studying the culture of control, rather than control practices, Garland creates a blind spot where any deviation in actual institutional practices from the cultural formation escapes the scholarly gaze.

This criticism is perhaps a little unfair on Garland. Given the oceanic sweep of his analytical canvas—all crime-control practices in the late twentieth century in the United Kingdom and the United States—it would require a multi-volume book series to include a detailed analysis of practice in both countries as well. This, we would suggest, though, is the value of carrying out highly focused studies of particular policy domains in specific times and places, as we have done. As we hope we have demonstrated, this still allows for an engagement with the 'big questions' but avoids the problem Garland encounters of being unable to see beyond the level of governmental discourses (important though they are).

We would argue also that there is a balance to be struck between the eschewal of explanation that Jonathan Simon espouses in *Governing Through Crime*, on the one hand, and Garland's grand effort to find a framework that can explain (almost) everything, on the other. Our own approach, which we have attempted in this book, is a micro–macro method, partly inspired by work by John Braithwaite and colleagues at the Australian National University (eg Braithwaite and Drahos, 2000; Braithwaite et al, 2010). In Braithwaite's view, there is a need to allow for the analytical lens to sweep across levels and to synthesize the micro and macro: 'The methodological prescription is to gather data on the most macro phenomena possible from the most micro source possible— individuals, especially individuals who act as agents for larger collectivities' (Braithwaite and Drahos, 2000: 14). So, for example, in our own study we gathered data about macro-level change in national drug policy over a period of decades by interviewing individual policy actors. Similarly, our observations of micro-interactions between actors in police stations and magistrates' courts generated insights about the nature of the risk-security nexus in contemporary governance. This is one way of resolving the dilemma that Garland (2001: vii–viii) identifies in the preface to *The Culture of Control*, where he argues that there is an 'unavoidable tension between broad generalization and the specification of empirical particulars' (2001: vii), in which significance and simplification are traded against each other in an apparently zero-sum game. While we do not claim we have necessarily avoided the trap in this book, we are certain that Garland is mistaken to say that individual studies can never escape this dilemma, although it is undoubtedly exceptionally difficult to achieve. One rare but outstanding example of a work that transcends this micro–macro divide is Braithwaite and Drahos's book *Global Business Regulation*, which manages to deliver a sweeping account of the big picture through a set of detailed case studies.

Counter-law and the governance of security

In his final book, *Crime in an Insecure World*, the late Richard Ericson (2007) sets out a powerful and compelling argument about the place of security in neo-liberal governance. He argues that the intensification of security measures at the turn of the twenty-first century is rooted in the obsession of neo-liberal political cultures with the problem of uncertainty. Limited and uncertain knowledge is productive of insecurities and anxieties. And in the face of these insecurities, the dominant response has been the 'urge to criminalize', leading to what he describes in his stirring opening sentence as the 'alarming trend across Western countries of treating every imaginable source of harm as a crime' (2007: 1).

For Ericson, the ratcheting up of security has been achieved through legal transformations. Adapting a Foucauldian concept (see Foucault, 1977: 221–3), he sets out the idea of *counter-law* as the central mechanism for security:

> There are two types of counter-law. Counter-law I takes the form of laws against law. New laws are enacted and new uses of existing law are invented to erode or eliminate traditional principles, standards, and procedures that get in the way of pre-empting imagined sources of harm. Counter-law II takes the form of surveillant assemblages. New surveillance infrastructures are developed and new uses of existing surveillance networks are extended that also erode or eliminate traditional standards, principles, and procedures of criminal law that get in the way of pre-empting imagined sources of harm.
>
> [Ericson, 2007: 24]

It is easy to see how this argument resonates with the criminal justice turn in British drug policy. The RoB, which we described in chapter five, for instance, is an example of counter-law I. A new law (section 19 of the Criminal Justice Act 2003) is enacted to circumvent the protections in the Bail Act 1976 (the presumption in favour of bail), which are felt to hinder the prevention of drug-related offending on bail. Similarly, the infrastructure for the production and communication of risk knowledge that we described in chapters four and six respectively, could be usefully understood as an example of counter-law II, that is as the creation of a new surveillant assemblage.

Ericson's thesis is a powerful one and has been highly influential within criminology. But we wish to suggest here that our study indicates it stands in need of some refinement. At the heart of our argument is the claim that Ericson's emphasis on the centrality of counter-law not only overplays the importance of law within strategies for the government of conduct but also rests on a limited and narrow conceptualization of what law is. Let us take the first of those points to start with. In our research in the three local sites, described in chapters four to six, we repeatedly observed that what was actually done in police stations and criminal courts was the product of a complex amalgam of inputs and factors. It could not be accurately characterized as the simple 'implementation' of legal powers. Taking again the example of the RoB, although the legal provision functions as an example of 'law against law' or counter-law I, decision-making by the courts was much more variable than this would imply. We saw instances of magistrates unwilling to reverse the presumption in favour of bail for minor offenders even if they bore the risk marker of the positive test, and others unprepared to remand in custody even after repeated breaches. And breaches were only presented to them after drug workers had decided to do so, with varying practice in different locations as to what constituted 'good reason' for missing an appointment and so on. So, rather than the application and enforcement of legal powers, what we were observing was more akin to what regulation scholars have termed regulatory space (see Hancher and Moran, 1989; Scott, 2001).

The regulatory space metaphor conveys the idea that regulation involves a complex set of interactions, processes, and relationships involving multiple institutions, networks, and actors. It moves away from a model of regulation as something done by one party (the regulator) to another (the regulatee) and decentres the state as the sole or even primary focus for analysis (Black, 2001). This resonates also with more Foucauldian perspectives associated with the governmentality framework (Foucault, 1991; Rose et al, 2006). In a much-cited paper, Rose and Valverde (1998) argue for the importance of studying 'legal processes' or the 'legal complex', rather than the 'law':

To investigate the legal complex from the perspective of government is to analyse the role of legal mechanisms, legal arenas, legal functionaries, legal forms of reasoning and so on in strategies of regulation. It is not merely that the law has no unity […] It is also that the law has no privilege […] The codes, techniques, discourses and judgements of law are only one element in the assemblages that constitute our modern experience of subjectivity, responsibility, citizenship.

[Rose and Valverde, 1998: 546]

What, then, are we to make of the concept of counter-law, given these ideas of regulatory space and the legal complex that seem to fit our empirical findings much more closely? In our view, the centrality Ericson gives to counter-law and to legal transformations is misplaced. They are just one element within a wider multi-stranded regulatory or governmental assemblage. Counter-law may actually be more significant at the level of political rhetoric, rather than in relation to specific regulatory strategies and practices on the ground. Ericson himself hints at this when he observes:

> Criminalization through counter-law has become *the* way of expressing authoritative certainty. For political authorities, it is the strongest expression of state authority in face of a lack of trust in public institutions and an increasing sense of ungovernability [...] [G]overning through crime sends a strong signal of certainty.
>
> [Ericson, 2007: 207, emphasis in original]

In other words, counter-law may be, in large part, an expressive intervention aimed at communicating that policy predicaments and social anxieties are being taken seriously and dealt with firmly. So the label 'Tough Choices', and messages about bail being refused for drug-using offenders who will not engage with treatment, operate additionally or even primarily as political communication, while in practice the picture is more variegated, as we saw in chapter five. As should be evident from our discussions in chapters two and three, we do not mean by this that counter-law is 'mere' politics and of no significance. The political realm is a vital one to grasp in understanding any area of social policy. Our empirical research suggests though the need to view the idea of counter-law from a different vantage point than the one Ericson puts forward.

Our second point concerns the way that Ericson understands what (counter-)law is. Here, we draw on the work of the legal theorist Gunther Teubner. In his landmark article, 'How the Law Thinks', Teubner puts forward a radical 'constructivist epistemology of law' in which he argues that law should be understood as a communicative process that has 'its own autonomous order and creates the world of legal meaning' (Teubner, 1989: 740). Teubner's theory, and the systems theory on which it is based (see Luhmann, 1995), are notoriously abstract and complex and we do not need to get embroiled in the details of their work. For our purposes here, we draw out a key insight from Teubner that is particularly relevant to teasing out the implications of our study for Ericson's counter-law thesis.

This concerns the nature of law as 'communication and nothing but communication' (Teubner, 1989: 739). For Teubner (and fellow systems theorists like Luhmann), law cannot be defined or understood either as a 'set of rules constraining individual action' (1989: 739) or, more radically, as made up of the actions and decision-making processes of legal actors (judges, magistrates, lawyers, etc). Instead, legal communications are the 'cognitive instruments by which the law [...] is able to "see" the world' (1989: 740). But this 'seeing' consists entirely of construction rather than reception or translation or interpretation:

Legal communications cannot reach out into the real outside world [...] Any metaphor about their access to the real world is misplaced. They do not receive information from the outside world which they would filter and convert according to the needs of the legal process. There is no instruction of the law by the outside world; there is only construction of the outside world by the law.

[Teubner, 1989: 740]

This process of construction does not involve an arbitrary 'invention' of social reality by an entirely isolated realm of law. Legal communications acknowledge the 'environment' in which law exists but autonomously construct 'legal models of reality under the impression of environmental perturbations' (1989: 740). Or, more pithily, they create 'legal order from social noise' (1989: 740). Among these 'perturbations', Teubner includes what he calls the 'psychic processes' of lawyers and other legal actors.

This radical constructivist view of law is difficult to grasp, in particular Teubner's treatment of the place of 'real people' within the law. When he states that actors in the legal process—defendants, plaintiffs, lawyers, judges—are 'mere constructs, semantic artefacts produced by the legal discourse itself' and 'role-bundles, character-masks, internal products of legal communication' (1989: 741), many social scientists and criminologists may find themselves in strong disagreement or simply bewildered. In many respects, we share this scepticism and we by no means fully sign up to a systems theory perspective. Yet, in our view, applying it to some aspects of our empirical findings does help to cast new light on the counter-law thesis. As we have noted, Ericson's argument is that counter-law involves the passing of new laws, in order to counteract, evade, or circumvent standards or restrictions posed by an existing law, that are deemed to impede the prevention of harms. This implies a strategy to use law to erode the rights of 'risky' individuals for the public good of enhanced security. But this does not really match what we found in our three sites, as described in earlier chapters. In practice, the application of the RoB, for example, was routine—defendants who would have been remanded on bail anyway simply had the restriction applied to their bail if they had a positive test result. So these defendants were not so much people with legal rights that were being circumvented but rather a 'role-bundle' created by legal discourse. In other words, for a given individual defendant, it mattered little what their actual patterns of drug-related offending were, provided they satisfied the legal criteria for eligibility under section 19 of the 2003 Act (aged 18 or over, positive test, etc). The status of 'drug-using offender' in this sense resembles the internal product of legal communication that may be 'perturbed' by social reality but is invented autonomously. It is a form of 'juridical "hyperreality" that has lost contact with the realities of everyday life and at the same time superimposes new realities to everyday life' (Teubner, 1989: 742). Again, what this implies is that the counter-law thesis applies more at the level of political or policy purpose than in relation to actual legal processes on the ground. This leads us to question how helpful a label counter-*law* really is.

We suggest, then, that Ericson's grand narrative about the ascendancy of security in late modern societies is a powerful contribution in that tradition of ambitious and sweeping accounts of the nature of contemporary governance. Within his narrative, the concept of counter-law appears, on the face of it, to provide a tool that can link the high-level narrative with a detailed understanding of regulatory activity in diverse domains. Our study supports a contrary view: the idea of counter-law is much better understood as an expressive intervention within neo-liberal political cultures, rather than as a mechanism or instrument for the execution of security measures.

Conclusions

Our critical intent in this book has been to provide a penetrating analysis and diagnosis of this policy domain and we hope that our account has offered some important insights into recent British drug policy. The Drug Interventions Programme has been little researched to date, aside from government-funded evaluations that, however rigorous and well executed (and many are), are inevitably constrained in scope. As far as we are aware, this is the first book-length independent analysis of this area. Given the impact DIP has had on the criminal justice system alone, as we discussed in chapter seven, this should be of considerable interest to criminologists and scholars of criminal justice. And drug policy researchers will no doubt be interested in what we have had to say, too, even if some of our claims will be seen as controversial. We are also sure that even if British drug policy is taking a new turn towards a focus on recovery, the infrastructure of drug interventions in the criminal justice system will remain intact for many years to come and so the policy and practice issues we have discussed here will be relevant well into the future.

But our intellectual ambition, of course, has been much greater than this. We have argued throughout the book that our study of a specific policy domain in a specific cultural and historical context has cast new light on the big picture of how we are governed in the early twenty-first century. In this concluding chapter, we have attempted to bring together this grander claim by considering how our research has indicated a need to revise and refine three stellar criminological contributions to this debate by, respectively, Jonathan Simon, David Garland, and Richard Ericson. At the heart of our argument, and strongly influenced by a classic early piece on risk by Pat O'Malley (1992), has been the idea that the risk-security nexus is a highly malleable assemblage that in specific contexts is aligned to particular political projects. It is only by understanding this political dimension—that is the distinctive politics of risk and security within a given policy domain—that we can fully grasp the nature of contemporary governance strategies.

In certain respects, such an approach bears some resemblance to the call by Loader and Sparks (2004) for an 'historical sociology of crime policy'. But, we suggest, a closer affinity is with the Foucauldian notion of genealogical analysis (Foucault, 1984, 1991; see also Shearing and Johnson, 2010). In that sense, we have been following Valverde's (2011: 19) sage advice that it is unproductive to think about risk-security as a 'noun as if it designated an entity, and that it is instead more useful to turn our attention to the myriad [risk-]security projects and mechanisms that can in fact be empirically studied'. One perennial, Habermas-inspired, criticism of this type of Foucauldian analysis is that it evades the responsibility to engage in normative debate (see Habermas, 1986) and indeed it is true that we have largely refrained in this book from discussing what direction we think policy *ought* to go in, in favour of developing a detailed critical account of the rationalities, strategies, and practices that have made up the policy and its implementation. In this regard, we might be felt to have failed to heed Stan Cohen's (1985: 238) stern admonition that 'it is a simple matter of intellectual integrity and honesty to clarify the policy implications of social-problem analysis'.

There is certainly much to admire about scholars like Cohen, who have such a powerful sense of moral obligation in their role as intellectuals but we are less sure that it is a 'simple matter' to read off these implications for policy from our analysis. We take our lead instead from another admirable and moral scholar, Clifford Shearing, who, perhaps more than any other, has demonstrated the potential for using the unique critical power of Foucauldian analytical approaches in the service of a practical engagement with efforts to enhance social justice and human rights (eg Shearing and Froestad, 2010). Inspired by Shearing (and others), our intention in this book has been to develop a critical analysis of this specific risk-security project, diagnosing precisely what this project is and the political field within which it is located, as a prelude to the development of alternative policy approaches. Indeed, we suggest that this diagnostic work is an essential form of ground-clearing, which provides a much more analytically secure platform for arguments about policy development. We end here by extending an invitation to the scholarly community to build on the study we have presented in this book by taking seriously the normative questions for which we have hopefully prepared the ground.

Appendix 1
List of Trigger Offences

Act	Offence
Theft Act 1968	Theft (section 1) [plus attempts]
	Robbery (section 8) [plus attempts]
	Burglary (section 9) [plus attempts]
	Aggravated burglary (section 10)
	Taking motor vehicle (section 12)
	Aggravated vehicle-taking (section 12A)
	Handling stolen goods (section 22) [plus attempts]
	Going equipped for stealing (section 25)
Misuse of Drugs Act 1971	In respect of Class A drugs only:
	Production and supply (section 4)
	Possession (section 5(2))
	Possession with intent to supply (section 5(3))
Fraud Act 2006	Fraud (section 1) [plus attempts]
	Possession of articles for use in frauds (section 6)
	Making or supplying articles for use in frauds (section 7)
Vagrancy Act 1824	Begging (section 3)
	Persistent begging (section 4)

Appendix 2
Required Assessments—Extracts from Drugs Act 2005

9 Initial assessment following testing for presence of Class A drugs

(1) This section applies if–
   (a) a sample is taken under section 63B of PACE (testing for presence of Class A drug) from a person detained at a police station,
   (b) an analysis of the sample reveals that a specified Class A drug may be present in the person's body,
   (c) the age condition is met, and
   (d) the notification condition is met.

(2) A police officer may, at any time before the person is released from detention at the police station, require him to attend an initial assessment and remain for its duration.

(3) An initial assessment is an appointment with a suitably qualified person (an 'initial assessor')–
   (a) for the purpose of establishing whether the person is dependent upon or has a propensity to misuse any specified Class A drug,
   (b) if the initial assessor thinks that he has such a dependency or propensity, for the purpose of establishing whether he might benefit from further assessment, or from assistance or treatment (or both), in connection with the dependency or propensity, and
   (c) if the initial assessor thinks that he might benefit from such assistance or treatment (or both), for the purpose of providing him with advice, including an explanation of the types of assistance or treatment (or both) which are available.

(4) The age condition is met if the person has attained the age of 18 or such different age as the Secretary of State may by order made by statutory instrument specify for the purposes of this section.

(5) In relation to a person ('A') who has attained the age of 18, the notification condition is met if–
   (a) the relevant chief officer has been notified by the Secretary of State that arrangements for conducting initial assessments for persons who have attained the age of 18 have been made for persons from whom samples have been taken

(under section 63B of PACE) at the police station in which A is detained, and
  (b) the notice has not been withdrawn.
  (6) In relation to a person ('C') who is of an age which is less than 18, the notification condition is met if–
      (a) the relevant chief officer has been notified by the Secretary of State that arrangements for conducting initial assessments for persons of that age have been made for persons from whom samples have been taken (under section 63B of PACE) at the police station in which C is detained, and
      (b) the notice has not been withdrawn.
  (7) In subsections (5) and (6), 'relevant chief officer' means the chief officer of police of the police force for the police area in which the police station is situated.

10 Follow-up assessment
  (1) This section applies if–
      (a) a police officer requires a person to attend an initial assessment and remain for its duration under section 9(2),
      (b) the age condition is met, and
      (c) the notification condition is met.
  (2) The police officer must, at the same time as he imposes the requirement under section 9(2)–
      (a) require the person to attend a follow-up assessment and remain for its duration, and
      (b) inform him that the requirement ceases to have effect if he is informed at the initial assessment that he is no longer required to attend the follow-up assessment.
  (3) A follow-up assessment is an appointment with a suitably qualified person (a 'follow-up assessor') –
      (a) for any of the purposes of the initial assessment which were not fulfilled at the initial assessment, and
      (b) if the follow-up assessor thinks it appropriate, for the purpose of drawing up a care plan.
  (4) A care plan is a plan which sets out the nature of the assistance or treatment (or both) which may be most appropriate for the person in connection with any dependency upon, or any propensity to misuse, a specified Class A drug which the follow-up assessor thinks that he has. [...]
[...]

11 Requirements under sections 9 and 10: supplemental
  (1) This section applies if a person is required to attend an initial assessment and remain for its duration by virtue of section 9(2).
  (2) A police officer must–

    (a) inform the person of the time when, and the place at which, the initial assessment is to take place, and

    (b) explain that this information will be confirmed in writing.

(3) A police officer must warn the person that he may be liable to prosecution if he fails without good cause to attend the initial assessment and remain for its duration.

(4) If the person is also required to attend a follow-up assessment and remain for its duration by virtue of section 10(2), a police officer must also warn the person that he may be liable to prosecution if he fails without good cause to attend the follow-up assessment and remain for its duration.

(5) A police officer must give the person notice in writing which—

    (a) confirms that he is required to attend and remain for the duration of an initial assessment or both an initial assessment and a follow-up assessment (as the case may be),

    (b) confirms the information given in pursuance of subsection (2), and

    (c) repeats the warning given in pursuance of subsection (3) and any warning given in pursuance of subsection (4).

(6) The duties imposed by subsections (2) to (5) must be discharged before the person is released from detention at the police station.

(7) A record must be made, as part of the person's custody record, of—

    (a) the requirement imposed on him by virtue of section 9(2),

    (b) any requirement imposed on him by virtue of section 10(2),

    (c) the information and explanation given to him in pursuance of subsection (2) above,

    (d) the warning given to him in pursuance of subsection (3) above and any warning given to him in pursuance of subsection (4) above, and

    (e) the notice given to him in pursuance of subsection (5) above.

(8) If a person is given a notice in pursuance of subsection (5), a police officer or a suitably qualified person may give the person a further notice in writing which–

    (a) informs the person of any change to the time when, or to the place at which, the initial assessment is to take place, and

    (b) repeats the warning given in pursuance of subsection (3) and any warning given in pursuance of subsection (4).

12 Attendance at initial assessment

(1) This section applies if a person is required to attend an initial assessment and remain for its duration by virtue of section 9(2).

(2) The initial assessor must inform a police officer or a police support officer if the person–
  (a) fails to attend the initial assessment at the specified time and place, or
  (b) attends the assessment at the specified time and place but fails to remain for its duration.

(3) A person is guilty of an offence if without good cause–
  (a) he fails to attend an initial assessment at the specified time and place, or
  (b) he attends the assessment at the specified time and place but fails to remain for its duration.

(4) A person who is guilty of an offence under subsection (3) is liable on summary conviction to imprisonment for a term not exceeding 51 weeks, or to a fine not exceeding level 4 on the standard scale, or to both.

(5) If a person fails to attend an initial assessment at the specified time and place, any requirement imposed on him by virtue of section 10(2) ceases to have effect. […]

13 Arrangements for follow-up assessment

(1) This section applies if—
  (a) a person attends an initial assessment in pursuance of section 9(2), and
  (b) he is required to attend a follow-up assessment and remain for its duration by virtue of section 10(2).

(2) If the initial assessor thinks that a follow-up assessment is not appropriate, he must inform the person concerned that he is no longer required to attend the follow-up assessment.

(3) The requirement imposed by virtue of section 10(2) ceases to have effect if the person is informed as mentioned in subsection (2).

(4) If the initial assessor thinks that a follow-up assessment is appropriate, the assessor must–
  (a) inform the person of the time when, and the place at which, the follow-up assessment is to take place, and
  (b) explain that this information will be confirmed in writing.

(5) The assessor must also warn the person that, if he fails without good cause to attend the follow-up assessment and remain for its duration, he may be liable to prosecution.

(6) The initial assessor must also give the person notice in writing which—
  (a) confirms that he is required to attend and remain for the duration of the follow-up assessment,
  (b) confirms the information given in pursuance of subsection (4), and
  (c) repeats the warning given in pursuance of subsection (5).

(7) The duties mentioned in subsections (2) and (4) to (6) must be discharged before the conclusion of the initial assessment.

(8) If a person is given a notice in pursuance of subsection (6), the initial assessor or another suitably qualified person may give the person a further notice in writing which–

  (a) informs the person of any change to the time when, or to the place at which, the follow-up assessment is to take place, and

  (b) repeats the warning mentioned in subsection (5).

14 Attendance at follow-up assessment

(1) This section applies if a person is required to attend a follow-up assessment and remain for its duration by virtue of section 10(2).

(2) The follow-up assessor must inform a police officer or a police support officer if the person–

  (a) fails to attend the follow-up assessment at the specified time and place, or

  (b) attends the assessment at the specified time and place but fails to remain for its duration.

(3) A person is guilty of an offence if without good cause–

  (a) he fails to attend a follow-up assessment at the specified time and place, or

  (b) he attends the assessment at the specified time and place but fails to remain for its duration.

(4) A person who is guilty of an offence under subsection (3) is liable on summary conviction to imprisonment for a term not exceeding 51 weeks, or to a fine not exceeding level 4 on the standard scale, or to both. […]

15 Disclosure of information about assessments

(1) An initial assessor may disclose information obtained as a result of an initial assessment to any of the following–

  (a) a person who is involved in the conduct of the assessment;

  (b) a person who is or may be involved in the conduct of any follow-up assessment.

(2) A follow-up assessor may disclose information obtained as a result of a follow-up assessment to a person who is involved in the conduct of the assessment.

(3) Subject to subsections (1) and (2), information obtained as a result of an initial or a follow-up assessment may not be disclosed by any person without the written consent of the person to whom the assessment relates. […]

16 **Samples submitted for further analysis**

(1) A requirement imposed on a person by virtue of section 9(2) or 10(2) ceases to have effect if at any time before he has fully complied with the requirement–

(a) a police officer makes arrangements for a further analysis of the sample taken from him as mentioned in section 9(1)(a), and

(b) the analysis does not reveal that a specified Class A drug was present in the person's body.

(2) If a requirement ceases to have effect by virtue of subsection (1), a police officer must so inform the person concerned. [...]

Appendix 3
Restriction on Bail—Legal Provisions

Section 19 of the Criminal Justice Act 2003 amended the Bail Act 1976 to provide a power for the courts to impose a Restriction on Bail. The following is extracted from Crown Prosecution Service guidance.

Section 19 applies when a defendant:

- is aged 18 or over; **and**
- has tested positive for a specified class A drug (namely heroin, cocaine or crack cocaine); **and**
- resides in a relevant Petty Sessions Area where the provision applies. (If the person is of no fixed abode, then it is open to the court to deal with that person as if he is a resident of the area in which he was arrested); **and**
- where the defendant has been charged with an offence under sections 5(2) or 5(3) of the Misuse of Drugs Act 1971 (possession/possession with intent to supply) relating to a specified class A drug; **or**
- where the defendant has been charged with an offence which the court is satisfied was caused, wholly or partly, by the defendant's misuse of a specified class A drug or was motivated, wholly or partly, by his intended use of a specified class A drug.

If a defendant falls within the criteria above and:

- has either been offered an assessment, to which he agrees; **or**
- following an assessment has had relevant follow-up proposed to him, and he agrees to participate in the relevant follow-up;

the court, if it grants bail, has a duty to impose as a condition of bail that the individual undergo the assessment and/or participate in any relevant follow-up.

The court may not grant bail unless it is satisfied that there is no significant risk of his committing an offence whilst on bail (whether subject to conditions or not) if the defendant either:

- refuses to undergo an assessment of their dependency on or propensity to misuse class A drugs; **or**
- having undergone such an assessment, and having had follow-up action proposed to address their dependency/propensity, refuses to undergo such follow-up.

References

Advisory Council on the Misuse of Drugs (ACMD) (1988) *AIDS and Drug Misuse. Part 1*. London: HMSO.

Advisory Council on the Misuse of Drugs (ACMD) (1991) *Drug Misusers and the Criminal Justice System: Part I: Community Resources and the Probation Service*. London: HMSO.

Advisory Council on the Misuse of Drugs (ACMD) (1994) *Drug Misusers and the Criminal Justice System: Part II: Police, Drug Misusers and the Community*. London: HMSO.

Advisory Council on the Misuse of Drugs (ACMD) (1996) *Drug Misusers and the Criminal Justice System: Part III: Drug Misusers and the Prison System*. London: HMSO.

Aldridge, J., Measham, F., and Williams, L. (2011) *Illegal Leisure Revisited*. London: Routledge.

Anglin, M. (1988) 'The Efficacy of Civil Commitment in Treating Narcotic Addiction' in: C. Leukefeld and F. Tims (eds) *Compulsory Treatment of Drug Abuse: Research and Clinical Practice*. NIDA Research Monograph 86. Rockville, MD: National Institute on Drug Abuse.

Anglin, M., Longshore, D., and Turner, S. (1999) 'Treatment Alternatives to Street Crime: An Evaluation of Five Programs' *Criminal Justice and Behavior* 26(2) 168–95.

Auld, J., Dorn, N., and South, N. (1986) 'Irregular Work, Irregular Pleasures: Heroin in the 1980s' in R. Matthews and J. Young (eds) *Confronting Crime*. London: Sage.

Ayres, I. and Braithwaite, J. (1992) *Responsive Regulation: Transcending the Deregulation Debate*. Oxford: Oxford University Press.

Baker, O., Dorn, N., and Seddon, T. (1994) 'The Cost of Heroin-related Crime' *Druglink* 6 15.

Barker, J. (1992) 'A Positive Bust: Arrest Referral in Southwark' *Druglink* 7(4) 15–16.

Bauman, Z. (1988) *Freedom*. Milton Keynes: Open University Press.

—— (1998) *Globalization: The Human Consequences*. Cambridge: Polity Press.

—— (2007) *Liquid Times: Living in an Age of Uncertainty*. Cambridge: Polity Press.

Beck, U. (1992) *The Risk Society: Towards a New Modernity*. London: Sage.

—— (2009) *World at Risk*. Cambridge: Polity Press.

Beck, U., Giddens, A., and Lash, S. (eds) (1994) *Reflexive Modernisation: Politics, Tradition and Aesthetics in the Modern Social Order*. Cambridge: Polity Press.

Becker, G. (1968) 'Crime and Punishment: An Economic Approach' *Journal of Political Economy* 76(2) 169–217.

—— (1976) *The Economic Approach to Human Behavior*. Chicago, IL: University of Chicago Press.

Belenko, S. (2001) *Research on Drug Courts: A Critical Review, 2001 Update*. Alexandria, VA: National Drug Court Institute.

Belenko, S., Foltz, C., Lang, M., and Sung, H.-E. (2004) 'Recidivism among High-risk Drug Felons: A Longitudinal Analysis Following Residential Treatment' *Journal of Offender Rehabilitation* 40 105–32.

Bennett, T. (2000) *Drugs and Crime: The Results of Second Developmental Stage of the NEW-ADAM Programme*. Home Office Research Study No. 205. London: Home Office.

Bennett, T. and Holloway, K. (2007) *Drug-Crime Connections*. Cambridge: Cambridge University Press.

Bennett, T., Holloway, K., and Farrington, D. (2008) 'The Statistical Association between Drug Misuse and Crime: A Meta-analysis' *Aggression and Violent Behavior* 13(2) 107–18.

Best, D., Sidwell, C., Gossop, M., Harris, J., and Strang, J. (2001) 'Crime and Expenditure amongst Polydrug Users Seeking Treatment: The Connection between Prescribed Methadone and Crack Use, and Criminal Involvement' *British Journal of Criminology* 41 119–26.

Best, D., Wood, K., Sweeting, R., Morgan, B., and Day, E. (2010) 'Fitting a Quart into a Black Box: Keyworking in Quasi-coercive Drug Treatment in England' *Drugs: Education, Prevention and Policy* 17(4) 370–87.

Bewley, T. (1965) 'Heroin Addiction in the United Kingdom, 1954–1964' *British Medical Journal* 2 1284–6.

—— (1966) 'Recent Changes in the Pattern of Drug Abuse in the United Kingdon' *Bulletin on Narcotics* 18 1–9.

Black, J. (2001) 'Decentring Regulation: Understanding the Role of Regulation and Self-Regulation in a "Post-Regulatory" World' *Current Legal Problems* 54 103–47.

—— (2002) 'Critical Reflections on Regulation' *Australian Journal of Legal Philosophy* 27 1–35.

Blackman, S. (2007) '"See Emily Play": Youth Culture, Recreational Drug Use and Normalisation' in M. Simpson, T. Shildrick, and R. MacDonald (eds) *Drugs in Britain: Supply, Consumption and Control*. Basingstoke: Palgrave Macmillan.

Bland, J. and Altman, D. (1994) 'Regression towards the Mean' *British Medical Journal* 308 1499.

Boother, M. (1991) 'Drug Misuse: Developing a Harm Reduction Strategy' *Probation Journal* 38 75–80.

Boreham, R., Fuller, E., Hills, A., and Pudney, S. (2006) *The Arrestee Survey Annual Report: Oct 2003–Sept 2004*. Statistical Bulletin 04/06. London: Home Office.

Brain, K., Parker, H., and Bottomley, T. (1998) *Evolving Crack Cocaine Careers: New Users, Quitters and Long Term Combination Drug Users in NW England*. Manchester: University of Manchester.

Braithwaite, J. (2002) 'Rewards and Regulation' *Journal of Law and Society* 29(1) 12–26.

—— (2003) 'What's Wrong with the Sociology of Punishment?' *Theoretical Criminology* 7(1) 5–28.

—— (2008) *Regulatory Capitalism: How it Works, Ideas to Make it Better*. Cheltenham: Edward Elgar.

Braithwaite, J., Braithwaite, V., Cookson, M., and Dunn, L. (2010) *Anomie and Violence: Non-truth and Reconciliation in Indonesian Peacebuilding*. Canberra: ANU Press.

Braithwaite, J. and Drahos, P. (2000) *Global Business Regulation*. Cambridge: Cambridge University Press.

Braithwaite, V. (1995) 'Games of Engagement: Postures within the Regulatory Community' *Law & Policy* 17(3) 225–55.

—— (2003) 'Dancing with Tax Authorities: Motivational Postures and Non-compliant Actions' in V. Braithwaite (ed.) *Taxing Democracy*. Aldershot: Ashgate.

—— (2009) *Defiance in Taxation and Governance: Resisting and Dismissing Authority in a Democracy*. Cheltenham: Edward Elgar.

Braithwaite, V., Murphy, K., and Reinhart, M. (2007) 'Taxation Threat, Motivational Postures, and Responsive Regulation' *Law & Policy* 29(1) 137–58.

Brehm, S. and Brehm, L. (1981) *Psychological Reactance: A Theory of Freedom and Control*. New York, NY: Academic Press.

Burns, N. and Grove, S. (2010) *Understanding Nursing Research: Building an Evidence-based Practice*. 5th edn. Maryland Heights, MO: Saunders.

Burr, A. (1987) 'Chasing the Dragon: Heroin Misuse, Delinquency and Crime in the Context of South London Culture' *British Journal of Criminology* 27(4) 333–57.

Burris, S., Drahos, P., and Shearing, C. (2005) 'Nodal Governance' *Australian Journal of Legal Philosophy* 30 30–58.

Burris, S., Kempa, M., and Shearing, C. (2008) 'Changes in Governance: A Cross-disciplinary Review of Current Scholarship' *Akron Law Review* 41 1–66.

Buzan, B., Waever, O., and de Wilde, J. (1998) *Security: A New Framework for Analysis*. Boulder, CO: Lynne Riener.

Cabinet Office (2011) *The Magenta Book: Guidance for Evaluation*. Revised Edition. London: Cabinet Office.

Caplan, A. (2006) 'Ethical Issues Surrounding Forced, Mandated or Coerced Treatment' *Journal of Substance Abuse Treatment* 31 117–20.

Castel, R. (1991) 'From Dangerousness to Risk' in G. Burchell, C. Gordon, and P. Miller (eds) *The Foucault Effect: Studies in Governmentality*. Hemel Hempstead: Harvester Wheatsheaf.

Castells, M. (1996) *The Information Age. Volume 1: The Rise of the Network Society*. Oxford: Blackwell.

—— (1997) *The Information Age. Volume 2: The Power of Identity*. Oxford: Blackwell.

—— (1998) *The Information Age. Volume 3: The End of Millennium*. Oxford: Blackwell.

Cohen, S. (1985) *Visions of Social Control*. Cambridge: Polity Press.

Coid, J., Carvell, A., Kittler, Z., Healey, A., and Henderson, J. (2000) *Opiates, Criminal Behaviour and Methadone Treatment*. London: Home Office.

Collison, M. (1996) 'In Search of the High Life: Drugs, Crime, Masculinities and Consumption' *British Journal of Criminology* 36(3) 428–44.

Corry, O. (2012) 'Securitisation and "Riskification": Second-order Security and the Politics of Climate Change' *Millennium: Journal of International Studies* 40(2) 235–58.

Crawford, A. (1994) 'The Partnership Approach to Community Crime Prevention: Corporatism at the Local Level?' *Social and Legal Studies* 3 497–519.

—— (1997) *The Local Governance of Crime*. Oxford: Clarendon Press.

—— (1998) *Crime Prevention and Community Safety: Politics, Policies and Practices*. Harlow: Longman.

—— (2007) 'Crime Prevention and Community Safety' in M. Maguire, R. Morgan, and R. Reiner (eds) *The Oxford Handbook of Criminology*. 4th edn. Oxford: Oxford University Press.

—— (2009) 'Governing through Anti-social Behaviour: Regulatory Challenges to Criminal Justice' *British Journal of Criminology* 49(6) 810–31.

Crawford, A. and Jones, M. (1995) 'Inter-agency Co-operation and Community-based Crime Prevention' *British Journal of Criminology* 35 17–33.

Dean, M. (1999) 'Risk, Calculable and Incalculable' in D. Lupton (ed.) *Risk and Sociocultural Theory: New Directions and Perspectives*. Cambridge: Cambridge University Press.

Deaton, S. (2004) *On Charge Drug Testing: Evaluation of Drug Testing in the Criminal Justice System*. Development and Practice Report No. 16. London: Home Office.

Dilts, A. (2008) 'Michel Foucault Meets Gary Becker: Criminality beyond *Discipline and Punish*' *Carceral Notebooks* 4 77–100.

Ditton, J. and Frischer, M. (2001) 'Computerised Projection of Future Heroin Epidemics: A Necessity for the 21st Century?' *Substance Use and Misuse* 36 151–66.

Ditton, J. and Speirits, K. (1981) *The Rapid Increase in Heroin Addiction in Glasgow in 1981. Background Paper No. 2.* Glasgow: University of Glasgow.

Dorn, N. (1994) 'Three Faces of Police Referral: Welfare, Justice and Business Perspectives on Multi-Agency Work with Drug Arrestees' *Policing and Society* 4 13–34.

Dorn, N., Baker, O., and Seddon, T. (1994) *Paying for Heroin: Estimating the Financial Cost of Acquisitive Crime Committed by Dependent Heroin Users in England and Wales.* London: ISDD.

Dorn, N. and Lee, M. (1995) 'Mapping Probation Practice with Drug Using Offenders' *Howard Journal of Criminal Justice* 34(4) 314–25.

Dorn, N., Murji, K., and South, N. (1990) 'Drug Referral Schemes' *Policing* 6(2) 482–92.

Dorn, N. and Seddon, T. (1996) 'Welfare, Partnership and Crime Reduction: Aspects of Court Referral Schemes for Drug Users' *Drugs: Education, Prevention and Policy* 3 59–71.

Douglas, M. (1992) *Risk and Blame: Essays in Cultural Theory.* London: Routledge.

Douglas, M. and Wildavsky, A. (1982) *Risk and Culture: An Essay on the Selection of Technological and Environmental Dangers.* Berkeley, CA: University of California Press.

Downes, D. (1988) *Contrasts in Tolerance: Post-War Penal Policy in The Netherlands and England and Wales.* Oxford: Clarendon Press.

Downes, D. and Morgan, R. (2007) 'No Turning Back: The Politics of Law and Order into the Millennium' in M. Maguire, R. Morgan, and R. Reiner (eds) *The Oxford Handbook of Criminology.* 4th edn. Oxford: Oxford University Press.

Duke, K. (2006) 'Out of Crime and into Treatment?: The Criminalization of Contemporary Drug Policy Since Tackling Drugs Together' *Drugs: Education, Prevention and Policy* 13(5) 409–15.

Dupont, R. and Wish, E. (1992) 'Operation Tripwire Revisited' *Annals of the American Academy of Political and Social Science* 521 91–111.

Edgar, K. and O'Donnell, I. (1998) *Mandatory Drug Testing in Prisons: The Relationship between MDT and the Level and Nature of Drug Misuse.* Home Office Research Study 189. London: Home Office.

Edmunds, M., May, T., Hearnden, I., and Hough, M. (1998) *Arrest Referral: Emerging Lessons from Research.* DPI Paper 23. London: Home Office.

Edmunds, M., May, T., Hough, M., Hearnden, I., and Van Rozeboom, R. (1997) *Get It While You Can: An Evaluation.* Sussex: SACRO.

Edmunds, M., Hough, M., Turnbull, P., and May, T. (1999) *Doing Justice to Treatment: Referring Offenders to Drug Services.* DPAS Paper 2. London: Home Office.

Elton, G. (1967) *The Practice of History.* London: Fontana.

Ericson, R. (1994) 'The Division of Expert Knowledge in Policing and Security' *British Journal of Sociology* 45 149–75.

Ericson, R. (2007) *Crime in an Insecure World*. Cambridge: Polity Press.

Ericson, R. and Haggerty, K. (1997) *Policing the Risk Society*. Clarendon Studies in Criminology. Oxford: Clarendon Press.

Ewald, F. (1991) 'Insurance and Risk' in G. Burchell, C. Gordon, and P. Miller (eds) *The Foucault Effect: Studies in Governmentality*. Chicago, IL: University of Chicago Press.

Farabee, D., Prendergast, M., and Anglin, M. (1998) 'The Effectiveness of Coerced Treatment for Drug-abusing Offenders' *Federal Probation* 62 3–10.

Farrall, S., Jackson, J., and Gray, E. (2009) *Social Order and the Fear of Crime in Contemporary Times*. Clarendon Studies in Criminology. Oxford: Oxford University Press.

Farrell, M. and Marsden, J. (2005) *Drug-related Mortality among Newly-released Offenders 1998 to 2000*. Online Report 40/05. London: Home Office.

Fazey, C., Brown, P., and Batey, P. (1990) *A Socio-demographic Analysis of Patients Attending a Drug Dependency Clinic*. Liverpool: University of Liverpool.

Feeley, M. and Simon, J. (1992) 'The New Penology: Notes on the Emerging Strategy of Corrections and its Implications' *Criminology* 30 449–74.

—— (1994) 'Actuarial Justice: The Emerging New Criminal Law' in D. Nelken (ed.) *The Futures of Criminology*. London: Sage.

Festinger, D., Marlowe, D., Lee, P., Kirby, K., Bovasso, G., and McLellan, A.T. (2002) 'Status Hearings in Drug Court: When More is Less and Less is More' *Drug and Alcohol Dependence* 68(2) 151–7.

Fischer, B. (2003) ' "Doing Good with a Vengeance": A Critical Assessment of the Practices, Effects and Implications of Drug Treatment Courts in North America' *Criminal Justice* 3(3) 227–48.

Fisher, E. (2007) *Risk Regulation and Administrative Constitutionalism*. Oxford: Hart.

Foucault, M. (1972) *The Archaeology of Knowledge*. London: Tavistock.

—— (1977) *Discipline and Punish: The Birth of the Prison*. London: Allen Lane.

—— (1982) 'Afterword: The Subject and Power' in H. Dreyfus and P. Rabinow (eds) *Michel Foucault: Beyond Structuralism and Hermeneutics*. Chicago, IL: University of Chicago Press.

—— (1984) 'Nietzsche, Genealogy, History' in P. Rabinow (ed.) *The Foucault Reader*. London: Penguin.

—— (1991) 'Governmentality' in G. Burchell, C. Gordon, and P. Miller (eds) *The Foucault Effect: Studies in Governmentality*. Chicago, IL: University of Chicago Press.

—— (1993) 'About the Beginning of the Hermeneutics of the Self: Two Lectures at Dartmouth' *Political Theory* 21(2) 198–227.

—— (2006) *Psychiatric Power: Lectures at the Collège de France, 1973–1974*. Basingstoke: Palgrave Macmillan.

—— (2007) *Security, Territory, Population: Lectures at the Collège de France, 1977–1978*. Basingstoke: Palgrave Macmillan.

—— (2008) *The Birth of Biopolitics: Lectures at the Collège de France 1978–1979*. Basingstoke: Palgrave Macmillan.

Fowler, L. (2002) *Drugs, Crime and the Drug Treatment and Testing Order*. Issues in Community and Criminal Justice Monograph 2. London: NAPO.

Friman, H.R. (2004) 'The Great Escape? Globalization, Immigrant Entrepreneurship and the Criminal Economy' *Review of International Political Economy* 11 98–131.

Gandossy, R., Williams, J., Cohen, J., and Harwood, H. (1980) *Drugs and Crime: A Survey and Analysis of the Literature*. Washington, DC: National Institute of Justice.

Garland, D. (1985) *Punishment and Welfare: A History of Penal Strategies*. Aldershot: Gower.

—— (1990) *Punishment and Modern Society: A Study in Social Theory*. Oxford: Clarendon Press.

—— (1995) 'Penal Modernism and Postmodernism' in T. Blomberg and S. Cohen (eds) *Punishment and Social Control: Essays in Honour of Sheldon Messinger*. New York, NY: Aldine De Gruyter.

—— (2001) *The Culture of Control: Crime and Social Order in Contemporary Society*. Oxford: Oxford University Press.

—— (2003) 'The Rise of Risk' in R. Ericson and A. Doyle (eds) *Risk and Morality*. Toronto: University of Toronto Press.

—— (2004) 'Beyond the Culture of Control' *Critical Review of International Social and Political Philosophy* 7(2) 160–89.

—— (2006) 'Concepts of Culture in the Sociology of Punishment' *Theoretical Criminology* 10(4) 419–47.

Garside, R. (2003) 'Nine Words That Shook the Criminal Justice World' *Safer Society* 16 2–4.

Giddens, A. (1984) *The Constitution of Society*. Oxford: Oxford University Press.

Gossop, M. (2005) *Drug Misuse and Reductions in Crime: Findings from the National Treatment Outcome Research Study (NTORS)*. NTA research briefing 8. London: National Treatment Agency.

Gossop, M., Marsden, J., and Stewart, D. (2001) *NTORS after Five Years: Changes in Substance Use, Health and Criminal Behaviour in the Five Years after Intake*. London: Department of Health.

Grabosky, P. (1995) 'Using Non-governmental Resources to Foster Regulatory Compliance' *Governance* 8(4) 527–50.

Granfield, R., Eby, C., and Brewster, T. (1998) 'An Examination of the Denver Drug Court: The Impact of a Treatment-Oriented Drug-Offender System' *Law and Policy* 20(2) 183–202.

Gunningham, N. and Grabosky, P. (1998) *Smart Regulation: Designing Environmental Policy*. Oxford: Clarendon Press.

Habermas, J. (1986) 'Taking Aim at the Heart of the Present' in D.C. Hoy (ed.) *Foucault: A Critical Reader*. Oxford: Blackwell, 103–8.

Hacking, I. (2003) 'Risk and Dirt' in R. Ericson and A. Doyle (eds) *Risk and Morality*. Toronto: University of Toronto Press.

Hammersley, R., Forsyth, A., Morrison, V., and Davies, J. (1989) 'The Relationship between Crime and Opioid Use' *British Journal of Addiction* 84 1029–44.

Hancher, L. and Moran, M. (eds) (1989) *Capitalism, Culture and Regulation*. Oxford: Oxford University Press.

Harocopos, A., Dennis, D., Turnbull, P., Parsons, J., and Hough, M. (2003) *On the Rocks: A Follow-up Study of Crack Users in London*. London: CPRU, South Bank University.

Hart, D. and Webster, R. (1994) *Great Expectations. Drug Services and Probation: A Guide to Partnership*. London: SCODA.

Haw, S. (1985) *Drug Problems in Greater Glasgow*. London: SCODA.

Hawken, A. (2010) 'Behavioral Triage: A New Model for Identifying and Treating Substance-abusing Offenders' *Journal of Drug Policy Analysis* 3(1) Article 1.

Hawken, A. and Kleiman, M. (2009) *Managing Drug-involved Probationers with Swift and Certain Sanctions: Evaluating Hawaii's HOPE*. Washington, DC: National Institute of Justice.

Hay, G., Gannon, M., Casey, J., Millar, T., Williams, K., Eastwood, C., and McKeganey, N. (2008) *National and Regional Estimates of the Prevalence of Opiate Use and/or Crack Cocaine Use 2006/07: A Summary of Key Findings*. London: Home Office.

Hayes, P. (1992) 'Requirements as to Treatment for Drug or Alcohol Dependency' *Probation Journal* 39 82–6.

Heale, P. and Lang, E. (2001) 'A Process Evaluation of the CREDIT (Court Referral and Evaluation for Drug Intervention and Treatment) Pilot Programme' *Drug and Alcohol Review* 20(2) 223–30.

Hearnden, I., Harocopos, A., and Hough, M. (2000) *Problem Drug Use and Probation in London: An Evaluation*. London: Inner London Probation Service.

Hebdige, D. (1975) 'The Meaning of Mod' in S. Hall and T. Jefferson (eds) *Resistance Through Rituals*. London: Hutchinson.

Held, D., McGrew, A., Goldblatt, D., and Perraton, J. (1999) *Global Transformations: Politics, Economics and Culture*. Cambridge: Polity Press.

HM Inspectorate of Probation (HMIP) (1997) *Tackling Drugs Together: Report of a Thematic Inspection on the Work of the Probation Service with Drug Misuse*. London: Home Office.

HM Inspectorate of Probation (HMIP) (2003) *A Long Way in a Short Time: Inspection of the Implementation of Drug Treatment and Testing Orders by the National Probation Service*. London: Home Office.

Holloway, K. and Bennett, T. (2004) *The Results of the First Two Years of the NEW-ADAM Programme*. Home Office Online Report 19/04. London: Home Office.

Holloway, K., Bennett, T., and Lower, C. (2004) *Trends in Drug Use and Offending: The Results of the NEW-ADAM Programme 1999–2002*. Research Findings 219. London: Home Office.

Home Office (2002) *Updated Drug Strategy*. London: Home Office.

—— (2006a) *Key Messages for the Drug Interventions Programme—August 2006*. London: Home Office.

—— (2006b) *DIP—Tough Choices Project FAQs*. 9 June version. London: Home Office.

—— (2008) *Drugs: Protecting Families and Communities. The 2008 Drug Strategy*. London: Home Office.

—— (2009) *Operational Process Guidance for Implementation of Test on Arrest, Required Assessment and Restriction on Bail*. (April reissue). London: Home Office.

—— (2010) *Drug Strategy 2010: Reducing Demand, Restricting Supply, Building Recovery: Supporting People to Live a Drug-free Life*. London: Home Office.

Hough, M. (1996) *Drug Misuse and the Criminal Justice System: A Review of the Literature*. DPI Paper 15. London: Home Office.

—— (2001) 'Balancing Public Health and Criminal Justice Interventions' *International Journal of Drug Policy* 12 429–33.

—— (2002) 'Drug User Treatment within a Criminal Justice Context' *Substance Use & Misuse* 37(8–10) 985–96.

Hough, M., Clancy, A., McSweeney, T., and Turnbull, P. (2003) *The Impact of Drug Treatment and Testing Orders on Offending: Two-year Reconviction Results*. Findings 184. London: Home Office.

Hubbard, R., Craddock, S., and Anderson, J. (2003) 'Overview of Five-year Follow-up Outcomes in the Drug Abuse Treatment Outcome Studies (DATOS)' *Journal of Substance Abuse Treatment* 25(3) 125–34.

Hucklesby, A. (1994) 'The Use and Abuse of Conditional Bail' *Howard Journal of Criminal Justice* 33(3) 258–70.

—— (1996) 'Bail or Jail? The Practical Operation of the Bail Act 1976' *Journal of Law and Society* 23(2) 213–33.

—— (1997) 'Court Culture: An Explanation of Variations in the Use of Bail by Magistrates' Courts' *Howard Journal of Criminal Justice* 36(2) 129–45.

—— (2009) 'Keeping the Lid on the Prison Remand Population: The Experience in England and Wales' *Current Issues in Criminal Justice* 21(1) 3–23.

Hucklesby, A., Eastwood, C., Seddon, T., and Spriggs, A. (2005) *The Evaluation of the Restriction on Bail Pilot: Implementation Lessons from the First Six Months*. Online Report 36/05. London: Home Office.

Hucklesby, A., Eastwood, C., Seddon, T., and Spriggs, A. (2007) *The Evaluation of the Restriction on Bail Pilot: Final Report*. Online Report 06/07. London: Home Office.

Hughes, P. (1977) *Behind the Wall of Respect*. Chicago, IL: University of Chicago Press.

Hughes, P. and Rieche, O. (1995) 'Heroin Epidemics Revisited' *Epidemiologic Reviews* 17 66.

Hunt, L. and Chambers, C. (1976) *The Heroin Epidemics: A Study of Heroin Use in the United States*. New York, NY: Spectrum.

Hunt, N. and Stevens, A. (2004) 'Whose Harm? Harm Reduction and the Shift to Coercion in UK Drug Policy' *Social Policy & Society* 3(4) 333–42.

Inner London Probation Service (ILPS) (1989) *Drug and Alcohol Survey*. London: ILPS Demonstration Unit.

—— (1990) *Chief Officer's Statement on Drugs*. ILPS Circular 21/1990. London: ILPS.

Institute for Criminal Policy Research (ICPR), Kings College London, University of Bristol, Imperial College, London School of Economics (2007) *National Evaluation of Criminal Justice Integrated Teams*. London: ICPR.

Jameson, F. (1984) 'Postmodernism, or the Cultural Logic of Late Capitalism' *New Left Review* 146 53–93.

—— (1991) *Postmodernism, or the Cultural Logic of Late Capitalism*. Durham, NC: Duke University Press.

Johnson, B., Goldstein, P., Preble, E., Schmeidler, J., Lipton, D., and Miller, T. (1985) *Taking Care of Business: The Economics of Crime by Heroin Users*. Lexington, MA: Lexington Books.

Jones, A., Donmall, M., Millar, T., Moody, A., Weston, S., Anderson, T., Gittins, M., Abeywardana, V., and D'Souza, J. (2009) *The Drug Treatment Outcomes Research Study (DTORS): Final Outcomes Report*. Research Report 24. London: Home Office.

Jones, A., Weston, S., Moody, A., Millar, T., Dollin, L., Anderson, T., and Donmall, M. (2007) *The Drug Treatment Outcomes Research Study (DTORS): Baseline Report*. Research Report 3. London: Home Office.

Jones, M. (2004) 'Anxiety and Containment in the Risk Society: Theorising Young People and Drug Prevention Policy' *International Journal of Drug Policy* 15 367–76.

Jordana, J., Levi-Faur, D., and Marin, X. (2011) 'The Global Diffusion of Regulatory Agencies: Channels of Transfer and Stages of Diffusion' *Comparative Political Studies* 44(10) 1343–69.

Keynes, J.M. (1920) *The Economic Consequences of the Peace*. New York, NY: Harcourt Brace.

Kilmer, B. and Pacula, R. (2009) 'Estimating the size of the Global Drug Market: A Demand-side Approach' in P. Reuter and F. Trautmann (eds)

A Report on Global Illicit Drugs Markets 1998–2007. Brussels: European Commission.

Klima, N., Dorn, N., and Vander Beken, T. (2011) 'Risk Calculation and Precautionary Uncertainty: Two Configurations within Crime Assessment' *Crime, Law and Social Change* 55 15–31.

Kohn, M. (1987) *Narcomania*. London: Faber & Faber.

—— (1992) *Dope Girls: The Birth of the British Drug Underground*. London: Granta.

Lee, M. (1993) 'The Unspoken Sentence? Treatment Conditions for Drug Using Offenders under the 1991 Criminal Justice Act' *Criminal Justice Matters* 12 15.

—— (1994) 'The Probation Order: A Suitable Case for Treatment?' *Drugs: Education, Prevention and Policy* 1(2) 121–33.

Lee, M. and Mainwaring, S. (1995) 'No Big Deal: Court-ordered Treatment in Practice' *Druglink* Jan/Feb 14–15.

Lemke, T. (2001) '"The Birth of Bio-politics": Michel Foucault's Lecture at the Collège de France on Neo-liberal Governmentality' *Economy and Society* 30(2) 190–207.

Levi-Faur, D. (2005) 'The Global Diffusion of Regulatory Capitalism' *Annals of the American Academy of Political and Social Science* 598(1) 12–32.

Levine, H. (1978) 'The Discovery of Addiction: Changing Conceptions of Habitual Drunkenness in America' *Journal of Studies on Alcohol* 39(1) 143–74.

Liddle, M. and Gelsthorpe, L. (1994a) *Inter-agency Crime Prevention: Organising Local Delivery*. Crime Prevention Paper No. 52. London: Home Office.

—— (1994b) *Crime Prevention and Inter-agency Co-operation*. Crime Prevention Paper No. 53. London: Home Office.

—— (1994c) *Inter-agency Crime Prevention: Further Issues*. Crime Prevention Paper No. 54. London: Home Office.

Lippert, R. and Stenson, K. (2010) 'Advancing Governmentality Studies: Lessons from Social Constructionism' *Theoretical Criminology* 14(4) 473–94.

Loader, I. and Sparks, R. (2004) 'For an Historical Sociology of Crime Policy in England and Wales since 1968' *Critical Review of International Social and Political Philosophy* 7(2) 5–32.

Luhmann, N. (1995) *Social Systems*. Stanford, CA: Stanford University Press.

Lyle, G. (1953) 'Dangerous Drug Traffic in London' *British Journal of Addiction* 50(1) 47–55.

McDermott, P. (2005) 'The Great Mersey Experiment: The Birth of Harm Reduction' in J. Strang and M. Gossop (eds) *Heroin Addiction and the British System. Vol 1: Origins and Evolution*. London: Routledge.

McGlothlin, W., Anglin, M., and Wilson B. (1977) *Evaluation of the California Civil Addict Program*. Washington, DC: National Institute of Justice.

MacGregor, S. (1989) 'The Public Debate in the 1980s' in S. MacGregor (ed.) *Drugs and British Society: Responses to a Social Problem in the 1980s*. London: Routledge.

McGrew, A. (2000) 'Power Shift: From National Government to Global Governance?' in D. Held (ed.) *A Globalizing World? Culture, Economics, Politics*. London: Routledge.

McIvor, G. (2009) *Review of the Glasgow and Fife Drug Courts: Report*. Edinburgh: Scottish Government.

McSweeney, T., Stevens, A., Hunt, N., and Turnbull, P. (2007) 'Twisting Arms or a Helping Hand? Assessing the Impact of "Coerced" and Comparable "Voluntary" Drug Treatment Options' *British Journal of Criminology* 47(3) 470–90.

—— (2008) 'Drug Testing and Court Review Hearings: Uses and Limitations' *Probation Journal* 55(1) 39–53.

Makkai, T. and Braithwaite, J. (1993) 'Praise, Pride and Corporate Compliance' *International Journal of the Sociology of Law* 21 73–91.

Mallender, J., Roberts, E., and Seddon, T. (2002) *Evaluation of Drug Testing in the Criminal Justice System in Three Pilot Areas*. Findings 176. London: Home Office.

Marlowe, D., Festinger, D., Dugosh, K., and Lee, P. (2005) 'Are Judicial Status Hearings a "Key Component" of Drug Court? Six and Twelve Months Outcomes' *Drug and Alcohol Dependence* 79(2) 145–55.

Matrix and Nacro (2004) *Evaluation of Drug Testing in the Criminal Justice System*. Home Office Research Study 286. London: Home Office.

May, C. (2005) *The CARAT Drug Service in Prisons: Findings from the Research Database*. Findings 262. London: Home Office.

Mazerolle, L. and Ransley, J. (2005) *Third Party Policing*. Cambridge: Cambridge University Press.

Measham, F., Aldridge, J., and Parker, H. (2001) *Dancing on Drugs: Risk, Health and Hedonism in the British Club Scene*. London: Free Association Books.

Measham, F., Newcombe, R., and Parker, H. (1994) 'The Normalization of Recreational Drug Use amongst Young People in North-West England' *British Journal of Sociology* 45 287–312.

Melossi, D. (1985) 'Punishment and Social Action: Changing Vocabularies of Punitive Motive within a Political Business Cycle' *Current Perspectives in Social Theory* 6 169–97.

Miles, S. (1998) *Consumerism as a Way of Life*. London: Sage.

—— (2000) *Youth Lifestyles in a Changing World*. Buckingham: Open University Press.

Millar, T., Beatty, S., Jones, A., and Donmall, M. (2002) *Outcome of Arrest Referral: Treatment Uptake, Treatment Retention and Behaviour Change amongst Drug Misusing Offenders Referred for Drug Treatment.* London: Home Office.

Millar, T., Jones, A., Donmall, M., and Roxburgh, M. (2008) *Changes in Offending Following Prescribing Treatment for Drug Misuse.* NTA Research Briefing 35. London: National Treatment Agency.

Miller, P. and Rose, N. (1990) 'Governing Economic Life' *Economy and Society* 19 1–31.

—— (1997) 'Mobilising the Consumer: Assembling the Subject of Consumption' *Theory, Culture and Society* 14(1) 1–36.

Ministry of Health (1926) *Report of the Departmental Committee on Morphine and Heroin Addiction.* 'The Rolleston Report'. London: Ministry of Health.

—— (1965) *Drug Addiction. Second Report of the Interdepartmental Committee.* 'The Second Brain Report'. London: HMSO.

Mold, A. and Berridge, V. (2007) 'Crisis and Opportunity in Drug Policy: Changing the Direction of British Drug Services in the 1980s' *Journal of Policy History* 19(1) 29–48.

Mott, J. (1991) 'Crime and Heroin Use' in D. Whynes and P. Bean (eds) *Policing and Prescribing: The British System of Drug Control.* Basingstoke: Macmillan.

Mugford, S. (1993) 'Social Change and the Control of Psychotropic Drugs— Risk Management, Harm Reduction and "Postmodernity"' *Drug and Alcohol Review* 12 369–75.

Murphy, K., Tyler, T., and Curtis, A. (2009) 'Nurturing Regulatory Compliance: Is Procedural Justice Effective when People Question the Legitimacy of the Law?' *Regulation & Governance* 3(1) 1–26.

Mythen, G. and Walklate, S. (eds) (2006) *Beyond the Risk Society: Critical Reflections on Risk and Human Security.* Maidenhead: Open University Press.

National Audit Office (NAO) (2004) *The Drug Treatment and Testing Order: Early Lessons.* London: NAO.

National Treatment Agency (NTA) (2010) *Drug Treatment in 2009–10.* London: National Treatment Agency.

Nee, C. and Sibbitt, R. (1993) *The Probation Response to Drug Misuse.* Research and Planning Unit Paper 79. London: Home Office.

Newcombe, R. (1987) 'High Time for Harm Reduction' *Druglink* 2(1) 10–11.

—— (1992) 'The Reduction of Drug-related Harm: A Conceptual Framework for Theory, Practice and Research' in P. O'Hare, R. Newcombe, A. Matthews, E. Buning, and E. Drucker (eds) *The Reduction of Drug-Related Harm.* London: Routledge.

Nurco, D., Ball, J., Shaffer, J., and Hanlon, T. (1985) 'The Criminality of Narcotic Addicts' *Journal of Nervous and Mental Disease* 173 94–102.

Oerton, J., Hunter, G., Hickman, M., Morgan, D., Turnbull, P., Kothari, G., and Marsden, J. (2003) 'Arrest Referral in London Police Stations: Characteristics of the First Year. A Key Point of Intervention for Drug Users?' *Drugs: Education, Prevention and Policy* 10 73–85.

O'Malley, P. (1991) 'Legal Networks and Domestic Security' *Studies in Law, Politics and Society* 11 171–90.

—— (1992) 'Risk, Power and Crime Prevention' *Economy and Society* 21(3) 252–75.

O'Malley, P. (ed.) (1998) *Crime and the Risk Society*. Aldershot: Ashgate.

O'Malley, P. (1999a) 'Volatile and Contradictory Punishment' *Theoretical Criminology* 3(2) 175–96.

—— (1999b) 'Governmentality and the Risk Society' *Economy and Society* 28(1) 138–48.

—— (2004) *Risk, Uncertainty and Government*. Abingdon: Routledge-Cavendish.

O'Malley, P. (ed.) (2006) *Governing Risks*. Aldershot: Ashgate.

O'Malley, P. (2011) 'Security after Risk: Security Strategies for Governing Extreme Uncertainty' *Current Issues in Criminal Justice* 23(1) 5–15.

Osborne, D. and Gaebler, T. (1992) *Reinventing Government*. New York, NY: Addison-Wesley.

Parker, C. (2002) *The Open Corporation*. Melbourne: Cambridge University Press.

Parker, H. (2005a) 'Pathology or Modernity? Rethinking Risk Factor Analyses of Young Drug Users' *Addiction Research & Theory* 11(3) 141–4.

—— (2005b) 'Heroin Epidemics and Social Exclusion in the UK, 1980–2000' in J. Strang and M. Gossop (eds) *Heroin Addiction and the British System. Volume 1 Origins and Evolution*. Abingdon: Routledge.

—— (2007) 'Drug Strategy Loses its Way' *Drink and Drugs News* 7 May 6–7.

Parker, H., Aldridge, J., and Measham, F. (1998a) *Illegal Leisure: The Normalization of Adolescent Recreational Drug Use*. London: Routledge.

Parker, H., Bakx, K., and Newcombe, R. (1988) *Living with Heroin: The Impact of a Drugs 'Epidemic' on an English Community*. Milton Keynes: Open University Press.

Parker, H., Bury, C., and Egginton, R. (1998b) *New Heroin Outbreaks amongst Young People in England and Wales*. Crime Detection and Prevention Series Paper 92. London: Home Office.

Parker, H., Measham, F., and Aldridge, J. (1995) *Drugs Futures: Changing Patterns of Drug Use amongst English Youth*. Research Monograph 7. London: ISDD.

Parker, H. and Newcombe, R. (1987) 'Heroin Use and Acquisitive Crime in an English Community' *British Journal of Sociology* 38(3) 331–50.

Parker, H., Williams, L., and Aldridge, J. (2002) 'The Normalization of "Sensible" Recreational Drug Use: Further Evidence from the North-West England Longitudinal Study' *Sociology* 36 941–64.

Patel, K. (2010) *The Patel Report: Prison Drug Treatment Strategy Review Group*. London: Department of Health.

Pearson, G. (1987a) *The New Heroin Users*. Oxford: Blackwell.

—— (1987b) 'Social Deprivation, Unemployment and Patterns of Heroin Use' in N. Dorn and N. South (eds) *A Land Fit for Heroin?* London: Macmillan.

—— (2001) 'Drugs and Poverty' in S. Chen and E. Skidelsky (eds) *High Time for Reform: Drug Policy for the 21st Century*. London: Social Market Foundation.

Pearson, G., Blagg, H., Smith, D., Sampson, A., and Stubbs, P. (1992) 'Crime, Community and Conflict: The Multi-Agency Approach' in D. Downes (ed.) *Unravelling Criminal Justice*. London: Macmillan.

Pearson, G., Gilman, M., and McIver, S. (1986) *Young People and Heroin: An Examination of Heroin Use in the North of England*. London: Health Education Council.

Peck, D.F. and Plant, M.A. (1986) 'Unemployment and Illegal Drug Use: Concordant Evidence from a Prospective Study and National Trends' *British Medical Journal* 293 929–32.

Prison Service (1995) *Drug Misuse in Prison*. London: Prison Service.

Raynor, P. and Honess, T. (1998) *Drug and Alcohol Related Offenders Project: An Evaluation of the West Glamorgan Partnership*. DPI Paper 14. London: Home Office.

Read, J. (2009) 'A Genealogy of Homo-Economicus: Neoliberalism and the Production of Subjectivity' *Foucault Studies* 6 25–36.

van Ree, E. (2002) 'Drugs, the Democratic Civilising Process and the Consumer Society' *International Journal of Drug Policy* 13 349–53.

Reichman, N. (1986) 'Managing Crime Risks: Towards an Insurance-based Model of Social Control' *Research in Law, Deviance and Social Control* 8 151–72.

Reuter, P. and Greenfield, V. (2001) 'Measuring Global Drug Markets: How Good are the Numbers and Why Should We Care about Them?' *World Economics* 2(4) 159–73.

Robertson, R. (2005) 'The Arrival of HIV' in J. Strang and M. Gossop (eds) *Heroin Addiction and the British System. Vol 1: Origins and Evolution*. London: Routledge.

Rock, P. (1995) 'The Opening Stages of Criminal Justice Policy Making' *British Journal of Criminology* 35(1) 1–16.

—— (1996) *Reconstructing a Women's Prison: The Holloway Redevelopment Project 1968–1988*. Oxford: Clarendon Press.

Rodger, J. (2008) *Criminalising Social Policy: Anti-social Behaviour and Welfare in a De-civilised society*. Cullompton: Willan.

Rose, N. (1999) *Powers of Freedom: Reframing Political Thought*. Cambridge: Cambridge University Press.

—— (2000) 'Government and Control' in D. Garland and R. Sparks (eds) *Criminology and Social Theory*. Clarendon Studies in Criminology. Oxford: Oxford University Press.

Rose, N. and Miller, P. (1992) 'Political Power beyond the State: Problematics of Government' *British Journal of Sociology* 43(2) 173–205.

Rose, N., O'Malley, P., and Valverde, M. (2006) 'Governmentality' *Annual Review of Law and Social Science* 2 83–104.

Rose, N. and Valverde, M. (1998) 'Governed by Law?' *Social & Legal Studies* 7(4) 541–51.

Rossman, S., Roman, J., Zweig, J., Rempel, M., and Lindquist, C. (2011) *The Multi-Site Adult Drug Court Evaluation*. Vols 1–4. Washington, DC: Urban Institute.

Rumgay, J. (1994) *Drug and Alcohol Treatment Requirements in Probation Orders: A Survey of Developments Since October 1992. Report to the Home Office Research and Planning Unit*. London: Home Office.

Russell, J. (1994) *Substance Abuse and Crime (Some Lessons from America)*. Harkness Fellowship Report. New York, NY: Commonwealth Fund of New York.

Sachs, J. (2000) 'Globalization and Patterns of Economic Development' *Review of World Economics* 136(4) 579–600.

Sampson, A., Stubbs, P., Smith, D., Pearson, G., and Blagg, H. (1988) 'Crime, Localities and the Multi-agency Approach' *British Journal of Criminology* 28 478–93.

Schaub, M., Stevens, A., Berto, D., Hunt, N., Kerschl, V., McSweeney, T., Oeuvray, K., Puppo, I., Santa Maria, A., Trinkl, B., Werdenich, W., and Uchtenhagen, A. (2010) 'Comparing Outcomes of "Voluntary" and "Quasi-Compulsory" Treatment of Substance Dependence in Europe' *European Addiction Research* 16 53–60.

Scott, C. (2001) 'Analysing Regulatory Space: Fragmented Resources and Institutional Design' *Public Law* 329–53.

Seddon, T. (1996) 'Drug Control in Prisons' *Howard Journal of Criminal Justice* 35 327–35.

Seddon, T. (2000) 'Explaining the Drug–Crime Link: Theoretical, Policy and Research Issues' *Journal of Social Policy* 29(1) 95–107.

—— (2005) 'Searching for the Next Techno-fix: Drug Testing in the Criminal Justice System' *Criminal Justice Matters* 58 16–17.

—— (2006) 'Drugs, Crime and Social Exclusion: Social Context and Social Theory in British Drugs-Crime Research' *British Journal of Criminology* 46 680–703.

—— (2007a) 'Coerced Drug Treatment in the Criminal Justice System: Conceptual, Ethical and Criminological Issues' *Criminology & Criminal Justice* 7(3) 269–86.

—— (2007b) 'The Regulation of Heroin: Drug Policy and Social Change in Early Twentieth century Britain' *International Journal of the Sociology of Law* 35(3) 143–56.

—— (2008a) 'Drugs, the Informal Economy and Globalization' *International Journal of Social Economics* 35(10) 717–28.

—— (2008b) 'Women, Harm Reduction and History: Gender Perspectives on the Emergence of the "British System" of Drug Control' *International Journal of Drug Policy* 19(2) 99–105.

—— (2010a) *A History of Drugs: Drugs and Freedom in the Liberal Age.* Abingdon: Routledge.

—— (2010b) 'Regulating Markets in Vice' *Criminal Justice Matters* 80 6–7.

—— (2010c) 'Drugs and crime' in J. Barlow (ed.) *Substance Misuse: The Implications of Research, Policy and Practice.* Research Highlights in Social Work 53. London: Jessica Kingsley.

—— (2011) 'Court-ordered Treatment, Neo-liberalism and *Homo economicus*' in S. Fraser and D. Moore (eds) *The Drug Effect: Health, Crime and Society.* Cambridge: Cambridge University Press.

Seddon, T., Ralphs, R., and Williams, L. (2008) 'Risk, Security and the "Criminalization" of British Drug Policy' *British Journal of Criminology* 48(6) 818–34.

Shaffer, D. (2006) *Reconsidering Drug Court Effectiveness: A Meta-Analytic Review.* Las Vegas, NV: University of Nevada.

Shearing, C. (2001) 'Punishment and the Changing Face of Governance' *Punishment and Society* 3(2) 203–20.

Shearing, C. and Froestad, J. (2010) 'Nodal Governance and the Zwelethemba Model' in H. Quirk, T. Seddon, and G. Smith (eds) *Regulation and Criminal Justice: Innovations in Policy and Research.* Cambridge: Cambridge University Press.

Shearing, C. and Johnston, L. (2010) 'Nodal Wars and Network Fallacies: A Genealogical Analysis of Global Insecurities' *Theoretical Criminology* 14(4) 495–514.

Sherman, L., Gottfredson, D., Mackenzie, D., Eck, J., Reuter, P., and Bushway, S. (1997) *Preventing Crime: What Works, What Doesn't, What's Promising.* Rockville, MD: National Institute of Justice.

Shiner, M. (2009) *Drug Use and Social Change: The Distortion of History.* Basingstoke: Palgrave Macmillan.

Shiner, M. and Newburn, T. (1997) 'Definitely, Maybe Not? The Normalisation of Recreational Drug Use among Young People' *Sociology* 31 511–29.

Shiner, M. and Newburn, T. (1999) 'Taking Tea with Noel: The Place and Meaning of Drug Use in Everyday Life' in N. South (ed.) *Drugs: Cultures, Controls and Everyday Life*. London: Sage.

Sibbitt, R. (1996) *The ILPS Methadone Prescribing Project*. Home Office Research Study 148. London: Home Office.

Simon, J. (1987) 'The Emergence of a Risk Society: Insurance, Law and the State' *Socialist Review* 95 61–89.

—— (1988) 'The Ideological Effects of Actuarial Practices' *Law and Society Review* 22 771–800.

—— (1998) 'Managing the Monstrous: Sex Offenders and the New Penology' *Psychology, Public Policy and Law* 4 452–67.

—— (2007) *Governing Through Crime: How the War on Crime Transformed American Democracy and Created a Culture of Fear*. Oxford: Oxford University Press.

Simpson, M. (2003) 'The Relationship between Drug Use and Crime: A Puzzle inside an Enigma' *International Journal of Drug Policy* 14 307–19.

Singleton, N., Pendry, E., Taylor, C., Farrell, M., and Marsden, J. (2005) *The Impact of Mandatory Drug Testing in Prisons*. Online Report 03/05. London: Home Office.

Skinner, Q. (2002) *Visions of Politics: Volume 1—Regarding Method*. Cambridge: Cambridge University Press.

Skodbo, S., Brown, G., Deacon, S., Cooper, A., Hall, A., Millar, T., Smith, J., and Witham, K. (2007) *The Drug Interventions Programme (DIP): Addressing Drug Use and Offending through 'Tough Choices'*. Research Report 2. London: Home Office.

Sondhi, A., O'Shea, J., and Williams, T. (2002) *Arrest Referral: Emerging Findings from the National Monitoring and Evaluation Programme*. London: Home Office.

South, N. (1999) 'Debating Drugs and Everyday Life: Normalisation, Prohibition and "Otherness"' in N. South (ed.) *Drugs: Culture, Controls and Everyday Life*. London: Sage.

Southwark Arrest Referral Pilot Project Monitoring Group (1991) *Report to the Home Office on the Southwark Arrest Referral Pilot Project. (A Study into the Feasibility of Working with People who Have Been Arrested and Want Help for Their Problem Drug Use). January 1989 to March 1991*. London: Southwark Drug Prevention Team.

Sparks, R. (1992) 'Reason and Unreason in "Left Realism": Some Problems in the Constitution of the Fear of Crime' in R. Matthews and J. Young (eds) *Issues in Realist Criminology*. London: Sage.

—— (2000) 'Perspectives on Risk and Penal Politics' in T. Hope and R. Sparks (eds) *Crime, Risk and Insecurity: Law and Order in Everyday Life and Political Discourse*. London: Routledge.

—— (2001) 'Degrees of Estrangement: The Cultural Theory of Risk and Comparative Penology' *Theoretical Criminology* 5(2) 159–76.

—— (2006) 'Ordinary Anxieties and States of Emergency: Statecraft and Spectatorship in the New Politics of Insecurity' in S. Armstrong and L. McAra (eds) *Perspectives on Punishment: The Contours of Control.* Oxford: Oxford University Press.

Spear, H.B. (1969) 'The Growth of Heroin Addiction in the United Kingdom' *British Journal of Addiction* 64 245–55.

Stevens, A. (2007) 'When Two Dark Figures Collide: Evidence and Discourse on Drug-related Crime' *Critical Social Policy* 27(1) 77–99.

—— (2008) 'Weighing Up Crime: The Overestimation of Drug-related Crime' *Contemporary Drug Problems* 35 265–90.

—— (2011a) *Drugs, Crime and Public Health: The Political Economy of Drug Policy.* Abingdon: Routledge.

—— (2011b) 'Are Drugs to Blame?' *Criminal Justice Matters* 83 24–5.

Stevens, A., Berto, D., Heckmann, W., Kerschl, V., Oeuvray, K., van Ooyen, M., Steffan, E., and Uchtenhagen, A. (2005a) 'Quasi-Compulsory Treatment of Drug Dependent Offenders: An International Literature Review' *Substance Use & Misuse* 40 269–83.

Stevens, A., McSweeney, T., van Ooyen, M., and Uchtenhagen, A. (2005b) 'On Coercion' *International Journal of Drug Policy* 16 207–9.

Stimson, G. (1987) 'British Drug Policies in the 1980s: A Preliminary Analysis and Some Suggestions for Research' *British Journal of Addiction* 82 477–88.

—— (2000) '"Blair Declares War": The Unhealthy State of British Drug Policy' *International Journal of Drug Policy* 11 259–64.

Stimson, G., Alldritt, L., Dolan, K., Donoghoe, M., and Lart, R. (1988) *Injecting Equipment Exchange Schemes, Final Report.* London: Goldsmiths' College.

Stimson, G. and Lart, R. (2005) 'The Relationship between the State and Local Practice in the Development of National Policy on Drugs between 1920 and 1990' in J. Strang and M. Gossop (eds) *Heroin Addiction and the British System. Volume 1: Origins and Evolution.* Abingdon: Routledge.

Strang, J. and Yates, R. (1982) *Involuntary Treatment and Addiction.* Strasbourg: Council of Europe (Pompidou Group).

Teubner, G. (1989) 'How the Law Thinks: Towards a Constructivist Epistemology of Law' *Law & Society Review* 23(5) 727–58.

Thompson, G. (2000) 'Economic Globalization?' in D. Held (ed.) *A Globalizing World? Culture, Economics, Politics.* London: Routledge.

Thornton, S. (1995) *Club Cultures: Music, Media and Subcultural Capital.* Cambridge: Polity Press.

Tully, J. (ed.) (1988) *Meaning and Context: Quentin Skinner and His Critics.* Princeton, NJ: Princeton University Press.

Turnbull, P.J., McSweeney, T., Hough, M., Webster, R., and Edmunds, M. (2000) *Drug Treatment and Testing Orders: Final Evaluation Report.* Home Office Research Study 212. London: Home Office.

Turnbull, P.J., Webster, R., and Stillwell, G. (1995) *Get It While You Can: An Evaluation of an Early Intervention Project for Arrestees with Alcohol and Drug Problems*. DPI Paper 9. London: Home Office.

Turner, R. (2004) 'The Impact of Drug Treatment and Testing Orders in West Yorkshire: Six-Month Outcomes' *Probation Journal* 51(2) 116–32.

Tyler, T. (1990) *Why People Obey the Law: Procedural Justice, Legitimacy, and Compliance*. New Haven, CT: Yale University Press.

Urada, D., Hawken, A., Conner, B., Evans, E., Anglin, D., Yang, J., Teruya, C., Herbeck, D., Fan, J., Rutkowski, B., Gonzales, R., Rawson, R., Grella, C., Prendergast, M., Hser, Y.-I., Hunter, J., and Poe, A. (2008) *Evaluation of Proposition 36: The Substance Abuse and Crime Prevention Act of 2000. 2008 Report*. Sacramento, CA: California Department of Alcohol and Drug Programs.

Urbanoski, K. (2010) 'Coerced Addiction Treatment: Client Perspectives and the Implications of Their Neglect' *Harm Reduction Journal* 7: 13.

Valverde, M. (2007) 'Genealogies of European States: Foucauldian Reflections' *Economy and Society* 36(1) 159–78.

——(2011) 'Questions of Security: A Framework for Research' *Theoretical Criminology* 15(1) 3–22.

Webster, C. (1986) 'Compulsory Treatment of Narcotic Addiction' *International Journal of Law and Psychiatry* 8 133–59.

Webster, R. (1996) *The Courting Game: A Handbook for Drug Service Intervention in a Court Setting*. London: SCODA.

Williams, L. and Parker, H. (2001) 'Alcohol, Cannabis, Ecstasy and Cocaine: Drugs of Reasoned Choice amongst Young Adult Recreational Drug Users in England' *International Journal of Drug Policy* 12 397–413.

Wilson, D., Mitchell, O., and MacKenzie, D. (2006) 'A Systematic Review of Drug Court Effects on Recidivism' *Journal of Experimental Criminology* 2(4) 459–87.

Wincup, E. (2011) 'Carrots And Sticks: Problem Drug Users and Welfare Reform' *Criminal Justice Matters* 84 22–3.

Wish, E. and Gropper, B. (1990) 'Drug testing by the Criminal Justice System: Methods, Research and Applications' in M. Tonry and J. Wilson (eds) *Drugs and Crime*. Chicago, IL: University of Chicago Press.

Yates, R. (1979) 'An Experiment in Multi-facility Induction' *Addiction Therapist* (Special Edition) Winter 3 25–30.

Young, J. (1999) *The Exclusive Society: Social Exclusion, Crime and Difference in Late Modernity*. London: Sage.

——(2002) 'Crime and Social Exclusion' in M. Maguire, R. Morgan, and R. Reiner (eds) *The Oxford Handbook of Criminology*. 3rd edn. Oxford: Oxford University Press.

——(2003a) 'Search for a New Criminology of Everyday Life: Review of *The Culture of Control* by David Garland' *British Journal of Criminology* 42(1) 228–43.

—— (2003b) 'Merton with Energy, Katz with Structure: The Sociology of Vindictiveness and the Criminology of Transgression' *Theoretical Criminology* 7(3) 389–414.

Zedner, L. (2002) 'Dangers of Dystopias in Penal Theory' *Oxford Journal of Legal Studies* 22(2) 341–66.

—— (2003) 'Too Much Security?' *International Journal of the Sociology of Law* 31 155–84.

—— (2007) 'Pre-crime and Post-criminology?' *Theoretical Criminology* 11(2) 261–81.

Zinn, J. (ed.) (2008) *Social Theories of Risk and Uncertainty*. Oxford: Blackwell.

Index